The Neutering of the American Male

by

Jim Wysong

Published by JPW Inc.

13-Digit ISBN: 978-0-9843950-0-2

1. Men - Masculinity 2. Women 3. Relationship
4. Self-help 5. Psychology

Cover Design, Dineen Miller
Cover Illustration, Duncan Long

Table of Contents

Forward
by
Barton Foster

Congratulations

By picking up *The Neutering of the American Male,* you have already made a choice not to accept the status quo: to look at yourself and the events of your past and their results, and to enact change in order to create a rich and compelling destiny for yourself and those you love.

Jim Wysong's book empowers people to enjoy, indeed to celebrate rather than endure or suffer in, their lives and relationships.

As the owner of the Barton Group, an executive recruiting and coaching firm, I talk to a wide range of individuals: people who build companies from start-ups to multi-billion dollar businesses, and people who seem to struggle their way through life and careers. I watch people lead their companies, families, and themselves to spectacular success, and others who lead them to disaster. I also see people who have truly fabulous marriages and careers who are very comfortable with themselves, and I observe high functioning people who spend their lives struggling in confusion, aggravation and frustration. As I've coached and worked with all of these people, I evaluate what makes them tick. I examine the factors that take them to success or failure in order to have the means to implement what works in myself and teach it in my coaching to others.

I am a person who has taken, and continues to take, an incredible journey of growth. I have wrestled with limiting beliefs and perspectives and have transformed them in my life so I am making major contributions to others. While reading *The Neutering of the American Male,* I was facing difficult challenges in many areas of my life and career. Jim gave me the tools to face those challenges, which brought a renewed zest for life.

Do you ever get overwhelmed and wish you could break free and be empowered? Do you ever want to be strong, decisive, confident, or self-assured? Jim takes us down a path that makes sense of why and how to break free, and enables us to begin that shift instantly, leading us to empowerment.

Since I have embarked on my own journey, as well as coaching others, I believe each of us can be our own captain. We can chart our own course, change directions, and have rich relationships, living life to its fullest. Navigating this journey successfully requires knowing what is behind the forces that drive us and how to connect and alter them. People can take charge of their beliefs, emotions, actions, and results by understanding what the building blocks and components are that make them up and by getting a plan of how to assemble them and even exchange the parts that need replacing.

Changes in our society and culture are accelerating as time progresses and these shifts have altered the masculine and feminine roles and dynamics within us, as well as between men and women. These changes cause conflict, confusion, aggravation, and frustration. Understanding what makes up our perceptions, relationships, and life enables us to change them to create the results we desire. Our perceptions can limit us, and if they do, we can change them so they drive us to our dreams.

We have both masculine and feminine dynamics within us and these powerful forces create opposition and attraction in relationships between men and women. What does this mean and how do we access the empowering parts of both when we want to? Jim breaks this down so we can understand it. We can shift and use the appropriate emotions to create wanted results.

In order to make changes that are effective and lasting in our lives, it is critical that we gain an understanding of how the many aspects of being human interact with and influence each other and how they in turn affect us as individuals.

Within these pages are insights revealing forces that drive us as individuals, but which are rarely recognized. Jim teaches us what that means in a step-by-step approach. We also learn the why and how, what influences these traits have, and how to transform them into healthy, rewarding results.

This book illuminates the way to become more successful fathers, mothers, husbands, wives, and leaders. It is for men to understand themselves and the women in their lives, as well as for women to understand themselves and the men in theirs.

I see Jim driven with passion, guiding us on a journey of growth and change in us and our relationships with others. He gives us an armory of tools, enabling us to enjoy our lives and dreams. His insight into the masculine and feminine aspects, and how they influence and interrelate to the human experience, gives his readers an understanding and ability to shift to a stronger, more appropriate state.

The Neutering of the American Male takes us on that journey. In a powerful presentation, Jim guides us from being incongruent and how we became that way, to understanding our roles and becoming congruent, operating from our true selves and creating the life and relationships of our dreams.

Barton T Foster CPC

Introduction

Without question, something has happened to the American male within the last hundred years. Whether some want to admit this or not, something *has* changed. Many men are not as sure of themselves and lack self-confidence. Although many men and women feel that something isn't right, they can't see clearly what is behind it or how to correct it.

Some see a conspiracy as a planned attack against men in general. Some blame the feminist movement, and still others blame a list of other things. But what does blame do? It is an attempt to justify where someone is, or what they have, or have not done.

Someone might say that it's the war between the sexes, and the women have gotten the upper hand. The challenge with that line is, the war between the sexes has been going on for thousands of years, and women have, in many ways, always had the upper hand on men. Think about it, women have always played men, they just let the men think it was his idea all along. So, what is new?

This book is not about pointing a finger and placing blame. In order to discover what has happened, we must first go backward and explore what has changed so we can understand how those changes have affected men and women.

The elements or forces that we are going to be examining in this book are at work all the time. They don't take holidays and they don't sleep in on Saturday. It doesn't matter whether someone believes in them or not. Like gravity, they are invisible, and like gravity, you can ignore it if you want, but watch your step, because sooner or later you will be picking yourself off the floor, wondering what happened.

These forces do not respect cultural, ethnic boundaries, or language barriers. What we are going to explore is at work in the lives of men as well as women.

What we are looking at is not a war between the sexes, but a very complex system of intertwining aspects that exist within each person. As the roles of men and women have shifted, the side-effects of the shifts have been felt, but because these side effects have not been seen clearly, people have not been able to address their new challenges directly. As a result men and women have been fighting the symptoms and each other, rather than the cause of their problems.

Men and women have always had challenges that each have faced throughout history. History teaches that mankind is known to swing like the pendulum of a clock, from one extreme to the other. My goal with this book is to help people understand how they can achieve a balance in their life.

Although the title of this book is the Neutering of the American Male, many men and women throughout the world are dealing with the same challenges that are addressed within these pages.

Note from the Author

When I was a young man of eighteen I asked my grandfather if he ever wondered who he was when he was my age. I was quite taken back by his response. "Wonder who I was? Why, I've never heard of such a silly question! Of course I knew who I was! We all knew who we were. What do you mean you're not sure of who you are?"

To be honest, I really felt stupid for asking him that question, and wished I had not been so open. But what came out of the conversation was a series of questions that have taken me on a journey that has led me to some wonderful, and at the same time, sobering discoveries.

For many years of my life, I worked to be the man I knew I should be, but regardless of how hard or what I tried, it seemed as though I lacked something. I, like millions of others, felt like I was beating my head against a wall when it came to making changes in my life. I longed to be the man, the husband and father that my wife and children need me to be.

There is nothing more discouraging than to work to make real changes in your life, simply to do the very thing you no longer wanted to do and end up back where you started.

What is contained within these pages has changed my life. I wish someone had taken me aside and taught me these concepts when I was younger. My life would have been totally different.

There is one element of life that is recognized by many but is not addressed within this book. That element is the spiritual. Most people believe there is a God, but differ greatly on their beliefs about God. Personally I am a Christian. If you would like to know more about Christianity there is a link on my web site. The elements that are examined within these pages are just like gravity in that they affect those who believe in God as well as those who do not.

As you read this book, you will discover keys that you can use to set yourself free from things that have held you back in the past. When a person does not understand what is happening in their life, they are powerless to make the changes they desire. But, when they understand what has been happening in their life, they can begin making real and lasting changes. Wherever you are when you pick this book up, is where you are. It is also where you begin the rest of your life.

Acknowledgements

There are many people who have come into my life who have helped me learn and grow personally as well as intellectually. As I think about how this book came into being, there are several people who have had an impact. Of all the people I have met, Collynn Pearl was the first to encourage me to see life differently than I had learned growing up. If it had not been for her thought provoking questions and her encouragement, I would not have begun a journey that has led to a new life for myself. Thanks, Collynn.

Many years ago, I met a young lady from Minnesota at a seminar. She mentioned that her husband was a worrier. As she and I talked, she commented, "It doesn't make sense. Why would anyone worry?" Reflecting on our short conversation over the years has produced many questions, which have led down an interesting path of discovery, some of which is in this book.

Mandy Pratt was the first person to really encourage me to write about what I was learning. Thank you also to Duncan Long our illustrator, Dineen Miller for designing our cover, and Robert Pierce for his generous assistance in the areas of formatting, publishing and marketing.

I would like to thank my friends who were patient with me as I asked questions that seemed to be out of this world. A special thanks to Joanne Sher and Donna Gerth who have done a great job editing. Above all, I would like to thank my wife, Patty, who continually encouraged me as she waded through my rough drafts and continues putting up with me after all these years.

I would like to thank my children for their patience and for what they have taught me, their father. One of the greatest educations a person can get is from being a parent. Alex, Abigail, Esther, Ivan, and Isaac, I love you and I am exceedingly proud of each of you.

A special thank you to Dudley and JoAnn Sargent, and to my father and mother who always did the best they could with what they had, and were the best parents they knew how to be. I love you and always will. Thank you all.

Disclaimer

No real names have been used. As with all books, this contains opinions and ideas of the author. It is intended to provide helpful and informative material on the subjects which are addressed within this publication. It is sold with the understanding that the author and publisher are not engaged in rendering medical, health, psychological, or any other kind of personal, professional service or therapy in this book. The reader should consult his or her medical health, psychological or other competent professional before adopting any of the concepts in this book or drawing references from it.

The content of this book by its very nature is very general. Where each readers situation is unique therefore as with all books of this nature the purpose is to provide general information rather than to address individual situations which books by their very nature cannot do.

The author and publisher specifically disclaim all responsibility for any liability, loss, or risk, personal or otherwise, which is incurred as a consequence, directly or indirectly, of the use and application of any of the contents in this book.

Change as Never Before

Have A Large Number of American Men been Neutered, As the Title of this Book Implies?

If so, how? It is obvious that, physically, men are still male and women are still female. So what is different?

Change comes in all forms; it can be physical or intellectual in nature. Change can be abrupt and alter the world in an instant or it can happen so slowly that it is unnoticed until one day everyone wonders what happened.

Technology has changed our world forever. The world is a different place than it was a hundred years ago. The roles of men and women have become blurred beyond recognition during that time. People of today have been affected by many of those changes in ways they have not seen or understood, but they have felt the changes all the same.

If we were to look back in history and examine how men and women related to each other, we would find that for thousands of years, their interactions were pretty much the same. Basically, the man was the provider for his family while the woman took care of their children at home.

If people disagreed with these roles, it did not necessarily mean they could break free of them. For thousands of years, physical limitations dictated roles to both men and women. As technology eliminated many of the physical boundaries that had limited women, they began to take on new roles.

Change, when it happens, can be far reaching. For example, in the process of manufacturing new technologies, by-products have been produced that have had devastating long-term effects on people in those areas. In some cases water tables have been polluted and people have suffered, not realizing that they were consistently poisoning themselves every time they took a drink of water.

Is Change Bad?

That depends on the change and which side of the fence you are on. With change comes the unknown. It is easier to see physical by-products of a new technological advancement. The psychological by-products, however, are more challenging to see because psychological by-products take much longer to come about and are not seen clearly.

History has never before seen the technological advances that have taken place in the last hundred years. The up front changes that technology has created have been obvious as the individual advancements have been incorporated into our lives.

The after-effects or by products of technological changes are not always seen clearly because they sometimes take generations to come to the surface. Unfortunately once the by-products have surfaced, they don't hold up a sign declaring what has brought them into existence or how to correct them.

It is much easier to see how changes affect the environment and how animals react to each other, but it is another thing to see how technological advances have affected how people relate to, and interrelate with, each other over a hundred years of great technological advancements.

Let's consider some of the changes that have taken place and their by-products in how people relate to each other.

For thousands of years the world remained essentially unchanged. People were farmers, herdsmen and tradesmen. Each generation did basically what their parents and grandparents did.

After all, there wasn't much to change. The discovery of copper was the first of many changes that would alter the world for ever.

Since the discovery of copper, technology has been shifting the balance of power. Those who had the technology replaced those who did not. Each time there was a new breakthrough in metals--copper, bronze and then iron--it resulted in power shifting from one group of people to another.

The technological advances that were experienced in metals were hundreds of years apart, but when they did happen, it did not take long for the groups who had the new technology to incorporate it into their armies, thus shifting the power equation between nations.

Gun Powder Changed The World Forever

Aside from how metals affected international relations, one of the most significant discoveries was that of gunpowder. This new weapon brought an end to the knights and kingdoms that had lasted for hundreds of years. This discovery, plus the invention of guns, brought power into the hands of the people who possessed them.

Later, steam engines provided the power that made possible labor saving inventions that had been only dreamed about in the past. Discovery after discovery changed the lives of people. Gas and diesel engines replaced steam, making smaller engines possible. Edison invented the electric light bulb and Bell the telephone. The technological changes that once altered only how nations related to each other, were now touching the common person's life.

One man with the use of tractors and other labor saving inventions could do more than twenty men could in the past. These new labor saving inventions were not confined to work life; many new discoveries were directed at making work in the home easier also.

The Depression hit the United States and put a hold on growth and technological advancements. The country worked to regroup and dig its way out of the Depression.

When the United States was forced into World War II, it was far behind in its military readiness due to its naval losses at Pearl Harbor and the fact that its enemies had been gearing up for war for almost ten years before it began. If you were to judge the outcome of the war based on the superior technology and number of weapons that were represented on each side at the beginning of the war, the United States would have been declared lost and without hope.

Life was changing not only for the men who were getting shipped out to fight, but also for those who remained here in the States. All pitched in doing what they could, from recycling metal to buying war bonds. Legions of women took to the factories to support the men they loved and wanted home with them. Women exchanged their aprons and petticoats for drills, rivet hammers, torches and welding equipment. Dresses and skirts were replaced with slacks and work clothes. Today that doesn't sound like much of a change, but back then it was a major shift. Some women found themselves wearing pants for the first time in their lives.

There were not enough workers to build the needed supplies. The largest relocation in history took place during World War II. Including military personnel, over 25 million people were mobilized and moved during the war. Many of the factories that were building the military hardware were confined to certain areas. Some towns' populations were increased by 500-600% almost overnight. One town had its population increase by 400%, and 80% of the new workers moving in were women working in the plant.

Rosie the Riveter made her debut. In reality, there were millions of Rosies: women who set their aprons aside and took up war time jobs. Without the monumental efforts expended by these millions of women, the United States would have lost the war. World War II was won on two fronts: at home in the manufacturing plants and on the battlefields.

Women who were not accustomed to the idea of going to work in a factory made the change. Many were not welcome by those already in the factories. Supervisors, as well as men working in the plants, were against having women working with them. But there was no choice. The women proved themselves to be not only able, but proved that they could do as well as, or in some cases a better job than, some of the men who had worked there for some time.

When their husbands left for the war, the women had to take care of their families and work at the same time. Rarely could a family live on what they received from the government. These women made decisions and were forced to stand up in the face of whatever they had to overcome in taking care of their families. The men, on the other hand, were told what to do. They were not faced with figuring out for themselves. You did as you were ordered.

Women for all Practical Purposes had to become Men

During World War II, while countries were fighting for their lives, and to keep Hitler from taking over the world, something was happening on a huge scale that had never happened before. Many women, like my grandmother, discovered new beliefs about themselves that were very different from what they believed in the past. They were no longer the same women they were before the war began. They knew, without doubt, that they could do what men did and do it well. This was a new identity for many women. They realized (some of them for the first time) that they were capable of doing whatever they set their minds to.

Once a person's mind has expanded, it cannot become less than it has grown to be. This is also true with identity. A great many women had discovered a new identity for themselves that had them on equal terms with the men whom they had replaced during those war years. This equality was only from the women's perspective. The men had not realized that life, and the women they left behind, were no longer the same. The world and the people in it had changed, and many were unaware of the changes that had taken place.

It would have been nice if the war had been over when the war ended, but in some ways it wasn't. There were many adjustments ahead for everyone. Many women found themselves without jobs when the men came back. For some, that was fine. They went back to their families and worked to piece their lives back together again. Others found going back to their old roles very difficult.

Couples, when apart for long periods of time, typically dream about and fantasize of the time when they will be reunited. These fantasies are often exaggerated to the point that their lover is the image of perfection, resulting in reunions that frequently produced shock to both parties. Not only were they not how they were remembered, they had changed, which added to the confusion and frustration.

Husbands and wives came face to face and realized that each of them had changed a great deal. Fathers wanted love and acceptance from their children, only to be greeted by distance. Coupled with the after effects of the war, families were torn apart, not because of distance in miles but rather by fear and misunderstandings.

Some men imposed the same discipline on their families they had in the military, while others wanted nothing to do with discipline. Many men were scared to death of sudden loud noises. I remember hearing stories of how my grandparents always left the city where they lived for the Fourth of July so my grandfather would not have to deal with the firecrackers.

Men came home wanting to be the hero, and they discovered that was not the case. Yes, everyone was glad they were home, but things were different. Many of the soldiers didn't fit in and, for some, it took a long time before they were comfortable again. Recovering from the war was a slow process for many of the soldiers and their families.

Add together all of the adjustments that needed to be worked through, and couples were faced with many challenges that had to be overcome. Everyone did the best they could with what they knew at the time. We all owe a debt of gratitude to all those who served in the military and the men and women who worked in the defense plants during World War II. America would not exist as we know it today had they not done what they did.

While some women were quite content to return to their homes and resume the role that they'd had before the war began, for others things on the surface did not seem quite right. It was at this time that many more women started fighting for equal rights. Many women were outraged that they were being displaced and "put down by those men." Why would some be outraged and some be happy to return to what they had done in the past? This too shall be addressed in later chapters.

While the soldiers were fighting for their lives and their country, in the United States a shift in power was beginning to take place between men and women, the scale of which had never happened in history.

During the war, women were faced with doing things they had never done before. They had to stretch themselves and stretch they did. With many of the men gone, women had no choice but to step up and fill roles that were once only filled by men.

As technological advances were made in the medical field, the age-old concern of women turning up pregnant was no longer such a major issue. The pill, as it has come to be known, made it so women need not worry about getting pregnant. In the sixties, equal rights legislation was passed and the word sex was included just before the bill was passed into law. This new law, coupled with the medical advances, removed many final barriers that had held women back.

It is not the point or desire of this book to debate these issues. They are a part of our history and both men and women have been affected directly or indirectly by the many changes that have happened.

Men Need to be More Understanding

I was born in the sixties, so I did not experience the college demonstrations that took place, but I have seen and talked with many who were there during that time. I grew up hearing about the generation gap. With each new generation that comes along there is something new that they latch onto that sets them apart from the rest of the people.

One of the loudest themes I heard being shouted while I was growing up was that men needed to be more understanding; that a woman wants a man who will talk with her about his feelings. Women can, and do, talk about their feelings; why won't a man?

As I listened to that it made sense and didn't sound out of reason. I wasn't alone: many other men listened to what the women were saying and a lot of young men conformed to the women's requests.

Over time something happened. A lot of women didn't like it when a man talked about his fears or his insecurities. Men have always had fears and insecurities at times. It had always been something that guys simply didn't discuss freely with others. Many couples found themselves unhappy without knowing why.

The roles of men and women have become blurred and the distinctions that once existed are all but gone. The only place for people to get their understanding of what it is to be a man or woman anymore is by the people around them and what they see on television.

There are books out titled "Why Men Love Bitches" and "Why Men Marry Bitches." The subtitles of these books are

"From Doormat to Dream Girl – a woman's guide to holding her own in a relationship." In her books the author, Sherry Argov, promotes women taking charge in the relationship and in a (kind way) putting the man in his place.

Both books are filled with tips on how to take charge and keep control of your relationship. According to Argov, women should set the tune of the relationship, determine when they get together, and what a woman will do and won't do.

Without doubt, it is not healthy or right for either a man or a woman to let someone walk all over them. Some of you reading this may be saying 'Go Sherry,' while others might be thinking, 'Gee, I don't want a man who lets me boss him around.'

Whether a woman wants a strong man or an understanding one, that one thing is what matters to her. But what makes a man understanding or strong, and is it possible for a man to be both strong and understanding?

Men, do you find yourself being drawn to a woman who takes charge or to one that wants you to lead in the relationship? Do you understand why you are drawn to a certain type of woman? I know with one couple I worked with, the husband told me "I have always been attracted to women who are stronger than myself."

So what has happened that men are attracted to strong women, as this gentleman and Sherry Argov attest? That is one of the things that we will explore throughout this book. But, it is important to understand a distinction that is sometimes overlooked. There is a big difference between when a man is attracted to a woman who is feminine and confident in who she is, and when a man is attracted to a woman because he has learned to look to women for strength and leadership.

The Industrial Revolution Removed Fathers from Their Families

There are many changes that have taken place in how children are raised. One of them, and the earliest, is when fathers went to work in factories. As a result, fathers were unable to spend time with their families. This sort of thing has happened regarding a small percentage of people for as long as there have been ships and hunting parties. But prior to the Industrial Revolution the fathers would be gone part of the time and then would be home for periods of time.

When the Industrial Revolution came about, men went to work and spent all their work time away from their family while the wife took care of their children. One major change was that the son could not go to work with his father when he became old enough. He had to remain at home with his mother, and then would go to school.

Children were an Asset

Prior to this, father/son and mother/daughter teams would often work together when the children weren't in school. This was a great help to the parents and to the children as well. The children learned about life and how to do just about anything that needed to be done. Most of Americans lived on farms and life was simpler then.

Sons use to look to their fathers for instruction and teaching in every area of life. Much of the time working together was spent in conversation about every subject you could imagine. Not only did a son and daughter learn about how to do different chores that needed to be done, they learned about life and what it was to be a father and a mother from working with their parents.

A son learned that, as a father, it would be his place to teach his sons about life and about being a man. This is the way it had been for thousands of years. Sons learned what it was to be a man from their fathers. A hundred years ago teenage boys had a better understanding of what it was to be a man than most men today because it was spelled out and explained to them by their fathers.

When things fell apart they knew they could figure something out: after all, they had been through similar things with their father. Dads would teach their sons about business, making deals, how to read people and what to watch out for. Fathers would teach their sons how to plan and make their dreams a reality.

This all happened one on one in a true mentoring relationship. It gave young men starting out an advantage. They not only had more experience, they had confidence, and that is a major asset. They knew who they were and what they wanted to do, and proceeded to do just that.

When the Industrial Revolution began, it created a crack in the mentoring process. With each successive generation the crack widened a little more and, for the most part, went unnoticed by many of that day.

WWII Changed the World Forever

When World War II came into the picture, roles were altered: women had their identity stretched, and they embraced new roles. When the men came back from the war, they took back their places, pushing out the women who filled those spots during the war.

The traditional roles of men and women would never be quite the same again. Women had learned that they could do more than they ever had thought they could do. Many of these women started to rally and voice their feelings about what they saw as unfairness. Politicians learned that women could vote them in and out of office, and so the politicians started listening to them.

When families lived on the farm, children were an asset, but urbanization changed that since there weren't as many things for children to do. On a farm, children helped out with the chores and learned to do things for themselves that were a big help to their parents. In the cities, children could not just go to work with their father. Slowly the perspective of children being an asset shifted to children as a financial liability.

The separation of fathers from their sons was, and is, a very big thing even today. If you question this, find a man who did not get to know his father and ask him if he wishes that were different. The majority will answer yes: they wish they had gotten to know their dads.

There are many contributing factors that play a part in each of our lives. To look at any one and ignore the others would result in confusion and frustration for all involved. So I shall start with the basics first.

We have only to glance at technological advances to see how they have had an impact on people on the outside. As we continue, we will explore how technology and the shift in roles have impacted couples, families, and individuals.

There is no escaping the fact that technology has changed our lives in numerous ways. Throughout history, men and women each had certain roles and those roles were more or less dictated by the physical make-up of men and women. For instance, only recently, as in the last fifty to sixty years, has a man been able to feed a baby. For thousands of years that was not possible. It is not that anyone chose to set it up that way, it just was.

Whether a woman has ever thought of it, or believes it, a man has a desire to be a hero to the woman he loves. That is important to him. It is hard to do well and to impress the one you love when you are not sure what it is you are supposed to be doing, and you find yourself questioning your own abilities.

Some women I have talked with have said, "I just don't get it. Why do you men have to be the hero anyway? What is the big deal?" These women are telling the truth: they don't get it. But the nice thing is that men and women don't have to totally understand the opposite sex to have a great relationship together.

A man use to be able to be the hero for the woman he loved because he did what she could not do for herself. She would smile and truly appreciate what he had done. There is nothing more beautiful on a woman than a smile. But in the times in which we live, there is not much a man can do that a woman cannot.

Fathers use to pass on to their sons wisdom of what it is to be a man; that has not been happening for generations and generations. Added to that, the lines between men's and women's roles have been blurred beyond recognition. Boys physically grow into men and don't feel as though they have grown up yet. Part of them wants to be strong and bold, and another part is fearful and unsure of what to do or how to do it. Most men don't know how to relate to women because of the blurred lines between men's and women's roles.

There are certain approaches to life that are inherent to men that are foreign to women and vice-versa. We look at each other and say, "You've got to be kidding." This is nothing new. It has always been that way.

Most babysitters are female. From the time a boy is born until he is out of school, he has had women telling him what to do for the majority of his first eighteen years of life. Think about it: boys sit in school being taught by female teachers for most, if not all, of their days in school. This is not meant as a judgment toward the women teaching; far be it. But consider this: when a boy sits under a male teacher, that boy can envision himself becoming the teacher. When a boy sits under a female teacher, at the unconscious level there is a link made that women are teachers. It is more difficult for a boy to envision himself becoming the teacher when he grows up.

Technological advances have made our lives so much easier in many ways, but these advances have slowly removed the ways through which a man is able to be the hero and knight in shining armor to the woman he loves.

Electricity is one of the wonders of life and it has made our lives so easy. For men it has made life easier and, at the same time, more complicated. Because of electricity, a woman can, with the use of machinery, do anything a man can do. The ways for a man to distinguish himself have disappeared a little more with each new technological development. I have even heard some women say, “Men. Who needs them? We have sperm banks!”

There are some things about being a man that women just will not understand. A lot of men will not compete with a woman. It is not manly. Besides, if he gets beat, there is no worse thing. So as a result, he lets her do her thing and he does his thing.

Many women have found themselves carrying the leadership role and many are tired of it. I was working with an Australian couple. The woman said she was tired of being the man, and it was about time for him to take the role of leader. As it turned out, he refused to even try. We will visit this couple later.

Another man told me, “You know, in my heart I have always known I was a number one man, but I just couldn’t get beyond the number two spot. I have spent my whole life in the number two spot, while a part of me longed to stand up and take the role I have always known I should have, I was torn and doubted that I could do it.”

Many men feel as if there is a part of them that is missing, that somehow they lack what it takes to be a man. In reality, nothing could be further from the truth, but on the inside it feels like something is missing. Finding that something is one reason for writing this book. This book is not just for men, it is for all people no matter their sex or nationality.

I have not written this book to point fingers, to make accusations, or place blame. Life is life. No one asked for the hand they were dealt. The problem is when you are not sure how to play the cards that life has dealt you.

Wherever you are, there you are! Don’t judge yourself if you are not where you want to be. You have the opportunity to start where you are and go forward.

As I mentioned earlier, I am going to cover many aspects that contribute to and are intertwined into who a person perceives himself to be. I realize that for many some of this information will be new. What I have learned and am including in this book has taken me over thirty years to learn. I count it a privilege to teach it to my children and to share it with you. My life has been totally turned around as a result of incorporating this knowledge into my life.

We will start where everyone starts, in a home with parents. This may sound odd, but to understand how we come to be who we are, we must examine what happens within us as we grow.

Gender Dynamics

What is it to be Masculine?
&
What is it to be Feminine?

Where do we get our understanding of what it is to be manly or womanly? Initially each of us get our understanding from the people who raise us. We adopt our model of what masculinity and femininity are from our parents.

I will give you a brief definition of "model," as we will be referring to it throughout this book. A model is comprised of a person's beliefs and their perceptions/understandings of the world around them. Here's an example: a person who has been bitten by a dog will have a different model (understanding/perception) of the world than a person who has only known friendly and lovable dogs all their life. One will not be fearful of a dog approaching, while the other could very well have an altogether different reaction to the sight of it. Same world, different model, different emotional realities.

Take a few minutes. In a journal or tablet write out your thoughts, views and beliefs on masculinity and femininity as you understand them at this moment and from where/who did you get those beliefs. There are no right or wrong answers for this exercise. It is simply for later reference.

What did you find? Did it surprise you? To write things out is to separate yourself from them slightly. It also helps to clarify your own thoughts and beliefs.

Within a relationship between a man and woman there are seemingly opposing forces that are constantly in motion. Thus the term "gender dynamics." At first glance it would seem very straightforward: men are masculine and women are feminine. If that were the case, life would be totally different from what we experience. In actuality men and women possess both masculine and feminine qualities. This knowledge may or may not be new to you. There is a great deal for us to consider within gender dynamics.

All men and women have what is referred to as a core nature. Boys and girls are born with a core nature that is naturally congruent with their sex. Boys have a masculine core and girls have a feminine core. If children are put into a room with all kinds of toys and things to play with and left to themselves, the boys always go to the blocks and trucks. They would be building things and making all kinds of noises while always trying to outdo the others. Girls, on the other hand, will go play with the dolls. Their focus is on relationships and communication rather than on accomplishments.

There are some who appear to have a core that is opposite their physical sex. A girl with a very strong personality temperament may be mislabeled as having a masculine core or a boy with a softer personality temperament is mislabeled as having a feminine core. A major force in how a person's masculinity or femininity is lived out before the world is their personality temperament. A person's personality temperament is going to have a major influence in how a person is perceived and understood or misunderstood. Many people are living incongruent to their core nature on a regular basis.

Families are the greatest initial influence regarding gender dynamics. Each of us was taught or caught our beliefs from our family. Children are in a constant state of learning, even when they are not officially sitting under a teacher. A child's parents are his/her greatest teachers. Children look to their parents to learn what it is to be an adult. They copy their parents more than parents would like. Since parents are the initial sources of a child's learning, this is where we shall begin.

To understand how the overall masculine and feminine roles play out and affect those involved, I have included a set of diagrams to illustrate the inner workings of masculine and feminine aspects of gender dynamics in relationships. On the next page is a diagram that represents a husband and wife who are congruent with their core nature.

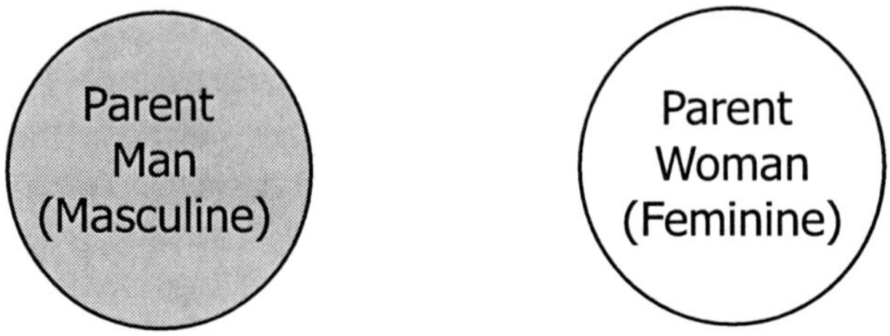

Their children will adopt the model that their parents live out before them as their own. The majority of learning that takes place at early ages is done through mimicking. When the parents are congruent with their core nature, it is picked up by their children who will in turn accept their parents' model as their own.

This diagram shows how being congruent with their own natural core is taught, if not consciously by the parents then by example, through how they live.

Magnets are a great analogy for how masculine/feminine energies work within gender dynamics. Magnets, like people, have two opposing energies within them. Magnets and people are attracted to opposite polarities.

When two of the same polarities come together there is a pushing away affect, instead of attracting each other.

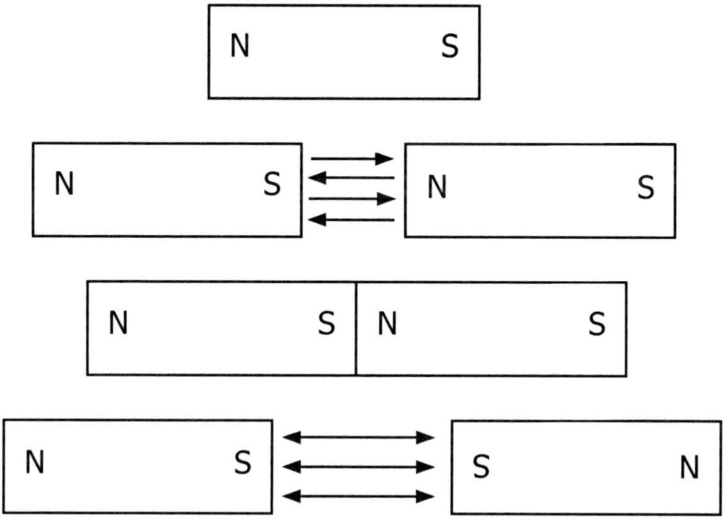

Just as with magnets, opposite energies (poles) are attracted to each other and two of the same energies (poles) push away from each other.

The same result plays out within gender dynamics: similar energies are repelled and opposites are attracted. The drawing below illustrates how the two opposing forces of masculinity and femininity are drawn to each other.

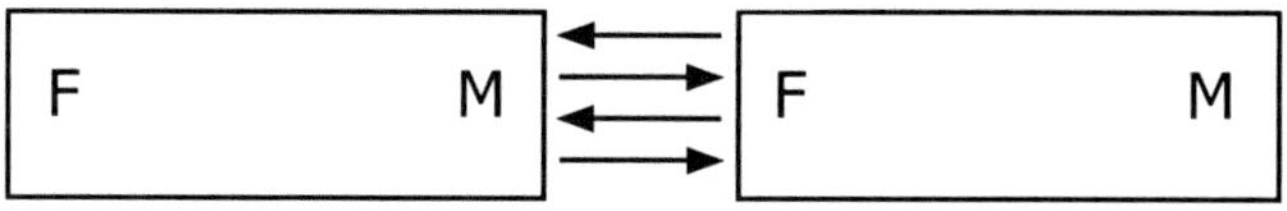

Depending on the home life and other elements a person experienced while growing up, they will either remain congruent with their core nature or they will adapt. In the drawing below, group "A" represents a man and woman who have grown up and remained congruent with their core nature. The larger letter represents the dominant energy while the underlined letter is their core nature.

Group "A"

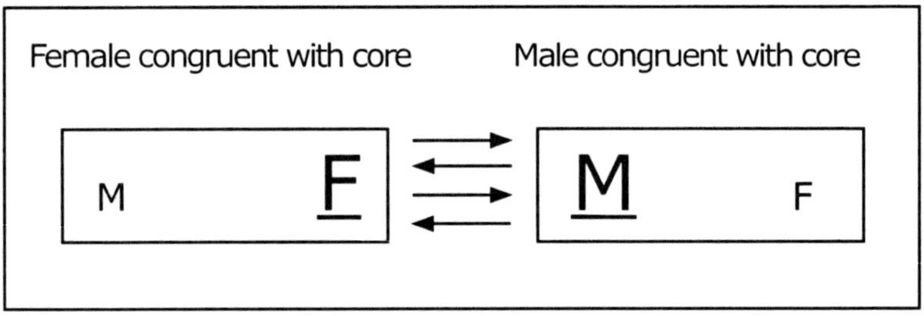

Group "B"

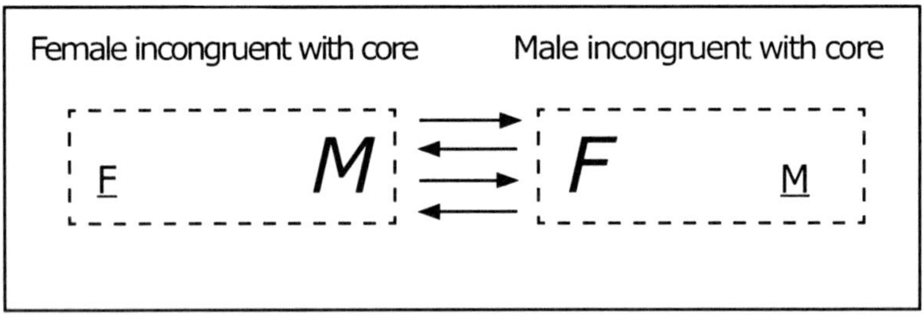

The group "B" drawing represents a couple who is incongruent with their core nature.

Masculine energy and feminine energy are attracted to each other irrespective of whether congruency or incongruency exists. If two of the same energy come near each other, they will push way from one another. But when two opposite energies come near each other, they will be drawn together through the attraction power of the complementary energies.

The man and woman in group A have adopted models which have kept them congruent with their core nature. The man and woman in group B have adopted models that have resulted in them becoming incongruent from their core nature.

Neither couple is better than the other, yet the congruent couple has many distinct advantages over the couple that is incongruent from their core.

When children are young, their feminine and masculine sides both exist. If left to themselves, they will gravitate to their core nature. Unfortunately, models that direct them toward incongruence are adopted instead of models that assist them in remaining congruent with their core nature.

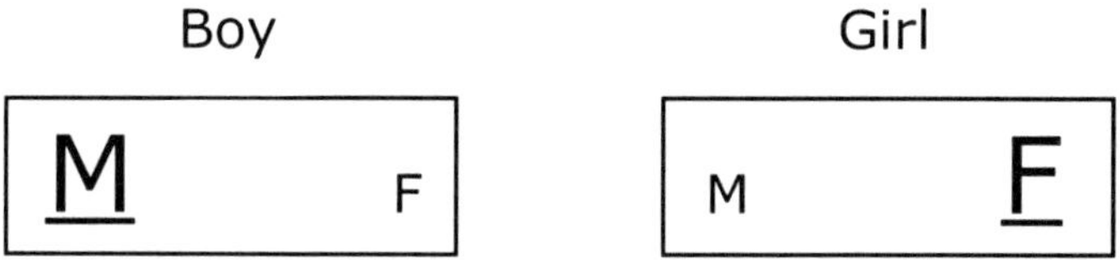

As children grow, they learn to adjust to the family environment in which they live. As mentioned earlier, children will look to their parents for information regarding what it is to be a man or woman. Children will mirror their parents. If both parents are congruent with their core natures, the children will follow their example. On the next page is a diagram representing a married couple where both members are incongruent with their core nature.

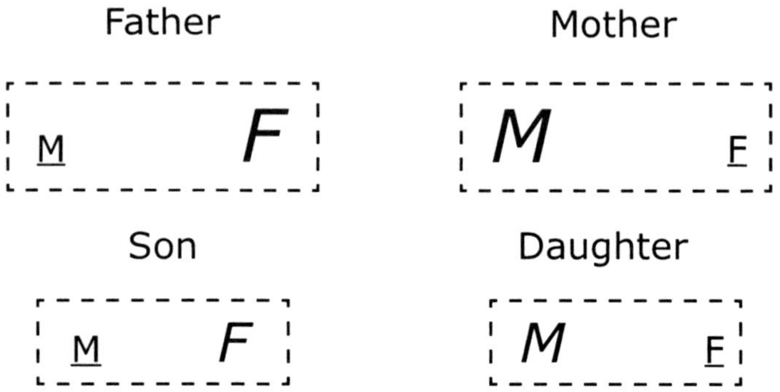

As this couple has children, the new generation will adapt their masculine/feminine energies to be accepted by their parents. Just as with the magnets, if the energies are of the same polarity, they will be pushed away from each other. In the family above, with the mother being the dominant masculine force, if the son does not want to get pushed away, he must adopt the complementary energy to the dominant mother. If the son does not adopt the complementary energy, there will be tension between him and his masculine mother. The daughter will follow the example of the mother and grow up incongruent to her feminine core.

It is important to understand that the bulk of what is going on happens at the unconscious level. It is often felt before it is understood. Every person has a need and a desire to not only be accepted, but also to receive love from their parents. This need for acceptance is important to children of all ages, and it works at the unconscious level coming to the surface as emotions.

The push and pull of masculine/feminine energy works at the unconscious level in children and adults as well. A man can be attracted to a beautiful woman and pursue her, but if they are both giving off the same energy there will be no attraction between the two of them other than a physical one. On the other hand, if they possess opposite energies, providing they have enough of the same interests and values, it is possible that they would choose to get married. This is often how people who work in proximity to each other find themselves drawn to each other.

If a man who is masculine meets an attractive woman who is also masculine, they may be physically attracted to each other at first, but they will find that the attraction soon disappears, because the masculine energies that they both possess will push them apart. Often these couples can't explain why the relationship didn't work: they just know it didn't.

On the other hand, if the woman is masculine and the man is feminine there are the correct ingredients for attraction between the two people. The fact that they are incongruent with their core nature does not take away from the attraction they feel toward each other.

* * *

In every home there has to be a leader. This leader is the dominant partner in the spousal relationship. The sex of the parent who is dominant will have far-reaching effects on the development of the entire family.

Remember our drawing earlier that represents a husband and wife who are congruent with their core natures.

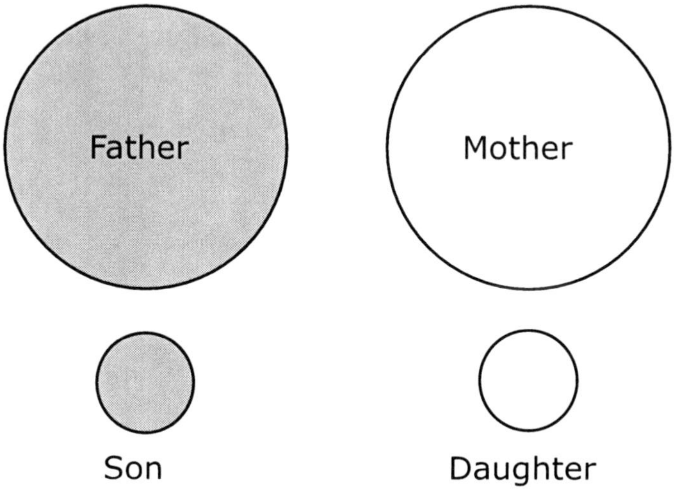

This shows how being congruent with their own natural core is taught. If not consciously by the parents, then by example through how they live. Because the son looks to the father as an example of what it is to be a man, the son will follow his father's example without question.

What happens when incongruence sets in as a result of upbringing? If two people meet who are incongruent with their core nature and they marry, it is not uncommon for them to remain incongruent: in other words, the woman is the leader of the family and the man is submissive.

Most people become stuck in an incongruent state as a result of copying the examples they had while growing up. There are other factors that contribute to a person remaining stuck in an incongruent state. We will go into these in greater detail later.

On the following page there is a drawing that shows what takes place within the gender dynamics of incongruent couples. This drawing shows four examples of couples with varying degrees of female dominance. Each of these couples will have different intensities of the same problems in their relationships.

The amount of overlap in the drawings represent the amount of support the man is receiving from the woman's leadership. As always the men have a masculine core and the women have a feminine core. They are living life incongruent with their core nature, so the women are the masculine force in the relationship.

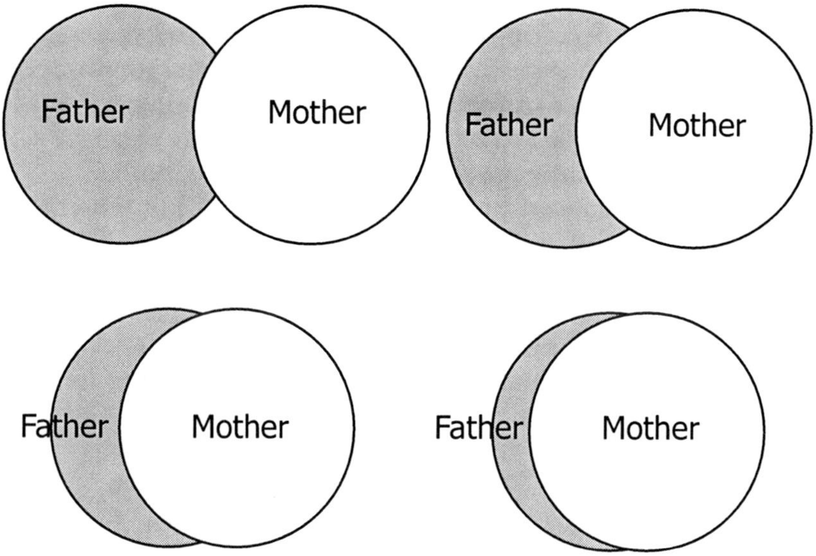

When a mother is dominant in a family, it changes the family dynamics dramatically. In the drawing above you see how the parents lived out their relationship. The son will learn his role as a man from his father. How his father relates to women is how the son will relate to women: he will look to women who are strong for leadership, and he will become feminine in his approach to life.

If this couple has a daughter, she will learn from her mother to take the dominant role and will assume the masculine role in her own life. Children who are raised in this home are trained to look to women for leadership and guidance. Because the woman was the dominant one of the parents, a son, through following the father's example, adapts the complementary feminine role.

The son grows up and adopts the feminine role model as his father did, and he, too, gets along with his mother and receives the love and acceptance that he needs and desires. (We will be exploring what drives this adaptation later.)

It is important to note that the mother doesn't just provide leadership and decision-making, but also an invisible external emotional support system. This external emotional support system is a by-product of incongruency and will influence much of the unexplainable attraction to members of the opposite sex who possess the same masculine qualities as the mother.

This may not seem to be a big deal at first, but when this male child gets out in the world and his mother is not there, the support that she provided for him is not there any longer either. This is depicted in a drawing shown below. The void is caused by the absence of the mother's leadership, decision-making, and emotional support that the child (who is now a man) has depended on in the past.

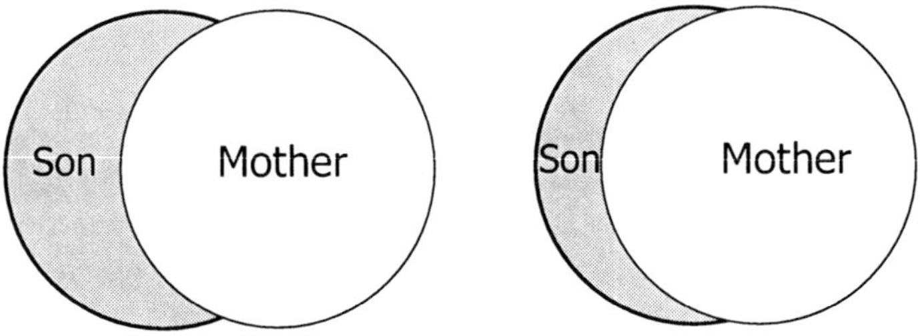

The circles above represent the effects of adaptation by a male child to a dominant mother. In each of the drawings, the amount of masculinity that is given up is in direct proportion to that of the dominant mother and passivity of the father. If the parents have a 70/30 split, with the mother being 70% dominant, the son will adapt to being only 30% on the masculine side. It is quite common for children to mirror their parent in this respect. Neither the children nor their parents have any idea of what is taking place in their lives.

In any family setting there is always a leader; there has to be for a home to function. This leader is looked up to for guidance, support and leadership. The void that is created when the dominant mother is not there is felt but often not understood. This void represents the absence of the support that was provided by the mother.

On the outside this invisible support is not seen. The first time I had an experience with someone who was in this position was approximately 30 years ago. At the time I didn't know how to explain what was taking place. But I have often reflected on what happened with a friend of mine.

Keith had a small construction company. He was doing okay: not great, but he was making ends meet. On the outside he seemed like everyone else. He was a likable guy who would do what he could to help people. I knew him for several years and then we went separate ways. About six months later his mother died. I had found this out approximately six months afterward. When I asked how Keith was doing, the answer was not good.

After his mother died, there was a time of grieving which everyone goes through, but Keith never seemed to come out of it. He was functioning at almost a survival mode. He couldn't make basic decisions, let alone major ones, for a long time.

It seemed as if he was on the edge of a breakdown. It took several years before he really recovered from the loss of his mother. I finally met up with Keith about four years after his mother died. We talked for a long time. He and his family had moved and was doing well by then. At the time none of us had any idea of what had happened with Keith.

Below is a drawing that shows what was going on for Keith at a level that other people could not see and Keith could not explain to himself or anyone else. When Keith's mother was alive, he was dependent on her for emotional support and leadership.

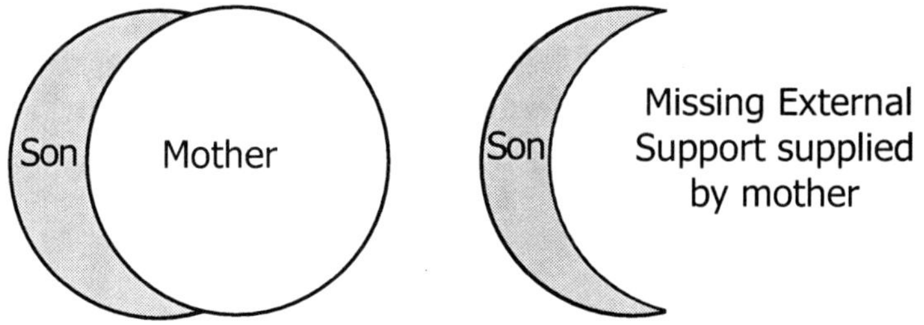

When Keith's mother died, the person whom he had leaned on literally his entire life was no longer there. I thought back on all the conversations we had during the time I was in contact with him. Not once did he mention his father. As it turned out, Keith had married a woman who was strong and leaned toward the masculine side until she had children. Then, after the children were born, Keith's wife returned to her core nature. This stopped her from filling the void that Keith's mother had filled when he was younger. Keith found himself trying to develop an internal masculine structure within himself while he was in his mid forties.

When a father is the dominant role model in a family, the male children see him as their model and will gain an understanding of what it is to be a man through their father's example. They will imitate the father's lifestyle, mannerisms, values and perspectives. As a father this is sobering, yet absolutely true.

A son can visualize himself becoming the leader if his father is the leader. Becoming a leader is part of the child's model of the world. If the mother is the leader, the son cannot see himself becoming the leader as clearly, if at all. The association is made that women are the leaders and men follow. When the mother is the leader (dominant parent), being the follower then becomes the son's model of the world.

Part of masculinity is conquering things. Why else would a boy climb some of the things that they climb? If you ask him why he climbed it, he will often say because it was there. This may seem strange to some, but consider how it can prepare a boy for life. The "IT"-- what ever it may be-- is an obstacle. A leader has many obstacles that must be overcome for victory to be won. This teaches ingenuity, tenacity, persistence, determination and confidence. These are real life experiences the child has to draw upon to inspire confidence and self-esteem.

In the diagram below, figure A represents a male who has been raised and is congruent with his core nature of masculinity. Figure B represents a man who has adopted a feminine role, incongruent with his core nature.

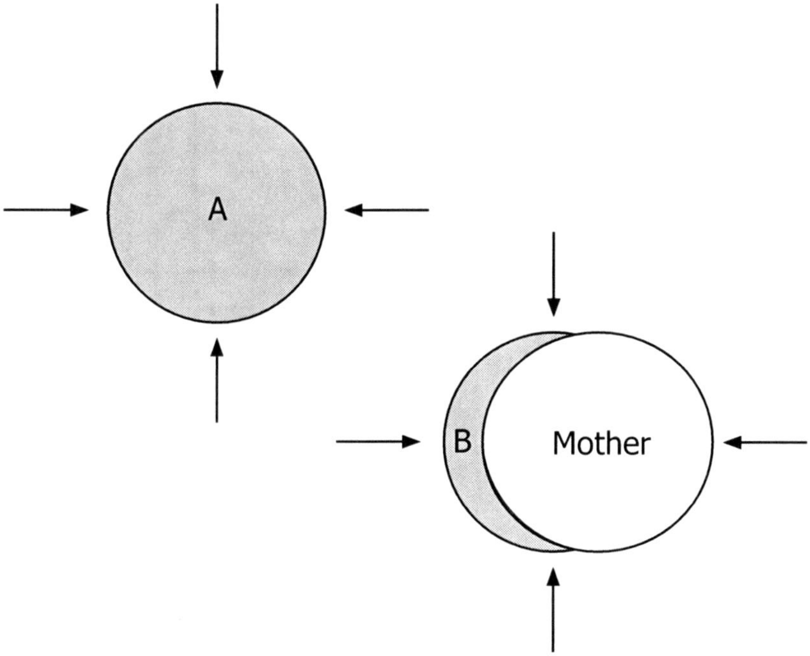

The arrows shown represent pressure that is common to life. When the pressure of life increases, person A, who is congruent with their core nature, will feel the pressure but will not be crushed or distorted by it. As long as person B has the external support they have become dependent on, they too, are able to withstand the pressure, but not as well as person A.

The diagram below shows what happens when the pressures of life are increased. Without the external support, person B is vulnerable. If the same pressure is applied to both A and B, A feels it and is able to deal with it, while B starts to cave in and is distorted under the same pressure that had very little effect on A.

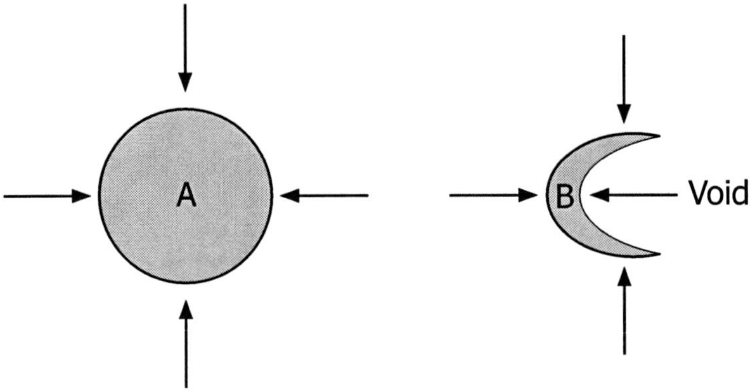

Keith was in the position of B. He did okay as long as his mother was there for support. Once his mother was gone, he felt the pressure as never before and he was emotionally being crushed under it (or so it felt). Keith's mother was not only his emotional support, but his confidence was in his mother. He never developed confidence in his own abilities and strengths. He had no history of making decisions without his mother. Then she was gone!

The man who is living his life incongruent to his core nature is represented by Figure "B." In a situation when normal pressures of life increase, it is more difficult for him to stand up under the pressure. Pressure that would not be a real problem for the congruent person can be devastating to the person who is incongruent with their core nature. This pressure at the emotional level can feel as though it is literally crushing and distorting the incongruent person who is experiencing it.

A boy who has been raised in a home where the woman was dominant will also be attracted to a strong woman as an adult. What happened to Keith? If what is stated is correct, Keith should have been attracted to a strong woman who would be able to support him.

Keith was attracted to and did marry a very strong woman. She did complement him and they made a wonderful team together. So, what happened? When Keith's wife started having children she went back to her feminine energy, which resulted in her becoming congruent with her core nature. Her focus went to nurturing and caring for their children. She actually became congruent with her core nature and loved it. Keith found himself in a bind. His wife was no longer the pillar of strength he married and he found himself leaning on his mother after all those years. When she passed away, he didn't know what to do or which way to turn.

Typically the man who is in this position has no idea what is happening to him. He feels stressed, he has very little self-confidence, and he looks to someone for help. The emotional turmoil that he is experiencing, compounded by the fact that he has no idea of what is going on, only continues the erosion of his self confidence and esteem. If something doesn't happen to halt the process that has already begun, his identity will shift, leaving him more certain of his inability to cope and to advance himself.

How does this affect him? Initially, you would not be able to distinguish him from any other man. Depending on personality temperament, the incongruence would manifest itself in totally different ways from one man to the next.

One of the many strong points this man has in his favor is that he is more in touch with his feelings. Unfortunately when a man is incongruent, he will find himself being emotionally pulled in two opposing directions. Part of him will know what he should do and want to do it, but another part of him senses that he is lacking in some way. Rarely does a man in this position realize what is happening and address the root of his problems, but rather addresses the symptoms that are visible on the surface. The intellectual and emotional tug-of-war that takes place within him causes emotions that are extremely confusing, which create even more self-doubt and the continued erosion of his self-confidence.

He can be tender and relationships are important to him, sometimes overly important. As a result he is easily hurt in relationships. He tries to be understanding and will go to great lengths to make a relationship work. Because he feels he needs others to guide him, he will not do some of what he needs to do to make the progress that he needs to make. He has abilities that he doesn't know exist because they are outside his model of the world.

Although this book is focused on men, it is impossible to get a good understanding of what has happened to men if we don't at the same time examine, if only briefly, what has been happening to women as well. What affects one sex affects the other.

A majority of women have been shifted into their masculine side as a result of many of the factors we covered earlier. Just as men suffer when they are incongruent with their core nature, so do women. As with men, personality temperaments will have a large influence in how much discomfort a woman will experience.

It is possible for a woman to be dependent on someone else for external support, just as Keith was. ***Both sexes need to achieve a level of independence from others in order to function in a balanced and healthy way. Without a healthy balance, men and women will live a more turbulent emotional life.*** It is possible for men to become congruent with their core nature and be able to access their softer emotions without becoming incongruent.

PERSONALITY

TEMPERAMENT

Personality Temperaments

What are they and where did they come from?

What do they have to do with you and me?

After much observation, Hippocrates (460-370 B.C.) concluded that there were four basic and distinct personality temperaments. The names he gave the four temperaments are the Sanguine, Choleric, Melancholy, and the Phlegmatic. There are many who have given different names to these same four categories, but I wanted to honor the man who originally thought of them and continue using the names he selected. Over the years new distinctions have been made, yet his four groups have held up and have not been improved upon or found faulty for thousands of years.

No one person is strictly one personality temperament, but rather a blend of at least two, if not more, of the four temperaments. Each of the four temperaments are great in their own right, containing both strong and weak points. We all like the idea of strengths, but we need to remember that any strength that is over done becomes a weakness.

Any weakness is an Opportunity for Growth in that Area

As you read through the different types, you will begin to discover aspects from some of them that fit you. The one that fits you the most will be your primary temperament and the next one in line will naturally be your secondary temperament. Keep an open mind as to how your blend of temperaments can be for your benefit.

At first, when I found out what my primary and secondary temperaments were, I was convinced that I had been dealt a bad hand. Don't do that to yourself. I now see the benefits that I have because of the blend of my temperaments. Another personal note is that as my wife and I were going over our temperaments, I was amazed. It gave me a much clearer understanding of why my wife did some of the things that she did. Several of the things I found to be very annoying. I thought she did them just to push my buttons, but I saw and understood that was not the case at all.

The four temperaments can be broken down into several groups. One set of groups would be the extroverts which are the Sanguine and Choleric, and the introverts which are Melancholy and the Phlegmatic.

Sanguine Extroverts	**Choleric** Extroverts
Melancholy Introverts	**Phlegmatic** Introverts

In another category the Choleric and Melancholy have internal frames of reference while the Phlegmatic and Sanguine have an external frame of reference.

Sanguine **External** Frame of Reference	**Phlegmatic** **External** Frame of Reference
Melancholy **Internal** Frame of Reference	**Choleric** **Internal** Frame of Reference

Although the four temperaments have both strengths and weaknesses, it is encouraging to know that your primary and secondary temperaments can actually have a balancing effect on each other. Some of the sharper edges of one temperament can be softened by the secondary temperament, just as some of the weak areas can be strengthened by the secondary temperament.

It is important to remember that once a weakness is discovered, it no longer has to remain a weakness. Each of us can, with persistence and determination, gain victory in areas where we once had difficulties. People are often misinformed about a weakness. This is often seen as something that is terrible or an area that they cannot master. On the contrary, unlike strengths that can be overdone and be devastating in their effects on others, weak areas can be strengthened to a point that they are no longer weaknesses, but rather are finely honed skills. When a person strengthens their weaknesses to the point they are strengths, the advantage is that what was a weakness and is now a strength is rarely, if ever, overdone to the point of doing harm to anyone.

SANGUINE

Strengths: Care-Free, Compassionate, Friendly, Personable, Warm, Enthusiastic, Outgoing and Talkative.

Weaknesses: Fearful, Exaggerates, Loud, Egocentric, Undependable, Restless, Undisciplined, Unstable, and Weak Willed.

The Sanguine man or woman loves to be in center light, they are the life of the party. As a super extrovert they are everyone's friend. They are just as comfortable talking with a total stranger as they are talking with an old friend. The Sanguine will give you their undivided attention as long as they are looking at you, but as soon as someone or something catches their attention then they are off. The Sanguine temperament loves to be around people and the more people the better. As you can probably guess, they detest solitude.

On the surface the Sanguine seems as confident as could be, but in reality they are insecure. The only temperament that is more emotional than the Sanguine is the Melancholy. This makes Sanguines susceptible to mood swings and angry outbursts. When a Sanguine gets angry, they typically will turn beet red and explode. Once he has blown up and gets it out of his system, he is his merry old self and your buddy once more, even if you are not feeling buddy-buddy yourself. Part of the Sanguine's moodiness can be attributed to their need for approval of others. Sanguines look to other people to find out if they are doing a good job. This puts them at a disadvantage in that they have a tendency to take people's comments personally. Sanguines tend to be disorganized and would rather "wing" something than sit down and plan it out in detail.

It is true that everyone has been given a dose of ego, but the Sanguine received a double dose, and his ego needs to be fed twice as much as the other temperaments. One of the most difficult challenges a Sanguine faces is the misuse of his ability to convince others to his way of thinking. If a Sanguine has a weak or flexible conscience he could easily slip down a path that he will later regret. Almost all of the world's greatest con-men have been Sanguines. Sanguines are known for touching people as they talk with them. This is comforting to some while aggravating to others. This tendency to touch can be misinterpreted by others as physical advances when it was not meant that way.

Sanguines can, and will, lead with enthusiasm as long as things are going well. But if things start going south, they will jump ship or gladly let someone else have the lead. After all, Sanguines love praise and glory, and they hate being shot at.

Sanguines have a double dose of the "externals." They are extroverts and they have an external frame of reference. This combination leaves the Sanguine more susceptible to the influence others. As extroverts, they love to be with others and to be accepted by others. Add that to their external frame of reference, and you have someone who, if they are not careful, will have a tendency to judge whether something is good to do from what others think about it rather than what they believe is correct. The Sanguine is more likely to go with the flow, rather than decide for themselves whether something is acceptable behavior. Many a Sanguine has found themselves in trouble, simply because they followed someone else's frame of reference.

MELANCHOLY

Strengths: Gifted, Analytical, Sensitive, Perfectionist, Aesthetic, Idealistic, Loyal, Self-Sacrificing.

Weaknesses: Self-Centered, Moody, Negative, Theoretical, Impractical, Unsociable, Critical, Revengeful, and Rigid.

Melancholy is one of the most creative, analytical, self sacrificing, and gifted of all the temperaments. They are rich in their abilities and are perfectionists with a sensitive emotional nature. This sensitive emotional nature paves the way for roller coaster rides on the Moody Express that will take the Melancholy to heights of ecstasy and then plummet them into gloom and depression. Melancholies are introverts by nature and prefer to let people come to him rather than going to them to make friends.

One of the Melancholy's greatest gifts is also one of their greatest challenges. They have a keen analytical mind that is difficult for them to turn off. They analyze everything. This gives them insights that many other temperaments miss, and at the same time, it can, if not controlled, cause them a great deal of turmoil.

Melancholies are not satisfied with simple self examination and reflection. Instead, Melancholies will dissect and analyze themselves until they have no self confidence or self esteem left. If Melancholies don't watch themselves, they will take the high standard they hold and will nit-pick themselves and everyone around them to death. If a Melancholy is not careful, he will focus on a few things that are not perfect and will be miserable. They will miss all the wonderful things that are going on and the people around them.

Melancholies enjoy the arts more than most of the temperaments. Melancholies enjoy the arts, and at the same time, they analyze them. The key is their focus and the meaning they give what they are looking at. This focus and meaning is a key area for every Melancholy to work on. The natural tendency of the Melancholy is to focus on what is not right according to their standards or expectations. This is the source of most, if not all, of the Melancholy's depression. It is critical that the Melancholy direct his or her focus in such a way as to encourage themselves rather than discourage themselves.

The Melancholy is more likely to marry when they are older. Mr. Melancholy forms a mental vision of an ideal wife. When he meets someone and finds himself caring for her, he then compares her to the ideal wife he has envisioned within his mind. Finding something wrong, he will either break up with her or continue to date her forever and hope that marriage never comes up. I know one Melancholy who wants to get married and has met many ladies who were good matches. But there was one thing wrong and that was the end of their relationship. Melancholy's are likely to develop cold feet for fear of making a wrong decision.

CHOLERIC

Strengths: Strong-Willed, Determined, Independent, Optimistic, Practical, Productive, Decisive, Leader, Confident, Courageous, and Self-Confident.

Weaknesses: Cold, Unsympathetic, Insensitive, Unemotional, Inconsiderate, Unforgiving, Domineering, Self-Sufficient, Sarcastic, Angry or Cruel, Opinionated, Prejudiced, and Proud.

The Choleric is decisive and determined, he easily sees the big picture and that is what he operates from. He does not enjoy details. To him, details only clutter things up. He is opinionated, bossy and loves activity--the more the better. He can have six to ten things going on all at once and be having a grand time. That is, as long as things are going well. People look at him and wonder how he keeps his sanity. The Choleric is not scared of challenges or adversity. In fact, he is often motivated by them.

Cholerics often succeed where others fail. Not because they are smarter or better than the next guy, but rather because he never gives up. He just keeps working and working toward his goals. It is not uncommon for a Choleric to see opportunities that others miss. Because Cholerics are so focused and determined to accomplish what they set out to do, they have a tendency to ride roughshod over people and do not hesitate to use people to get things done.

Most Cholerics have packed up their emotions in a shoe box and then misplaced the box. The one emotion that isn't in their shoe box is anger. That emotion stays right by their side. It is well oiled and is kept in good working order through frequent use. The Choleric can rip a person into shreds without batting an eye lash and wonder why people can be so emotional. The Choleric is an expert with sarcasm and can wound a person without being aware of just how obnoxious they have been toward someone.

The Choleric's greatest challenge is not from without, it is from within himself. His anger. Unlike the Sanguine who blows up and then is back to his normal jolly self, the Choleric can, and does, stay hot for a long time, some times for hours or even days. Cholerics are also capable of holding grudges but not as much as the Melancholy temperament. If a Choleric does not learn to get control of himself or herself it can cost them everything they hold dear.

It is not possible to control anger after it has erupted. That is the same as trying to stop a lighting bolt from hitting the ground or stopping water that has just broken through a dam. The way to deal with the anger is to deal with what is causing the emotion of anger. For the Choleric to succeed in dealing with his or her anger, they must focus on preventing the anger before it has a chance to explode. We will address the way to accomplish this in the section of "Models and Meanings."

Strengths That are Overdone Become Weaknesses

Phlegmatic

Strengths: Calm, Easy-Going, Dependable, Efficient, Conservative, Practical, Leader, Diplomat and Humorous.

Weaknesses: Stingy, Fearful, Indecisive, Spectator, Self-Protective, Selfish and Unmotivated.

A Phlegmatic will rarely confront a person or openly refuse to do something, but they will somehow manage to skirt around the issue they don't like or agree with. The Phlegmatic is more likely to stand there and agree with you and then walk away and ignore what you have said and what he agreed to. He simply will do it his way, as compared to some of the other temperaments who would be in your face while they are doing it their own way. Phlegmatics are more subtle and quiet in their approach. This is due to their desire to avoid confrontation. It is true that Phlegmatics want to avoid confrontation, but this is sometimes second to their stubbornness which is always creeping into the mix.

It is not uncommon for a Phlegmatic to marry a Choleric, opposites do attract and the Phlegmatics are about the only ones who can get along with the Choleric. Choleric's think that they have it easy, but they are in for a surprise. I wouldn't be surprised if the phrase "The irresistible force meets the immovable object" was first used to describe a Choleric - Phlegmatic marriage. This combination truly makes for an interesting marriage.

The Phlegmatic is diplomatically cool on the surface, but in reality he or she is usually fearful and indecisive. This is due to their desire to please everyone and not displease anyone. They want to avoid making waves at all costs, and this makes them prone to go with the flow regarding things that they would never agree to on their own.

Phlegmatics are, by their nature, very cautious and fearful of any kind of risk whether it be emotional, physical or financial in nature. It was probably a Phlegmatic who coined the phrase "a bird in hand is worth two in the bush." This tendency to be overly cautious can result in the Phlegmatics missing out on some wonderful opportunities that may come their way. This natural tendency to worry is a result of where they continually place their focus. As with each of the temperaments, our focus has far reaching effects on what we will or will not do.

Each of the different personality types have strengths that make it possible for a person to accomplish great things. It is important to remember that any strength that is over done becomes a weakness. This applies to all of the personality types and the blends that each of us is comprised of.

It is important to note that each person is not all of one personality type. Each of us is comprised of two to three of the personality types. Depending on the ratio of a person's primary and secondary temperaments, these descriptions will vary if a person has a different ratio. To give an example, a person may be 60/40 or 70/30 Choleric/Melancholy or any other ratio, there are no set percentages that people come in.

Whatever you have determined fits you, look at the strengths and weakness. Some of them will fit and some will not. Don't let that confuse you. Remember, some of the strengths of one will offset the weaknesses of the other.

Let's look at where the different personality temperaments place when comparing where their natural tendencies place them on a line between accomplishment orientation and relationship orientation. For the purpose of simplicity, this illustration is dealing with the different personality temperaments, and does not include temperament blends, models, incongruency or unmet needs which can move a person to a different position on the line.

Accomplishment Orientated			Relationship Orientated
* Choleric	* Melancholy	* Sanguine	* Phlegmatic

The Choleric can find themselves so far on the accomplishment side of the line that while they are pursuing an accomplishment they miss everything else around them. He or she is a force to be reckoned with and they make sure others know that they are to be in control. They are not concerned with how others feel. They are only concerned with what they want to accomplish and how you can help them. As a rule, Cholerics are more pointed to task accomplishment rather than relationships.

It is not that a Choleric does not care about people around them. Their focus is on what they are working to accomplish, and as a result, their relationships are secondary. The saying "out of sight, out of mind" summarizes the approach of a large number of Cholerics when it comes to relationships. Relationships are like the lights at home--they worked when I left this morning and they will be the same when I return after weeks of work, sports, conquering, vacation, whatever. Upon returning home, his understanding is that the lights and relationship will be burning just as brightly as when he left. A Choleric will often be surprised when there are difficulties in their relationships.

People often misunderstand weaknesses. They are thought to be a handicap and an area that they cannot master. Quite the contrary. Unlike strengths that can be overdone and be devastating in their effects on others, weak areas can be strengthened to a point that they are no longer weaknesses, but rather finely honed skills. When a person strengthens their weaknesses to the point they are strengths, the advantage is that what was a weakness and is now a strength, is rarely, if ever, overdone to the point of doing harm to anyone.

The diagram on the preceeding page represents where each individual temperament would be placed if they were not balanced with a secondary temperament. As you can tell, a person who is a Choleric-Sanguine would shift placement on this line dramatically. The fact that we each have a secondary temperament is a tremendous asset, in that it adds a whole new realm of talents and abilities that a person can access.

I once worked for a man who had adopted the model that you never compliment an employee. No matter how much they accomplish or how good a job was done, always find something that needed to be done better and point that out. He was being promoted and was training me to take his place. Can you guess what his primary personality temperament was? If you guessed Choleric, you're right on the money.

He was more focused on accomplishing a job than on relationships. This showed up at work and in his home life as well. People at work had to put up with him and so did his family, until they had enough. In both cases, as soon as people were able to get away from him, they did. The fifteen men who worked under him were thankful when he was gone, and they saw that I did not agree with his way of doing things. As soon as his children were able to move out on their own, they did. I remember him telling me how he didn't understand why they were acting the way they were toward him. "Look what I did for them!" he would say. "Don't they understand how much I love them?"

He missed the mark with his family and everyone who worked with him because he was only aiming at the target of accomplishments. He had never spent any amount of time focusing on his relationships with others and he simply never made relationships one of his priorities. When he did focus on his relationships with others, it was with the same approach he used in making some goal or project a reality. He was used to making things happen and that was how he approached everything and everyone.

Obviously, this man was strong in the area of accomplishments and weak in the area of relationships. He never made the connection that relationships cannot be approached the same way as a goal. Goals you make happen, relationships you allow to happen. Both goals and relationships require attention and focus. If you want a relationship to grow, it is helpful to do things that will encourage it to grow, but don't try to force it. The relationship must be allowed to grow.

Allowing a relationship to grow requires both strength and vulnerability. It means that you are not in control, yet you never lose control of yourself or what you believe in.

Once again this is not good or bad, it simply is.

Have you ever heard a person saying "That is just who I am?" For the person who is saying that statement, they are telling you the truth as they understand it. The problem is that they are deriving their identity from their behaviors. To understand this, consider the following scenario. What if a person who is normally honest tells a lie. Does that make them a liar? Some will say yes and some will say no.

Are they a person who told a lie, or are they now a liar? What you say will be determined by what you have been taught to believe. In reality, they told a lie, even if they told another lie, the lie is an event. If we start to see them as a liar, it will alter how we respond to them. If that person starts to believe they are now a liar, and embrace that as part of their identity, it will have far reaching ramifications. It is critical to make a distinction between a person's behavior and who they really are as an individual. This is a key distinction to make when you look in the mirror and are looking at yourself.

Two men who have different personality temperaments will experience different realities when congruent with their masculine core. The Choleric and the Phlegmatic are opposite each other and, as a result, are going to experience different worlds when they are congruent with their core nature. The reasons for this is that their personality temperaments are going to pull them in different directions.

CHOLERIC	PHLEGMATIC
1. Extroverts	1. Introverts
2. Internal Frame of Reference	2. External Frame of Reference
3. Confrontation No Problem	3. Confrontation BIG Problem
4. Very Opinionated	4. Very Agreeable
5. Wants to take Control	5. Does not want to be in Control
6. Makes Decisions Quickly & Easily	6. Prefers to pass on Decision making

As you can imagine, after reading through this comparison, these two men are going to live in different worlds. Even if they are in identical situations, they will each face different challenges that they will need to overcome if they are going to live a well balanced life.

The Choleric will find that getting in touch with his tender side may be a real stretch. The Choleric's internal frame of reference is a strength that is often overused and out of balance, resulting in their tendency to ignore what others think and/or feel.

I knew a Choleric whose wife was having some serious headaches. He refused to believe that she was experiencing pain. One day he and I were talking and he mentioned that his wife was lying to him about having headaches. I asked him what made him think she was lying to him. "Headaches are the biggest joke I have ever heard. I've never had a headache and I don't believe that anyone has headaches." I assured him that headaches are for real and that if he was fortunate enough to have never experienced a headache, he should be thankful. His response was "Are you serious?" It took several hours and four other people, whom he trusted, before he began to embrace the possibility that headaches existed.

This is a good example of how far out of balance a person's internal frame of reference can get. This man had never experienced a headache. False logic took over. The conclusion was that since he had never had one, they didn't exist. The information in our own conclusions is not evaluated as intensely as if someone else were to tell us the same thing. His understanding of the world did not include headaches because he had never experienced a headache.

For my friend, it took his wife and five other people whom he completely trusted before he accepted that headaches were for real. In reality, he accepted it as a possibility for a period of time before he actually accepted it as truth.

Typically, when a person's understanding of the world is challenged, and enough proof is offered, they may change their beliefs of the world. They accept the possibility that there might be something to what the others are saying. If this is the case, they will begin looking for evidence to validate this new possibility. If they find evidence that proves what has been stated is true, then they have what they need to change their model of the world. Years later, my friend had his first headache. He thought he was dying. He is now a believer--headaches are real.

The Phlegmatic, who may already be in touch with his tender side, will be stretched in the areas of making decisions and standing firmly behind his decisions. The reason this can be a stretch for the Phlegmatic is because of their strong desire to avoid confrontation. Someone may not agree with the decision and disagree with him, resulting in a confrontation.

The Phlegmatic is naturally an introvert with an external frame of reference causing them to second guess themselves about the decisions they make. It is always easier to do what others want from the beginning.

If you are having some challenges figuring out your personality temperament blend, we offer a personality temperament test through our website at www.TheNeuteringoftheAmericanMale.com

MODELS & MEANINGS

What do You Think of When You Hear the Word **Model?**

For many, the first thing that comes to mind is a miniature version of a real life thing. The quality of the miniature (model) can vary greatly. Some models look just like the real thing, down to the smallest detail. Some models are barely recognizable when they are compared to the real thing. Whether the model is of high quality and is an accurate representation of the real thing, or if the model is of poor quality and is distorted, they are both models nonetheless.

Galileo Was almost Burned at the stake for Embracing an Unaccepted Model in His day

What do you think would happen if someone had a model that was not the same as the real thing, but that model was the only thing they had to use as a reference to guide them? When they used the information they gathered from their model as a guide in real life, do you think they would run into some problems? People around them may be completely confounded by their actions and have no idea why that person is conducting themselves as they are.

We, as humans, develop models (our understandings) of the world in which we live. These models become our map or blueprint of our world. We live our lives according to the models we adopt. There are several good examples of this that are well known. One is Galileo's models that the earth revolved around the sun. He printed this in a book, and it would have cost him his life if he had not done some fast talking.

Everyone thought that Christopher Columbus was crazy for thinking that he could sail to India by going the opposite direction. After all, everyone knew that the world was flat, and if you sailed too far in the opposite direction, the ship and everyone on board would fall off the edge of the world and be lost forever.

A Person's Model is their Blueprint, or Map, that They use to Guide themselves Through Life

Christopher Columbus had noticed that when a ship was far away, all that was visible was the tops of their sails. When he was turning an orange that had a butterfly on it he noticed that as the orange revolved only the tops of the antenna were visible. As he turned the orange more, more of the butterfly became visible. This is when he considered the world was round.

Each of these men had a different model of the world than their contemporaries. History proved them right, and they are heroes in their own right.

Everyone knows that the world is round and that the earth revolves around the sun. These are proven facts. If you look at the lives of these men, their models of the world affected their behavior. If their model of the world was the same as everyone else's, they would have made different decisions and their actions would have been totally different. We would have never heard of them. Throughout the ages people have responded differently and sometimes with hostility toward people who have had different beliefs and models.

Each of us has our own models of the world. These models vary from one person to the next. The majority of a person's models of the world are taught by those who raise them. When a child starts out, they have no models and no point of reference through which to understand the world around them. Those who raise them will either intentionally, or unintentionally, lay before the child models that represent their understanding of the world and the many aspects of life according to how they see it.

There are different Kinds of Models

There are what I call umbrella models, and then there are more specific or sub-models. All models are made up of beliefs and thoughts. A model is never made up of just one belief, but rather all the beliefs you have on a particular subject. The models that are umbrella models will influence the models under them.

The beliefs a person has about a subject are going to affect their thoughts about that subject and, if it is an umbrella model, everything that is linked to the umbrella model will be flavored by the beliefs of that umbrella model.

A model that is under an umbrella model is not less important than the umbrella model. The sub-models deal with specific subjects in greater detail than an umbrella model would.

An umbrella model is general by its nature. Examples of umbrella models would be:

"Life is Great"
or
"Life is full of Hardships & Disappointments"

As you can tell, these two models are going to have an amazing impact on whoever embraces them. Umbrella models flavor a person's more specific models.

Consider how each of the umbrella models above would affect a person's life in the following specific/sub models that are listed below:

- Relationships
- Friends
- Work
- Relaxing
- Finding enjoyment

How do you think these two umbrella models would impact a person's life in those specific areas? The largest umbrella model that people have is about life. This model will flavor each of the models that they have under it.

Models consist of a person's beliefs and thoughts regarding that subject. Your model is your guide that will influence the meanings you give events, and, in turn, what will ultimately determine your actions. Your models will have a positive or negative leaning. The direction that your model leans will either encourage or discourage you. They will propel you forward, or chain you to where you are.

Consider two people who are born into poverty. Person A is taught that being poor is life and there is nothing much they can do about it. If they can get by, they are really doing something! Person B is taught that being poor is only temporary: that it is a stepping stone to better things. As Person B grows he continues hearing about and looking for opportunities to use as his stepping stones. Person A, on the other hand, is hearing that there are no opportunities and there is no way a person can get ahead. Person A often finds themselves fighting discouragement and depression, and he doesn't experience much enjoyment in life. On the other hand, B finds life to be exciting even when things don't go the way he wants.

A Person's Models & Beliefs will Affect the Quality of their Emotional life

Neither person A nor B has a history or point of reference to evaluate the models that are presented to them, so they accept what they are taught as reality. Person A believes that he will never be able to reach beyond poverty. Person B believes that poverty is only temporary. Even though he may be in poverty, his belief that poverty is only temporary will assist him in getting out it.

These two people have different models of the world in which they live. With this example, it is easy to see the difference on the surface. Person A is taught that being poor is a way of life and that there is no hope of getting ahead. There is no way a person can make it, without luck. "See those people? They are lucky and we are not." The beliefs that make up a person's model of the world are going to generate thoughts that are in line with their beliefs. Any thoughts that come along that are inconsistent with their model are rejected as irrelevant.

Person B believes that being poor is only temporary and is going to see a totally different world than Person A who believes that "being poor is life." They could physically live on the same block, yet they would see life as if they were actually living in different worlds. One will see opportunities that the other will not even notice.

A person's beliefs will encourage them to reach only as far as the edge of their model and no further. If a person reaches beyond their model, they are venturing out past what they believe is possible, and as a result of operating counter to their beliefs, they will sabotage themselves.

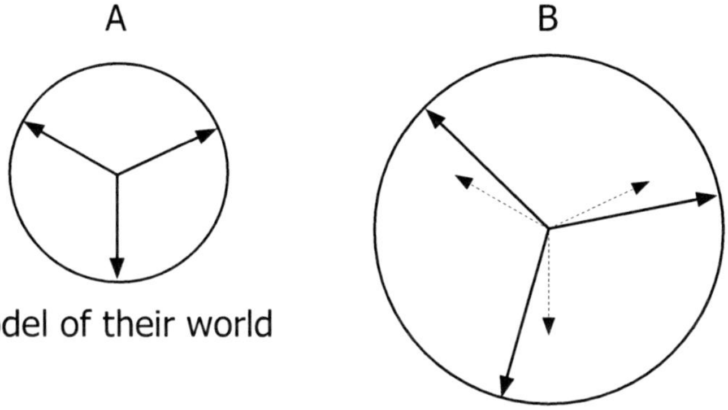

Model of their world

Expanded Model of their world

The drawing above illustrates a person's model of the world. The arrows represent the reach of an individual's beliefs. The boundaries of their model will be at the edge of what they believe is possible, as seen in circle A. Everything outside their model is believed to be beyond their reach. Circle B illustrates how much larger a person's model becomes when they change what they believe they can do.

What are the models that you have been taught?

In your journal write out and describe the models that have been handed down to you while you were growing up. If this seems challenging to you, don't be discouraged. It is often easier to see someone else's models at first.

When discovering your own models, it helps to write out your beliefs about an area of life. These beliefs will help you understand your models. Often as you examine your beliefs, you will begin to see your models outlined.

There are thousands of people who have been born poor and had nothing. But, they did not remain poor; they became very wealthy. What really made the difference? The model of the world that they adopted was the key. Yes, without doubt they worked hard and took action, but their actions would not have come about if they had not adopted models that contained beliefs that a person could get ahead and do well.

A Person's Model Becomes Their World

Every model of the world inherently contains beliefs. If you change your beliefs, you have begun the process of changing your models of the world. Each of us has many models that we employ every day. We have models for how people should treat each other, models for relationships, good driving, and what makes a person a great employee. You name it and you have a model for it. And if you don't, you will soon.

I remember a friend of mine who prided himself on his driving skills. He would see a space between two cars traveling down the highway doing 60-70 miles an hour and would cut through traffic, weaving back and forth, cutting in front of this car and that car. To hear him tell it he was the greatest driver there ever was. But that is not what other drivers thought of him. To them, he was probably the most reckless driver they had ever seen.

My friend, whom I did not like to ride with, had a different model of what made a person a great driver than did the majority of the people I know. Each of us drives according to the model we have adopted. What was the real difference between my friend and those who thought he was crazy? They had different models of driving and different beliefs. But there is one thing more. As a result of having different models, they gave different meanings to the same events.

The people whom my friend would cut off while executing his "great driving" gave it meanings like "he is crazy; he is trying to kill himself and us too." My friend, on the other hand, gave his driving meanings such as adventuresome, exciting, and a fun challenge.

Initially
A person's Models
are the Guides
that will
Influence the Meanings
They give Events

Occasionally he would be cut off by his rival: "the other guy." He would make a comment like "Wow, did you see that guy? Did you see how I avoided a wreck? That guy has got to be crazy. Why, if I weren't such a good driver we would have been in a wreck."

When my friend got to where he was going, he was excited and invigorated. Meanwhile, a great number of people were thankful to see him off the road. Much to everyone's surprise, he has never had a really bad accident. When I rode with him years later, I was glad to see he had become more considerate in his driving, although he still to this day sees driving as a real challenge and an adventure.

What is your model for driving? Write it down in your journal. Writing this out as we go will make it possible for you to have a clear picture of your models and how they are constructed. We will be referring back to this later. It is worth the time and effort.

We will examine meanings more deeply later. It is important to understand that models, beliefs, and meanings are all interrelated.

How do Models Work in our Lives & Why are they so Important?

A person's model becomes their blueprint, or map, of their world. If a person wants to go somewhere, they follow their map. If a person wants to accomplish something, they follow the guide they have come to trust--their model which consists of their beliefs.

Personality temperaments have an enormous impact in our lives. Each temperament has models that are compatible with its natural leanings. When we consider the Choleric and the Phlegmatic temperaments, which are at opposite ends from each other, a model that would be perfectly suited to a Choleric would be totally unacceptable to a Phlegmatic, and vice versa.

Our personality temperaments touch every aspect of our lives. This is not bad. The key is to understand how the many different aspects of a person all work together. If you are unaware of the intertwining of the aspects, they are not just confusing; they can result in frustration and discouragement as well.

Each temperament is going to have its own perspective. The Choleric will have a perspective that is totally different from the Phlegmatic and much different from both the Melancholy and the Sanguine. The Sanguine will have a perspective that is geared toward relationships and the approval of others. The Melancholy will have a perspective of looking at the details and finding out what is wrong or could go wrong with it. The Phlegmatic sees life as 'The one who gets along wins,' while the Choleric's perspective is 'Who cares? Let's get this thing done! Move. Move, faster.'

The natural tendency is for each person to approach an event from a perspective that feels natural to their particular temperament blend. This tendency is not fixed in stone, but until a person learns how to balance their temperament, they will naturally approach most things through their personality temperament's strengths. When this is done, what was once a strength can easily become a weakness.

When someone says to a child, 'Why don't you act like so and so?' The reason is often that they are wired differently. All of us can, and do, learn to make adjustments, but these adjustments take time. If there are unknown aspects that need to be addressed, you could very well feel as though you are beating your head against a wall. It takes time and understanding to make the right adjustments.

A person's beliefs (flavored as they are by their temperament) become their favored approach for how they operate in life. Each of us has the desire to be right--nobody likes to be told they are wrong. Sometimes a person grows up understanding the world to be a certain way, only later to learn that reality is different from what they thought. Often it is said that, that person was wrong. In reality, their information was wrong, but it is said that they are wrong, which personalizes it.

When we say "you are wrong", people take it personally. But, by showing that the information was wrong, the person is much less likely to internalize the situation, take it personally and respond as though they are being attacked.

It is always easier to make adjustments ourselves. We save face. No one likes losing face. This is especially true for certain temperaments, regardless of what culture you are from.

This being the case, everyone tests their models, but rarely from the perspective of them possibly being wrong. Most people test their model by examining its strengths. This is done through their lens, which sees only the strengths, but not the weaknesses, of their model.

Each of us is inside our models looking out and it is from that perspective that we test them. We see our models through the lens of our own personality temperament, which affirms our beliefs in their correctness because it is in line with the world we have come to know—the world that we understand as reality. From that perspective, it is hard to see clearly. This is where a good friend or mentor comes in and can give insight that we would otherwise have difficulty seeing.

Remember our example of two people born into poverty? It is possible for any temperament to adopt either of the two models that I have presented in this example. If a person with a more passive personality temperament adopts and embraces the model of poverty being an inescapable part of life, their passive Phlegmatic temperament will make it easier for them to live within that model and not become upset over their situation.

If a person with a more aggressive personality temperament (Choleric) were to adopt the same model, their temperament would have a more difficult time of comfortably living within that model. Their inner drive would be in opposition to the model they have been taught which contains beliefs that there is no way to change their situation. This would create a great deal of frustration within them. The result could very easily be anger over what is seen as an unfair situation and aggression that they would find difficult to control.

If you were to go strictly by which model naturally fits with each of the different temperaments, the natural fit would be that the model of poverty is life is more compatible with the more passive phlegmatic temperament, while the model of poverty is only temporary is more compatible with the more aggressive choleric temperament. It is important to understand that neither of the temperaments is locked into a particular model of the world.

Each could learn the model that leans opposite their temperament. Should a person adopt a model that is not in alignment with their personality temperament, they would find themselves being stretched. This does not mean that a person could not make the necessary adjustments. Without doubt, each temperament would have their own distinct approach to working through their challenges, but that does not lessen their ability to achieve success.

The person who adopts a model that is opposed to their personality temperament makeup will experience much more frustration because they will find themselves being pulled in opposite directions: one way by the beliefs that make up their model, and the other way by their personality temperament leanings. Any time there is a mismatch between the beliefs that make up their models and the natural leanings of their personality temperament, that person is going to experience a great deal more frustration than the person whose models, beliefs and temperaments are in harmony.

Many people have set goals and have even gone to goal setting workshops. At many of these workshops they encourage you to write out goals that are bigger than anything you have previously dreamed. For most, when it is all said and done, they look down at their list and it looks like someone else wrote it for them. If a person writes out a list of goals that are outside of their model of the world, those goals will be out of reach until they are able to adjust their model so that it is expanded enough, or shifted, to incorporate their new goals. If the goal is outside your model, it is outside of your identity. We will cover this later.

Your unconscious mind evaluates the following:

1. Beliefs within your models

2. Your beliefs about who you understand yourself to be, and not be

3. What you believe is possible for you

4. Your psychological needs (covered later)
5. How your psychological needs are being met currently
6. How they could be met in the future

So, if the goal is outside your model, it does not inspire. Instead, it results in more feelings of inadequacy and reinforces the thoughts that you will never be able to reach it.

Each model has what I call a center of gravity: where your model tends to pull you. Let's consider a drawing that illustrates how a model's center of gravity affects an individual. As with all models, the center of gravity is in the center, *but the individual is not always in the center.* There are two different instances when a person is not in the center of their model. They include when a person is first adopting the model as they are learning it from someone else, or when they are in the process of changing the beliefs that make up their models.

The models that we are going to illustrate are the two we considered earlier. Person A has adopted the model that being poor is life and there is nothing they can do about it. In other words, life is poverty and poverty is life. There is no escaping poverty.

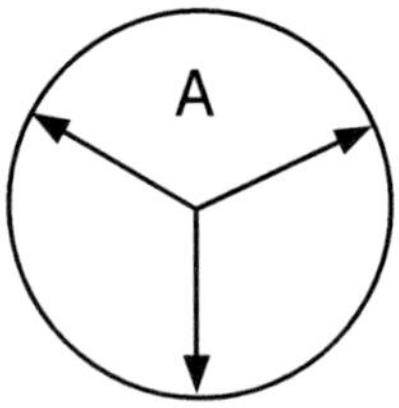

Poverty is Life

The beliefs that make up any model are going to be the power source for its center of gravity. The stronger the person holds on to the beliefs that are at the center of their model, the more intense the pulling power the model's center will have on the individual.

In the drawing on the preceding page, person A can move all around within the circle which represents poverty, but the beliefs that are at the center of their model will have a continual pulling effect that will keep bringing them back to the middle.

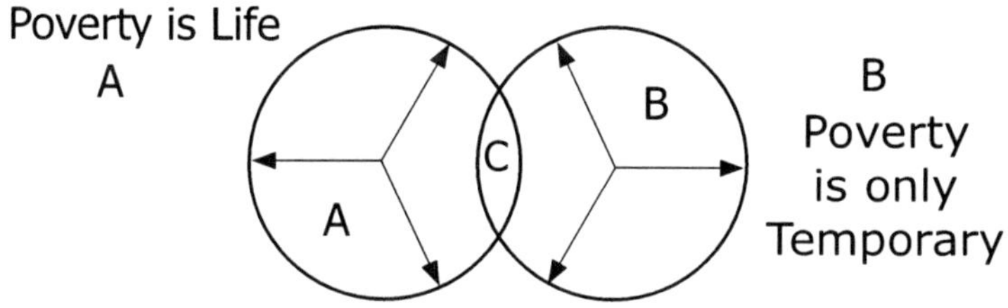

The drawing on this page shows both person A's and person B's models of the world together. Remember: person B believes that poverty is only temporary. Even though he may be in poverty, his belief that poverty is only a temporary part of life will assist him in getting out of poverty.

In life, people's models do overlap. Some models are almost identical while others like these have only a few similarities. In this case, these models both contain poverty, which is represented by the area marked C. Each individual can move around in the model, with the center of each model having a pulling effect on the individual toward the center. That being the case, even though person B may be living in poverty, it will be only a matter of time before they are no longer in poverty.

This principle does not only apply to someone who was born into poverty. Many people have lost everything they own and have found themselves with nothing, but they did not stay that way. They worked, and within a short time, they were doing well again.

How does this work? Person B's model contains beliefs that, if he works hard and applies himself, he will be able to get out of poverty. Persons A and B can both work very hard and be good people, but their results will be different. The reason for the different results is simple but often overlooked.

One Person will See More Opportunities than the Other Person Because In Their Model Opportunities Exist

Persons A and B are both born into poverty. Both are taught and they adopt the different models that are presented to them by their parents. Person A will see some opportunities as time passes, but because of his belief that life and poverty are inseparable, he will evaluate all opportunities that come his way through that perspective. His beliefs will discourage him from doing something with the opportunities that come his way. It is not uncommon for him to feel as though there is no use even trying.

Person B will see more opportunities than person A because person B's model has conditioned him to believe that opportunities are going to exist. He will be looking for, and open to, opportunities that will come his way. While the center of gravity is pulling person B *away* from poverty, the center of gravity of person A's model will be pulling him farther into a poverty mindset. Over time, this affects how people see themselves.

A person is not always located over their center of gravity. When a person is young and is adopting their models, their model's center of gravity is not yet established or strong enough to exert a pulling force on the individual. The other time when person is not over their center of gravity is when they are reforming their model. During this process, their center is moving and so are they, but not always at the same pace.

People don't usually venture outside their model. They will push themselves toward a goal and go right up to the edge of their model, just to find themselves being pulled back to where they were before. This is because a person's beliefs about what is possible go to the edge of their model: beyond their model their beliefs change to that of what is impossible for them.

Have you ever witnessed someone who was trying to advance themselves and they were doing great? Then all of a sudden, for no explainable reason, they just quit and fell back to where they were before. What you witnessed was someone who pushed themselves to the edge of their model and possibly a little further. They could not go any farther than that because they had reached the end of the chain that is their beliefs.

This happens when they are trying to escape their model but they have not dealt with their beliefs that make up their boundaries. So they work and work, stretch themselves only to find themselves back where they began, which reinforces their belief that they can't do it.

Everyone's model positions them somewhere in relation to the rest of the world. In the last diagram the two models shifted the individual to a different position compared to the world around them.

How Families contribute to Models

Earlier in the book we considered how the family we grow up in is a major contributor to the models of the world we adopt. Some of what we accept into our model of the world is taught and some is caught.

The greatest part of our models are caught. The exception to this rule is when there is a formal mentoring that goes on between an older man and younger man (this is also true for woman and girls). If there is a formal mentoring that takes place, it is with the intent of teaching understandings and wisdom that is not necessarily available any other way. It is a much more personal teaching as compared to a "classroom" type of teaching.

In mentoring, the teacher trains the student in different ways of looking at things: of looking beyond and through events in ways that shed new light and understanding. The best mentors teach the student how to see and operate in different models of the world, which would otherwise require years of experience.

This happened more readily in years past between fathers and their sons. But since World War II, the time fathers and sons have spent together has changed a great deal. Research has shown that parents and children spend very little time together, let alone in quality conversations.

When I was a child, I adopted a simple model of the world. It came directly from my parents. In that model, Santa was real. I had heard some things, but I didn't know for sure, so I remember asking my parents if Santa Claus was real. "Oh, yes, he is real." I believed in Santa Claus for many years. Then one day someone told me there was no such a thing as Santa Claus. I argued for Santa because I believed it to be true: my parents had always told me about him and they would not lie to me. To me Santa was real, and I was not going to listen to someone who was wrong and said that Santa didn't exist.

I went home and told my parents that a kid at school was lying and how I stood up for Santa. I was informed that the other kid was right. I had believed in a lie all those years. I was crushed. I wanted to believe that Santa was real. Santa was my friend. I learned some hard lessons that day. I don't remember which lesson hurt me more; no Santa or that my parents lied to me. Although I was not aware of it at that time, in my model of the world parents always told their children the truth and a boy could trust his parents. My model changed that day.

At that point in my life I had no idea of models or looking at things from another perspective. I didn't understand that my parents told me that Santa was real because they enjoyed watching the excitement in my face when Santa was in town. Or when we got up on Christmas morning and ran to find what Santa had left for us. My parents didn't sit me down and explain those things to me. I didn't know, so I went with what I did know—my conclusion. *Parents will lie to you for no reason. You can't trust them to tell you the truth.*

Our Own Conclusions are Often Embraced as "Facts"

I now understand how wrong I was. My parents didn't mean any harm. They wanted me to be happy. My conclusion then was based on the information I had at that time, not what I know now. I took the information I had then and I did the math. It added up that parents will lie to you for no reason. It was done. It was not screened or tested heavily; it was accepted.

Have you ever been around young children? They will believe just about anything they hear. I remember one time I said "When pigs fly!" to my oldest son. It was something that he knew was a joke. Later my wife told me that one of our younger children heard it and thought that pigs really did fly. I went to our daughter and explained that pigs really can't fly.

There is a distinct difference between these two examples. One model was caught by the child and the other was consciously taught to a child. The important key is that in both cases the child had no reference by which to judge the validity of what was being said. Without references, it was accepted as truth.

This is a funny example of how children will accept something they hear as reality. As time progresses, a child builds their set of references and beliefs. In other words, they adopt models of their world and use those models as references to determine if some thing they are being told is "correct" or not. It may indeed be true, but if it is in opposition to the references they have within their models, it will not be readily accepted, at least not without a great deal of proof.

If someone tells you something that does not fit right within your model, you may consider it. If you do consider it, you will test it before you change your belief about it. Does it make sense? Does it add up? You will seek out any reference of your own from which to verify the validity of it. It may be accepted more quickly depending on who told it to you and how your relationship is with that person.

If, on the other hand, you come to a conclusion yourself, unless you make special efforts to test your conclusion, that conclusion will be accepted as truth. The conclusions we personally come to do not go through the same evaluation process as do the things we are told by others. When a model is caught, that which is caught is an internal conclusion and not evaluated the same as if someone told you. Conclusions are often perceived and accepted as reality, without being tested or proven.

Sometimes when a couple who has children are splitting up, one of the children may blame himself for the parents breaking up. When an adult finds out that the child sees himself as responsible for the break up, it is very hard to convince the child that they are not responsible. The fact might be that the children may have been the thing that had kept them together much longer than they would have if there were no children. But the child believes that they are at fault, even though no one has ever told them that. Because it is a conclusion they have come to themselves, it is embraced as fact. The sad thing is that if a child continues to blame himself, embracing the blame will have adverse effects on the child. His identity will be affected by it.

I was on a trip in Ecuador, and as we were driving through the mountains we could look across the landscape and see ridge after ridge of what looked like little mountain ranges. On most of the slopes there were cattle and we were sure that it took them some time to learn to walk on the steep slope. As we talked about it, one of the younger guys, who was about sixteen, said something about the cattle looking odd. I chimed in that they weren't odd; they were a special breed of cattle developed for walking on the steep slope in this region. In fact, this breed of cattle was specially bred to have shorter legs on the right side and longer legs on their left side.

He looked at me like I was crazy, then at the cattle, then at me again and back at the cattle. For a long time he didn't know what to think. He looked at me and told me I was crazy. To this reply someone else made the comment "You mean to tell me you never heard of this world famous breed of cattle?" Now he was puzzled. He said if that was true then how can some of the cows be facing different direction on the same ridge? I explained to him that when they developed this breed, they made a right hand and a left hand cow. This brought a big smile to his face. "You're crazy," he said.

"Suit yourself," I said and then didn't say anything more about it. Later we were driving and he squealed, "Look at those, are they the right hand cows or the left hand cows?" He had spotted a ridge on which the cattle were all facing the same direction. Everyone in the car roared with laughter. He figured out what was up and he started laughing too.

This is a fun example of models. It shows a model that this young man had about cattle. It shows how models contain beliefs we have regarding something. In this example, this young man had his model challenged. He internally sorted through his references and rejected the new model that was presented to him, but because it did not end there, and this new model was presented again with some claim as evidence, he began reconsidering it. This happens every day.

Initially the models that we adopted were by default. These models seem to cling to us as if they were a second skin. Once a model is adopted it is incorporated into our identity. This is why if we simply try to get rid of it, we experience a great amount of discomfort. Our internal identity is linked to our models of the world.

If you know someone who has a model that is harmful to them, the worst thing to do is to call their model wrong. We are all attached to our models. To make a person's model wrong can come across as a personal attack.

If you say someone's model is wrong, you are making the only thing they know wrong. This leaves the person feeling as if they have nowhere to turn or go and thus boxes them into a corner. Understand that the only references a person has are what they have been taught. If you make them wrong for adopting their model, you lose any hope of helping them.

If you tell someone their model of the world is wrong, you have just set their heels in the dirt and you won't move them. Here is an important note: You don't want to move them. They have to move themselves. All anyone can do is to offer them something that will help them expand their model of the world.

Most models have been accepted and adopted by default. If you pressure someone to change they will resist. If you leave a way for a person to explain their past models, beliefs, and behaviors you open the door that allows them to make changes without feeling forced or pressured.

When a child becomes a young adult, they go through a questioning period. This process begins during their teen years or early twenties. All their life they have been told what to do, how to act, and what to believe. In short, they go through the process of making a belief, or value that they have been taught, their own, or they discard it as one would an unwanted item. This is not to say that a person will turn their back on what they have been taught, but at some point they have to decide if they are going to keep it as their own.

During this process they are weighing not only what they have been taught but also what they are feeling as a result. This goes in order from the strongest feelings to the weakest feelings. If they feel strongly about some value or belief, it stays. If not, it goes. Whatever they are considering, weighing out their emotions is going to be the tilting factor regarding their model of the world and themselves. At this point they are deciding who they are apart from their parents. They will cling to and own the models they have been taught or they will discard them and look for other models. We will cover much of this in greater detail in the section on needs.

As a person becomes more set in their beliefs, their models can become firm or even harden up like concrete, which can result in the individual being defined by their models. Their models can take over, in that they lose the ability to consider anything outside of their model.

Models have an enormous impact on an individual's perceived identity which we will examine in the identity section.

Person X adopted a model of the world in which they believed that everything that went wrong with life was something that had to be endured. Person Y, in comparison, adopted a model of the world that when things went wrong it was for the sole purpose of nudging them toward growth. Do you think that these two people would have the same amount of trials and challenges? From the outside perspective, the answer would be yes. If you were to ask persons X and Y, however, there would no comparison.

Person X, who believed that everything was against him, would perceive himself as having many times the number of trials and problems as person Y. In reality they may actually have almost the same amount. Person Y, who believed that everything was actually for their growth and ultimately for their good, would not see some of the challenges as stumbling blocks but would perceive them as opportunities.

In reality, things would go right and wrong for both people. The key is that the positioning of the person in the two models is different. Person X, who has adopted the model that everything is out to get him, has elevated life's circumstances above himself. In contrast, person Y, who believes everything is somehow meant to assist him in his own personal growth and is ultimately for their good, has elevated himself above life's circumstances. The difference in perspective is as different as night and day. There is literally a shift in power.

X's perspective will be to look up at whatever events he experiences as bigger than himself. As a result, he will experience certain emotions that are congruent with his model of the world. When an event is believed to be bigger than you are, you are more likely to experience the emotions of helplessness, being overwhelmed, and fighting depression as a direct result of your model of the world. You are more likely to feel as though life is something that has to be endured.

Person Y is going to be looking down on the events that they are experiencing. The events will appear smaller because of the shift in perspective. This model will result in the person experiencing certain emotions such as confidence, self-assurance and optimism. As you can see, the emotions that person Y will experience are totally different from those of person X. Person Y would be much more likely to view life as something that is to be enjoyed and savored. The perceptual shift between these two models literally creates different realities for each of them, even though they are living at the same time, experiencing many of the same, or similar, things in life.

Models can be Masculine or Feminine

Models are simultaneously simple and complex. They are made up of beliefs, perspectives and meanings which create our emotions. Models can also be categorized as masculine or feminine in nature. At the same time, our models reflect back on the people who hold them. The models we hold to can be restrictive and confining in their effects on us, or they can be inspiring and empowering, urging us forward to better things.

It is important to note here that just as there are masculine and feminine models, there are positive and negative models within each of them. What we are considering here is a positive masculine model in comparison to a negative feminine model. This is to show contrast, but also to recognize and address how models can, and do, affect a person's perspective and their life. A man who is incongruent will find himself experiencing the negative side of this example in varying degrees depending on his level of incongruency.

The negative side of this example is not desirable for either men or women. Simply because it falls under the feminine category does not mean that all women are, or should be like this. Just as there are negative masculine models in which a person is selfish, angry, hateful, and heartless, does not mean that all men are like that or should be like that.

Men and women have the ability to embrace many different models (positive or negative) and thus the emotions that are predominately associated with those models. This will be examined in greater depth in the MFD-R section.

The two models that were described in the preceding paragraphs are examples of both feminine and masculine models. Person X's model sees things as overwhelming and intimidating. Nothing goes right for them and it is common for them to feel as though they shouldn't even try. Their model places them in a vulnerable and weak position. The world and the events are viewed as bigger and more powerful. This model presupposes the individual to be helpless and at the mercy of what happens to them. Their model places them in the weaker feminine position with their problems in the stronger masculine position.

Person Y adopts a model of the world that when things go wrong it is ultimately for their good. If they look long enough they will find it, and in the long run they will be better off as a result of the challenge they went through. This person's model positions them in a spot that is opposite that of person X. In this model, person Y takes the stronger position which is the masculine position.

The emotions that these two people will experience as a result of the models they have adopted, will be radically different. Each will experience difficulties and challenges, but X's model will be discouraging and depressing, while Y is encouraged and inspired. They may face some of the exact problems: X will refer to them as stumbling stones, while Y refers to them as stepping stones.

Each of these people will have good and bad experiences. Do you think that person X will remember more good things or bad things? Do you believe these two people will experience a different quality of life?

Every model that puts a person in the position of being smaller than the event is going to have a negative affect on that individual. The presupposition is that you don't have a chance, and that will have an immense influence over you. That model will hinder you greatly and will restrict what you try, let alone what you will accomplish in your life.

The other option is to see the event as being smaller and weaker than you. If you were to adopt this model of the world, the presupposition contained within it is that you are stronger and will prevail. This would be evident not only in your beliefs, but in your actions as well. You would be more confident and have the belief that you were capable of accomplishing a great deal more. You would try things that you would not have otherwise, and as a result, you would be much more successful. Even when things were not going your way, your model would point you toward encouragement and faith that it was all going to work out wonderfully.

It is not What an Event
Does to a Person
But Rather
What the Person Does
With the Event
That makes the Difference

We have been considering models. There are adopted models, the ones we are handed and simply accept without our realizing what is taking place, and there are models that we have created. Existing models can be changed and recreated in such a way as to move a person from a weaker position to a stronger position.

Any time an event takes place, those involved give it a meaning. What does this event mean to me? Typically, any event that causes us some form of pain is given a negative meaning and, on the other side of the coin, any event that brings us pleasure is given good meanings. As discussed earlier, our unconscious mind looks to find ways to save work. One of the ways it does this is to link things together.

If you had a bad experience with a dog, your brain will link dog and pain together. The stronger the emotions were when you went through the experience, the stronger the link will be. The greater the emotional intensity during an event, the stronger the memory will be. It is possible, that if the event is intense enough, it could alter your model of the world.

How is it, then, that two people can go through the same experience and it have totally different effects on each of them? To find the answer to that question,we must look at the way the question is worded. It is not what an event does to a person, but what the person does with the event. The meanings you give the event will determine if you become stronger or weaker as a result of the experience.

If we take the perspective that the event affects the person, the person has to be smaller than the event, which would be the feminine position. If that is the case, the event is more intimidating and more powerful than the person, who might be crushed by it over time. But if the person takes the position of being bigger than the event, which would put them in the masculine position, they have positioned themselves to grow stronger as a result.

The Importance of Meanings

Each of us gives meaning to everything that happens in our lives. This is true whether it is something someone says or doesn't say to us or the events that take place in our daily lives.

If someone cuts us off on the freeway, each of us will give it usually one of two meanings, "Wow, that guy didn't see me. How lucky I am that he didn't hit me," or "That #%*# cut me off!" which could lead to "I'll show him."

In each case, the person gave meaning to the event. The different meanings that were given resulted in the creation of totally different emotional states within the individual. You may have never had the experience that I just described above. I know I have. I have been both the one being cut off and I have been the one who has honestly not seen someone and accidentally cut them off. After realizing what I had done, I felt really bad and have even said out loud "Oh my. Sorry, buddy, I really didn't see you." I've had this same person honk their horn as they cut me off to give the impression that they were really trying to hit me.

So what happened? I accidentally cut them off and they gave it the meaning that I had done it on purpose. (They had probably met my friend who thought he was a race car driver.) The person who I had accidentally cut off responded more to the meaning they gave the event than the event itself.

Have you ever had something happen that you thought was intentional and you were upset over it, only to find out it was a complete accident? As soon as you realized it was an accident, your emotions totally changed. What we focus on and the meanings we give to events are going to alter how we see our world and the emotions we experience on a daily basis.

I remember a time I went to pay my real-estate taxes at the courthouse. Our tax bills came out and they had the payment broken into two different installments. For fifteen years I had always waited until the second installment was due and paid the amount in full. When I got to the window the lady there informed me that I was going to have to pay a fine. I was somewhat surprised by this. Never before had there been a fine for paying it all at the end of the second installment.

I asked when this had been implemented in our county and the lady snapped at me that there was a notice on the tax bill this year. Well, I knew it was my own fault that I didn't know about it, because I had done as I had always done--I looked at the amount due and the second installment date that payment had to be made by, then proceeded to put it on the shelf with the date marked on the envelope as to when it needed to be paid.

I had run into this once in another county where I had purchased a house for resale, so I knew that the fine would not really amount to much at all. I asked what the total would be, and, to my surprise the lady snapped at me with the amount. I looked at her in disbelief and quietly suggested that she relax. "I'm the one paying the taxes and the fine, not you," I said to her. She told me, "You're the one who has made me uptight. You're the one who has made me feel this way by getting angry with me."

That statement really took me by surprise. Not only was I not the slightest bit angry, I had said nothing and had done nothing that would convey that I was. I honestly was not angry.

I realized what was going on. This poor lady had been dealing with every taxpayer who was accustomed to paying their taxes as they had in the past, and now they were being fined. The fact that the fine was almost nothing didn't matter (my fine was $3.47), but the idea of being fined had apparently wound some people into a tizzy, and this lady was catching the brunt of it. I tried as best I could to reassure her that I was not angry and that I didn't blame her for my fine.

I found that I was becoming somewhat perturbed with her for refusing to understand that I was not angry, until I realized there was nothing I could do to convince her. This lady had her mind made up, and clearly she was working hard to make her self-fulfilling prophecy come true. I decided to leave her to her own devices, and went on my way, thankful that I only had to pay a fine of $3.47 and not more.

Many, if not all, of us have been on both sides of an event similar to the one I described. It is amazing what a person can focus on and bring into reality. Occasionally, I find myself thinking about that lady and wondering how she is doing. It is easy for a person to get into a rut like she had. What I learned was worth far more than $3.47. The sad thing is I don't think she learned anything from it.

What did she do anyway? Let's consider what happened. There was a major change in how they were collecting the real estate taxes that year. I know some people who are never happy about paying taxes, so I can see how this lady might have had some difficult people to deal with.

People Remember the Emotion of Pain Louder and Longer than the Emotion of Pleasure.

People being creatures of habit as they are, I can guess that I wasn't the only one who waited to pay the whole amount at the end. I can image that many of those who were not thrilled about paying the taxes and normally didn't say anything had spoken up and complained about the change. It is easy for us to get upset with someone else when we made the error, isn't it?

Those who regularly came in and complained about paying their taxes most likely went through the roof, and I'm sure she heard far more than she should have. It might be safe to say that at the beginning of the tax paying season she had braced herself for what she believed was ahead.

Sometimes we anticipate how someone is going to react to an event or situation and we plan our responses ahead of time. I can imagine it at this moment. "*I'm tired of how these people get on my case. I'm not getting the money. Why are they always mad at me?*" Can you imagine what that lady went through from one day to the next? When I walked in there, she was ready for me. I wasn't going to catch her with her guard down.

As you read, I could not convince her to put down her sword and shield. She had formed her model of how people were going to react. She hung on to it so hard that she didn't even notice when someone was not following her model. She was living and responding according to her model and not according to what was happening. We do this too sometimes.

It is not uncommon for our models to get shifted for us. These shifts happen either quickly or slowly. If an event takes place and it is highly emotionally charged, it has the potential to shift our model to a degree. If it happens over and over again, and is highly charged, as it was for this lady, the shift can be sudden and extreme.

Typically, positive shifts require much more time and repetition than negative shifts do because, although pleasurable experiences contain emotions, those emotions are not as intense or powerful as the negative emotions that we often associate with things going wrong. People remember the emotions of pain longer and louder than the emotions of pleasure.

The emotions of pain and anger grab you by your throat and lift you off the floor. They have your total, undivided attention. Pleasurable emotions, in comparison, softly caress you. If a dog bites you while you are in pleasure, you move from pleasure to pain quickly. You forget your pleasure instantly as you discover yourself in pain. Though I am using an example of physical pain, emotional pain has the same effect. This example illustrates the immediate transition from pleasure to pain, regardless of whether it is physical or emotional.

The transition from pain to pleasure is not nearly as fast or as intense as is the transition from pleasure to pain. You can be experiencing pleasure, and without warning, pain can rip you out of your seat, throw you down on the floor, and try to stomp the life out of you. In contrast, if a person is in pain, pleasure doesn't come along and grab someone to the extent they totally forget the pain they were in. Pleasure can only coax a person to join it, while pain attacks.

What meanings do you think the tax collector had given events and people? We could guess, and that's all it would be. The best we could do is to put ourselves in her spot and think through what meanings we might give things. We could give meanings like: 1) People are such jerks! 2) Nobody likes me! 3) Why are people always getting mad at me? 4) I try to be nice and people just get upset and angry with me. 5) People are all just a bunch of #@*!%@#s!

Meanings create our emotions. The meanings you give events that come into your life are what determines the emotions you feel! Not only do I know it to be true in my life, but I have seen it countless times in the lives of others. Something happens and someone gives it the meaning that it was done intentionally. They start getting hot under the collar and then they find out it was an accident and they change the meanings they gave it. At that moment their emotions change also.

The difference between what some call a stumbling block and what others call a stepping stone is the meanings that each person gives the event. You and I don't have a choice. We have to give each event some kind of meaning. You may say that you'll not give it any meaning whatsoever. If that is the case you have just given it the meaning that it is unimportant to you and it doesn't matter. Any way you slice it, a meaning is given.

When each of us starts out, we don't have a great number of meanings to give. A child does not have a meaning for "hot" until they touch something hot. Once they do, the meaning is solid and it has the memory of pain linked to it, making it a powerful motivator.

Many of the first meanings a child gives events are a direct result of pain they have experienced. This is life and it isn't long until a child learns to figure out what some things mean without discomfort.

Each of us develops a system for giving things meaning. Once we have experienced something several times, or just once if the event was painful enough (like touching a hot stove), we have a meaning for it. At some point this system for giving meanings begins operating at the unconscious level. It becomes automatic and, to an extent, happens with little or no conscious thought. This need to give meaning to things stays with us all of our life.

When a situation arises and we don't have a meaning for it, it can be most unsettling. We are fearful that it might cause us pain, and how much is not known. Not knowing how much pain might be ahead is difficult emotionally.

If you are trying to give something a new and better meaning and it doesn't seem to be working, then you need to examine the beliefs that make up your models. Do they contain some beliefs that are at odds with the new meaning you are trying to give the event? An individual needs to reconcile their beliefs and their meanings.

The meanings that a person gives things and events are a result of comparisons we make in an instant. If someone says hot, you know what that means, and you are not going to be convinced otherwise.

I remember when I was in second grade walking to school in the winter. We lived in a Chicago suburb and winters were colder then than they are now. The sun was shining that day. I saw the sun glaring off the fender of a car and I was thinking about how hot cars get sitting out in the sun in the summer time.

As I walked past a car I reached out and touched it with my bare finger. To my surprise, my finger felt burned. I thought, "This is weird. It is in the middle of winter, and I just burned my finger on the car." I looked around and touched several other things that were so cold it hurt to touch them. It didn't fit, so I, very carefully, reached out and touched the car again. This time it felt very cold.

As a seven-year-old I was perplexed, to say the least. This did not fit into my model of how things were. It was so different that I never forgot it. In fact, I can still see the car and see myself looking at my finger.

Thirty years later I learned that the same nerves sense both hot and cold. That winter day, all those years ago, the sun was shining brightly just like it did in the summer, which was unusual for our winters. I had been thinking of the hot summer and how the cars are very hot when they sit in the bright sun. When I first touched the car, it was hot to my touch, which shocked me. I was thinking hot and when I touched it, it hurt. In reality, it hurt because it was so cold, but because I was thinking of how hot cars are in the summer time, the moment I touched it, it felt like I got burned instead of feeling the pain of the bitter cold.

This is a good example of how things can be misinterpreted in an instant, without any conscious thought. In this case, the wrong meaning was given to an event.

The Meaning You give an Event Is Going To Create Your Emotions.

Growing up many of us came to the conclusion that emotions were something that just happened to us. How did we come to believe this? Have you ever heard someone say "You made me angry?" If we take this statement at face value, someone else is responsible for that other person's anger. After all, they did it to them, right?

Remember when we were looking at false logic earlier? False logic never appears false at first. This is a perfect example of how false logic is employed. On the surface someone did something and the other person become angry.

Looks pretty simple and put into a mathematical equation it would look like this.

$$1 + 2 + 1 = 4$$

The ones represent the two people involved, the two represents the event and the four represents the outcome, in this case anger. Pretty simple and straightforward?

$$1 + 2 + 1 = 4$$

This appears to be both mathematically
and logically correct.

Have you ever watched a situation and not been able to figure out why someone reacted the way they did? Looking at everything, their reaction just didn't add up. To illustrate this in a mathematical equation it would look like this:

$$1 + 2 + 1 = -1$$

Just like the real life scenario, not only does this not look right, it is not right. So what happed? Let's look at the correct mathematical equation for what really happened. In reality what happened was this:

$$1 + 2 + \underline{\quad} + 1 = -1$$

This equation is written to represent what really happened. The blank is the unknown variable. The unknown variable is the key. What is it? In this case it is the "meanings" that the person who got angry gave the event. It would look like this:

$$1 + 2 + \underline{-5} + 1 = -1$$

Now we have a complete and correct understanding of what happened. In this example I have used the number (-5) for the meaning, because the meanings you give things carries enormous weight. This enormous weight can work for you, or against you. What determines whether it works for you or against you is the quality of the meaning you give the event.

If this same person were to give the same event a positive meaning it could very well look like this:

$$1 + 2 + \underline{5} + 1 = 9$$

In real life this too could confuse an onlooker because the 5 is not visible. A person's reactions to the meanings they give events are visible, but the meaning itself is not. To an observer, the reaction to the event is often attributed to the event itself, instead of to the meanings that the person gave the event.

If you were to question the person who gave the meanings, they might be able to explain the meaning that they gave, but chances are that unless you knew just what to ask, and how to ask it, the answer you would receive would be in the form of the emotions they were feeling at the time.

If you get an emotional response, it is possible that they may not understand their feelings and be confused by their emotions. This can be misleading unless you know how it all fits together. We will be working on these components throughout this book, but for now know that there are many contributing factors.

If your spouse is late getting home and it messes up your plans, then it is important to understand that, yes, your plans are messed up, but it is simply an event. It does not contain emotions until you give meaning to the event. You have the ability to give it whatever meaning you want and thus you have the ability to choose the emotions you experience.

It is impossible to feel emotions that are counter to the meanings you give the event. At best, you might be able to hide your emotions for a while, but the meaning you give the event will determine your emotional state.

Let's take a deeper look into this situation.

Someone's spouse is late coming home and the evening they had planned is not going to work out. What the spouse who is at home will say or do is going to be a continuance of what they had been mentally saying to themselves while their spouse was gone.

I will show two examples of both positive and negative meanings. As you read them, what emotions do you think they will create in the person who is thinking them? How do you think the spouse who is late will respond to the different approaches? What emotions do you think the statements to their spouse coming home late will nudge their spouse toward?

Negative response:

1. "Do you realize that our plans are all screwed up and the whole evening is ruined?"

2. "Do you know what time it is? Our whole #*&#@# evening is shot and I am so #%&*# angry about it!"

I am glad no one reading this has ever done anything like this. What emotions would these two examples create in the person who was saying them? Do you agree that number two would be in worse emotional shape than number one? How would you feel if you were the one who was listening to someone say that to you? You might feel like reaching out and touching that person (with a baseball bat).

Positive response:

1. "Do you know what time it is? I was worried that something bad might have happened. I sure am glad you're home."

2. "I'm glad you're home. I was really concerned. I couldn't image what it would be like if something happened to you. We have the rest of the evening. Here are your options.
What do you think?"

What emotions would these two examples create in the person who was saying them? From my perspective, number one would be neutral to low positive emotions. Do you agree that number two would be in better emotional shape than number one? How would you feel if you were the one who was listening to number two say that to you? You might feel like reaching out and touching that person with a hug or a kiss, but probably not a baseball bat.

There is an underlying difference behind the negative approach and the positive approach. The negative approaches are masculine in their origin. Masculinity, when not balanced, is very *self-oriented.*

Read through the negative approaches again. Do you see the underlying foundation of its construction is rooted in "self"? On the other hand, the positive responses are more relationship oriented. Now read through the positive responses again and see if you can tell the difference.

The positive responses are concerned about the other person and the relationship that exists between the two of them.

If you listen to yourself and others you can easily get an insight into where they are at that moment. It is important to realize that the self-orientation is not always bad. There are times when it is absolutely necessary. The key, as with everything in life, is balance. The examples I gave above are intentionally leaning to one side or the other to show their origins.

The more you focus on something, the greater its effect on you will be. If a person is driving and they look at the car in the other lane that is coming at them, their natural tendency is to move toward the object that they are looking at. Human beings have a way of following their focus. ***When your focus and your thoughts are in a certain direction, you are going to begin to experience the corresponding emotions that are linked to your thoughts and focus.***

From the positive and negative examples above, which would be the easiest for you to do? Which would be more of a challenge for you personally? The models that you have adopted will be a definite influence one way or the other.

You Can Choose The Emotions You Experience

Meanings are the major players in emotions. The meanings you tend to give will be influenced by your needs, which we will be looking at soon. The direction you find yourself going the majority of the time will give some great insights.

Models and meanings are intermingled and intertwined in that models have a tendency to flavor the meanings that a person gives to events. If your model is leaning toward the negative, that negativity is going to have a swaying power in what direction the meanings you give will have a tendency to go. Negative models have a way of influencing the meanings you give events toward the negative. Positive models have a way of influencing the meanings you give events toward the positive.

This is partly because humans follow their focus. Where your focus is, there you will find yourself. This is a key that we will come back to later. Also, the beliefs you form within your model are going to influence the meanings you give.

Models, overall, have a flavor to them. When you are inside your model you are experiencing the model, just as we saw in meeting the lady who was collecting the taxes. Her responses were based on her model rather than what was actually taking place.

The unfortunate person who was taught that being poor is a way of life will walk right past opportunities and not see them because their focus is on their model, and in their model there are no opportunities. They don't see them, just like the tax lady didn't hear me saying I was not upset about the little fine I had to pay. In other words, if your model has the flavor of chocolate and someone hands you vanilla, all you are going to taste is chocolate. They may even ask you how the vanilla is, and you will look at them strangely and say, "What are you talking about? This is chocolate." That is, if they even hear you at all.

The beliefs that are contained within our models affect how we see reality. They are our reality, just as it is for both people who were born poor, and just as it was for the tax lady. If a person believes that their spouse is cheating on them, do you think that they are going to consider evidence that might support their spouse's innocence? Or do you think they will interpret events that may simply be unexplainable as evidence for their belief? Remember, your beliefs and models will influence the meanings you give things and where you direct your focus is where you will find yourself.

If you are getting the impression that models can be prisons, you are correct. Your models can be the very walls that restrain you or they can empower and free you.

Get out your journal and write out different models that you have adopted. Remember, there are no right or wrong answers, and this list is for your eyes only. As we continue we will be referring back to this list. You'll be amazed at what you will discover, and how simple it is to make changes once you know how.

What have we learned so far?

Models, for the most part, especially in the early years, are adopted from the people who raise us. Some of what is adopted is literally taught and some of it is caught. What is caught does not go through the same evaluation procedure as that which is taught to us, simply because we came to the conclusion ourselves, and, to put it plainly, we know we are right. Don't we?

Let's consider for a moment a child who was raised in a family where the female was dominant and the male was submissive. Do you think that the child would have the tendency to adopt the model of the world that is being lived out before them? At least initially, yes. They don't have any other references to compare it to, so the child will most likely catch that the man is to be the submissive one in a relationship.

This can also play out in reverse. Let's say that a girl is raised in a home where the father is overbearing and obnoxious. Her mother is overly submissive and not much better than a slave in the eyes of the daughter. If this were the case, would you think the daughter would be treated much differently than her mother? Do you think that this daughter would want to mirror this model or do you think it might be painful enough that she would do anything to avoid it? These are examples of models that are caught through living life with others.

Remember the example of when pigs fly? One of my younger children overheard it and their conclusion was that since dad said it, it was true! PIGS FLY. It was accepted without question because Daddy said it. This too was caught, but is one of those things that would come to a point of being reevaluated later and changed. When my wife told me about our daughter thinking that pigs actually fly, I went and talked with her and explained that pigs really didn't fly. That was the easy part.

How many children do you think would have a hard time imaging that some people don't have a television in their home? The child would look at you and probably say, "What do you mean? Everyone has a TV. How can anyone live without a TV?" In the child's model of the world TVs are a must, simply because they don't know life without televisions, so everyone must have televisions. This is known as false logic. Unfortunately, it comes into play a great deal when children are catching things.

I saw a good example of this on an episode of "The Andy Griffith Show." In the show, Andy was a widower who had a young son named Opie. One day Opie and his friends were together, each boy telling stories, and, as boys will, each one was trying his best to top the others. After some silence because everyone was thinking how they could top the last guy, one of the boys made the claim that he knew what makes a woman have a baby.

All eyes and ears were glued to him. How? Was the response of all of them. "The other day we had salmon at our house and the next day my mom told all of us she was going to have a baby," was the response. Everyone's mouth fell open and no one had anything that would top that. "I always wondered how babies were made," one of them exclaimed. "Wow, salmon!" one of them said. Just as he said that somebody's parents started calling for them and the boys all went home.

Several days later Andy's girlfriend, who happened to be Opie's teacher, was coming over for dinner. Aunt Bee had made a special salmon dinner for the occasion. Opie's eyes got as big as saucers and his mouth about hit the floor. A look of sheer panic hit him as everyone started to sit down to eat. Opie was bound and determined to keep his teacher from eating the salmon. Needless to say, his behavior had everyone confused and bewildered. Finally, Andy took him out of the room to deal with him and the reason for the behavior was revealed.

The boy's behavior didn't make any sense at all to the adults until they were informed of the model of the world that he was operating from. Once that knowledge came out, it all made sense. The son was doing what he thought was the best thing to do because he cared for everyone there. Although his new knowledge could have been verified for truth, that had not occurred to him. When information comes from close peers, it is accepted more readily.

As crazy as it sounds, this type of false logic takes place every day. It is not confined to children. It can, and does, plague adults sometimes. It happens more than we would like to admit. We will look at this further in the section on NEEDS.

It is Possible to Change Your Models

If you want to change a model, you must start by evaluating the beliefs that make it up. If you are going to be successful at changing your model, you must start with your beliefs. As you change your beliefs, your model changes. As a result, it will become easier to give better meanings to the events that come into your life in the future.

Changing models and beliefs is only one important step that is involved in making lasting changes in your life. Models affect every area of our life, but they are not alone. ***It is possible to make changes in your models and beliefs, but if that is where a person stops making changes, they will find themselves back where they started in time.*** In the next two sections we will examine two other major factors that have an enormous effect in each of our lives.

Needs

What are "Needs" and are they Important?

If someone were to ask you what you need, what would probably come to mind is what you are lacking at this moment. If you haven't had lunch, food will come to mind. If you are cold, your first thought will be getting warm. Each of us has certain physical needs that must be met in order for us to live. If our physical needs aren't met, we can die.

A person's physical needs have to be met in a certain order. For example, air is the top physical need, we as humans, have. People can live for weeks without food, several days without water, but only several minutes without good air to breathe. Typically, the hierarchy of our physical needs are air, water, food, sleep, shelter from the elements and clothes (for most climates).

If a person has plenty of air but no food, their focus will be on what they lack, not what they have. The lack of our physical needs creates pain. Pain has a way of grabbing our attention and our focus. A person's top priority is what they are lacking even if it is third or fourth in the order of their physical needs list. This is true for all humans regardless of race, culture, or sex.

It is possible, too, for a person to meet their physical needs at many different levels. The quality and quantity of water, food and sleep will all impact a person's life. If all a person has is low quality food or contaminated drinking water, those items may keep them alive, but at the same time the quality of their life will be adversely affected as a result of meeting their physical needs with sub-quality nutrition.

Just as each of us has physical needs that must be met in order for us to be physically healthy, we, too have psychological NEEDS that must be met if a person is going to live a well balanced life. People have no choice but to attend to their physical needs first, then when those needs are met at satisfactory levels, they become aware of their psychological NEEDS.

There is a difference between physical needs and psychological NEEDS. Everyone has the same top physical need: that of air, followed by water and then food, but not everyone has the same top psychological NEED.

There is a great variety in the psychological NEEDS hierarchies from one individual to the next. This makes it more interesting when it comes to meeting people's psychological NEEDS. Couple the variety of NEEDS hierarchies with the different personality temperaments, and then throw on top of that the uniquely different models and beliefs that people have adopted, and it all makes for a wide range of ways people seek to meet their psychological NEEDS.

Let's look at the four psychological NEEDS everyone has.
They are:

1) CERTAINTY
2) VARIETY
3) LOVE & CONNECTION
4) SIGNIFICANCE

There is a distinction that is important to understand regarding the four psychological NEEDS. Several of the terms used for our psychological NEEDS are the same as some of the emotions we as humans experience. This is not to infer that humans need to experience all of the available emotions that are possible.

As we examine these psychological NEEDS, three of the five words used to describe our four psychological NEEDS are the same words used to describe emotions.

As individuals, we are all capable of experiencing a wide range of emotions. As for some of these emotions, our lives would be more pleasant if we never experience them. This is not true regarding the psychological NEEDS that each of us have. If a person does not get their psychological NEEDS met, they will experience a great deal of discomfort and trauma.

The Two Top Priorities of your Unconscious mind is to keep You Physically Alive & to Meet Your Psychological Needs

CERTAINTY is one that can be classified as an emotion or a state of being. The key to understanding how important CERTAINTY is, is to consider the lack of it. If CERTAINTY is lacking, it is often replaced by fear, which is a negative emotion that everyone wants to avoid.

LOVE has to do with a relationship with someone else. If there is no LOVE there, the next best thing is CONNECTION. We all desire to be loved, but when we feel unloved, CONNECTION will do. This plays out in many ways, as we will see. SIGNIFICANCE is another psychological NEED that is also considered an emotion.

Once physical needs are met, a person will seek ways to fill their psychological NEEDS. Just as people have different personality temperaments that influence their likes and dislikes, people value NEEDS at different levels. Every individual will have a different NEEDS hierarchy.

Every person will seek to meet their NEEDS in the order of their NEEDS hierarchy. Some may have as their top priority NEED of LOVE/CONNECTION while another person may have a top NEED of CERTAINTY.

Rarely do people consciously think about the NEEDS I have mentioned on the preceeding pages. They may experience a longing to be with someone or to accomplish something, or feel compelled to do something, but the underlying factor that is motivating them is rarely understood.

How Important is it for People to Have their Psychological NEEDS met?

People are wired so strongly at the unconscious level toward filling their psychological NEEDS that if they are unable to meet them in an acceptable manner, they will violate their own values, which they may have held for many years, so that they can meet their unmet NEED. Men have left women and vice versa for someone else. If you were to try to figure out why in the world they would leave their spouse for the other person, there does not appear to be a logical reason.

We will explore the NEED of CERTAINTY first. Even though CERTAINTY is a psychological NEED, one aspect of it is linked to our physical needs. If a person is unsure of how their physical needs are going to be provided for, they will experience some UNCERTAINTY that could reach levels of extreme fear, if circumstances were dire. If a person's physical needs are not met, it could result in their physical death, so it is naturally taken very seriously.

Imagine you are traveling by air or ship and it goes sour: the vessel you are on goes down in the water. You and several other people are in a life raft. You drift all night and all day, occasionally spotting sharks as they circle your raft. Darkness comes again, and you're the last one to fall asleep.

When you finally open your eyes you get a glimpse of land. Everyone is excited at the prospect, and after another half a day you and your companions reach land.

Once on land, you look back out at the ocean and see an occasional shark fin, and you think to yourself, *safe at last*. After breathing a sigh of relief, you and the others set out to explore the island and find some water. Everyone is hungry, but the most important thing to find is fresh water. Everybody knows they could go for weeks without food, but will only last several days without water, and that was already being pushed. As you search the island, it becomes very clear that if you don't find water soon, it will mean certain death. This drives everyone on with new vigor.

It is agreed that the group should split up, allowing more ground to be covered faster. At a certain time everyone will meet at a certain spot. For the rest of the day everyone searches. As the meeting time gets closer, everyone starts heading to the meeting place. One of the people spots another castaway and starts running as fast as he can. He trips and falls down a steep slope. When he finally lands at the bottom of the ravine with a crash, he feels pain all over his body. In a matter of minutes you join him, along with some of the other castaways. As he is helped up, he realizes that he is all wet and muddy. You look around and discover he had landed in a puddle of water.

Water at last. Everyone starts drinking. The water itself doesn't taste too good-- it has a muddy taste--but that doesn't bother them. This means they will live and that is what counts. As the days pass, it becomes clear that the island is deserted and you and your companions are the only people on it.

One of your group discovers a spot where fish can easily be trapped and then caught by hand. After a week on the island, much progress has been made. Thankfully it rains every other day and the puddle is adequate as a water supply, although it always has a taste to it. Another castaway is able to get a fire going, which he keeps feeding and won't let go out. Things are starting to settle down, and the sense of urgency is not as strong as it was before.

That night as everyone is sitting around a soothing fire, someone mentions his family back home. "I can't believe I forgot about my family back home for the last week." Everyone gets quiet. Even though their bellies are finally full for the first time since they crashed, they now feel a different kind of pain for the first time since they landed on the island.

Each one in the group feels it, yet each one is affected differently. This new pain that is felt reaches much deeper than the physical pain each of them experienced since landing on the island. This pain is not so easily remedied. Now they face their longest and most formidable challenge.

Days turn into weeks and then months. Several storms come through and all but destroy the shelters they have constructed. Most of the time they all keep busy simply staying alive. Some of their most challenging times are when things go well and they have more time on their hands to think. When they focus totally on what they are doing, the time goes fast and they are happiest. Occasionally, when they are doing things that don't require all their focus, they are hit with waves of emotion that feel like they might knock them over.

They all conclude that it is best for them to keep busy until they are rescued. Inwardly, each of them wonders if they are ever going to be rescued from the island.

Can you image actually being in that position? It would take all your efforts to live, something we take for granted. As you can see, once they were getting settled, they started thinking about other things. They were starting to feel their psychological NEEDS, which we will look at in detail now.

CERTAINTY

There are two aspects of CERTAINTY, as I mentioned, and each of us needs some amount of CERTAINTY regarding our physical needs being met.

People will focus first on the physical aspects of staying alive. Their need for CERTAINTY will always start in the area of the physical; once they have reached a level of CERTAINTY that they are comfortable with, they can then turn their attention to aspects of CERTAINTY that are not related to their physical existence.

What a Person Focuses on Will Either Create CERTAINTY within Themselves or Destroy the CERTAINTY They Already Have.

Sometimes CERTAINTY and SIGNIFICANCE become blurred. What some consider a luxury others will view as a necessity. If a person's living standard drops quickly one of the biggest challenges may very well be finding CERTAINTY in the transition period until they level out and adjust into the new standard of living.

Each of us possesses the need for CERTAINTY in varying degrees. The motivating factor behind this NEED is to eliminate or avoid stress, with the intent of increasing and intensifying pleasure.

The physical part of our CERTAINTY is derived from our surroundings and based on whether we ***believe*** we are safe. Will we freeze? Do we have water and food to eat? Our psychological NEED for CERTAINTY is, to a degree, hinged on our physical world in that our psychological NEEDS cannot be met until our physical needs are satisfied.

People's psychological NEED for CERTAINTY is affected by their models, perceptions and beliefs. Add to that the meanings they give events in their life and what they are focusing on, and they have the ingredients that will determine the level of CERTAINTY they will experience. All psychological CERTAINTY is created and destroyed by their focus and the meanings they give things in their life.

Because people have physical needs, it is easy to unconsciously link obtaining physical things with CERTAINTY. In reality, CERTAINTY is an internal state. Unfortunately, a large number of people have unconsciously linked physical things or the actions of others to the amount of CERTAINTY they experience on a daily basis.

Love and Connection

Each of us has our models of what love is and is not. This is true for all of the different relationships that exist between people: husband-wife, parent-child, child-parent, grandparents-grandchild, in-laws and out-laws. We all have our own beliefs and models about what love is and how it shows up in each of these relationships.

It is clear when people are not speaking the same language: when one is speaking Spanish and the other is speaking Chinese. It is quite another matter when both people are speaking the same words, in the same language, and they aren't understanding each other.

Because love is not always communicated with words, people get confused and frustrated. **Love is not exempt from meanings and interpretations.** Each of us has a preferred method of showing people that we love them. When someone shows love to us in the same manner that we prefer to show love, we understand and give the meaning that they love us. The reason is simple: it is spoken in our language or preferred style.

I know one couple who was near the point of splitting up. In talking with him, he told me he didn't feel loved. He said he would always tell her he loved her, but she never told him. His conclusion was that she didn't love him.

Remember how people treat their conclusions. If they came to the conclusion themselves, unless they make special efforts to test that conclusion, their conclusion will be accepted as truth. The conclusions people personally come to do not go through the same evaluation process as do the things they are told by others. This is especially true when emotions are high. Remember, conclusions are often perceived and accepted as reality without being tested or proven.

When I talked with her about their situation, she made it clear that she loved him a great deal. She even told me that if she didn't love him a tremendous amount she would have split up long before now. She went on to tell me "I show him I love him all the time. I love doing things for him, fixing him dinner, folding his socks, etc... Why does he always ask me if I love him anyway? I am showing him every day."

As you can see, they were both showing their love for the other, but they were communicating it in a way that the other didn't understand. When I talked with her husband, I asked him how his wife communicated her love.

"She doesn't," he said.

"Are you so sure?" I asked.

"Well if she does, I certainly don't see it."

When I asked him what she was always doing for him, he came up with a long list.

"Have you ever considered that these things are how she shows her love for you?"

"You've got to be kidding me," he said. "How in the world is folding my socks or cooking my dinner supposed to express love? It doesn't make sense."

I explained that to him it might not, because his approach to showing love is to speak it, while her preferred way to communicate love is through doing things for the one she loves. In reality, they both loved each other very much but were looking through their own model of how they communicate love.

Because what the other was doing did not fit into their model, they were missing it. Each was responding to their model of the world and the beliefs they held to of what love looks like and how it is communicated.

Everyone has a preferred way of showing that they love someone. When love is communicated to them using their preferred approach, they understand they are loved.

This is true of how love is shown between children and parents, also. Children can, and often do, have different ways of showing love, and it is in their preferred way to show love that they will understand when someone else is showing them love.

More couples & families have experienced heart-ache over love that was there, but was not recognized by the other party. People typically don't say, "This is how I am showing my spouse and family that I love them." Rarely do people go up to the ones they love and explain how they are trying to communicate their love for them. The person showing love usually doesn't ask the question "Do you accept and feel loved as a result of how I am expressing my love for you?"

In his book *The Five Love Languages*, Gary Chapman outlines five common ways that people communicate and understand love. They are:

1. Spending time together
2. Doing things for others
3. Saying how they feel
4. Giving gifts
5. Touching physically

Typically, the way a person shows love to others is the way they understand love that is shown to them.

One of the things that happens when a person feels loved is that they feel that they are significant, and understandably so. CERTAINTY and SIGNIFICANCE are by-products of love communicated in the preferred style of the other person, because it is understood clearly and it removes any doubt and questioning.

Love That is Unseen is Often Believed to Not Exist

One of the greatest challenges people face in the meeting of their psychological NEEDS is a result of misunderstandings and meanings that they give things. When a person is loved and that love is communicated but in a way that is not understood, the person feels unloved. This can affect their self-perceptions, and their inner identity.

When each spouse is showing love in ways that are not understood, it can have a snowball effect. I recently listened to a husband and wife. She was complaining that he didn't love her. I asked her how she knew. Her answer is below.

"He never gets me anything. If he would only bring me a card or something. It doesn't have to be expensive at all."

He countered with, "What do you mean I don't love you? I tell you every day that I love you. In fact you never tell me you love me, like I tell you. Instead you are always giving me little things. For what, I don't know."

Both of these people were showing love to the other in their own preferred style. The sad part was that because their spouse was not communicating it in their preferred style, they were giving the meaning that they were not loved. The whole time the other person was saying I love you, but it was not understood.

When a person has not felt LOVE for some time, their unconscious mind looks for LOVE, but when it can't find love, it will settle for CONNECTION, which is the next best thing in its understanding. (If LOVE is not available, CONNECTION will do.) When a person feels UNLOVED, the CONNECTION aspect is activated when one person is connected to another because of a negative event or activity that is taking place.

Something happens (a misunderstanding, perhaps, or an accident) and there is a disagreement. When this happens, the unconscious minds takes notes of how a disagreement meets many

Connection Can Exist in Both Positive and Negative Forms.

different NEEDS. Over a course of time, their unconscious mind incorporates disagreements as a viable method of meeting psychological NEEDS. Most couples who argue a lot are somewhere on this path. If they don't do something to reverse this process their relationship will be known by the motto: "Misery loves company."

Bonding through shared experiences is a common way that CONNECTION is made. Soldiers who serve and fight as a team build a very strong bond among themselves. The more intense and emotionally charged the situations are, the stronger the bond they experience.

Sometimes a man and a woman are in very intense situations where there is great danger. That type of situation will cause a bond to form between them. During that type of experience, they are experiencing VARIETY at high levels, they look to each other for CERTAINTY, and without doubt they are SIGNIFICANT to each other. Their situation causes them to bond to each other at a deep level.

If a man and a woman are in an intense situation and are wearing masculine and feminine hats that are naturally complementary, they will feel the natural drawing effects that exist within gender dynamics. Add to that the bonding that is taking place and they could very well find the other person totally irresistible and have no idea why.

When two people meet in the above situation and fall in love with each other and get married, once life returns to normal, it is possible that they could one day realize that they are not at all alike and wonder why they ever got together. If, by chance, one of them should change the masculine or feminine hat they are wearing, the natural drawing power within gender dynamics will reverse to a repelling power.

When a couple is in this position, their chances of staying together and enjoying life together are slim. If, on the other hand, they understand what is happening and they are open and willing to see what is at work behind the scenes, while making a few adjustments in their models and meanings, they can return to having a wonderful life together.

Rapport/Sameness is another way in which CONNECTION is made. This happens at a different level. When we perceive someone to be similar to ourselves, there is a level of rapport that is created. But beyond that, when someone is in many ways perceived as the same as we are, there is an unconscious CONNECTION that is created.

When a person meets someone who is like them and has made the same choices, those facts affirm each of them in their own decisions. They feel better about themselves as a result of meeting and getting to know this other person. As a result of meeting, both people can go away encouraged that they have made wise decisions. This commonality at the unconscious level deepens the level of rapport that is created.

The Need for SIGNIFICANCE is Multi-Layered in its Application to People

Everyone reading this is a unique individual and is significant for that very reason. In the movie "Fool's Gold," Moe refers to Alfonz as the "Ukrainian sidekick."

Alfonz's response was, "I don't think of myself in that way. I am the lead character in my own story."

That statement contains a great amount of truth that is so often overlooked. You are your own lead character. You are the star of your own show. Each person is significant. But the problem comes about when a person begins to feel insignificant as a result of the meanings they give events. If love is there but communicated in a way that you didn't understand, it would be easy to give meanings in the opposite direction and the emotions that would be experienced would be that of a lack of love and of being insignificant.

Everyone longs to be loved and accepted. This is true regardless of culture or geography. When a person first starts to question whether they are loved it is usually a result of the emotions they are feeling. Then they ask themselves a series of questions that they answer themselves. The answers and conclusions to those questions are almost always in agreement with the emotions they are feeling. People are wired at the unconscious level to remain consistent with who they perceive themselves to be; the challenge is that often how they perceive themselves to be is based on the emotions they are feeling.

The thought that "I have an unmet psychological NEED that is behind this emotion I am feeling" does not happen unless you have trained yourself to recognize the link that exists between unmet NEEDS and the corresponding emotions that are created as a result of the unmet NEEDS.

Parents are busy people. They have a million things to do and a short time to do them, not to mention the fact that they, too, are seeking to meet their NEEDS as well as take care of others. Spouses and children don't come with instruction manuals. It would be nice if they did. In fact, it would be nice if we came with an instruction manual for ourselves as well. But we, and they, do not. So everybody does the best they know to do.

Just as it is easy for a person to show love to their spouse in a way that is missed, it is just as easy to show love to a child in a way that is not understood as love by the child.

When a child does something that people respond to in the way the child understands love, the child will notice it, and will want to do it, or something like it, again. A man I know was traveling somewhere with his seven-year-old son. Their car broke down on the way, and while they were waiting for help to arrive the father and son sat in the hot car and talked. The dad was not only uncomfortable, but very irritated as well. Sweat was rolling off both of them for almost an hour while they talked about this and that.

Help finally arrived and they were on their way again. Several weeks later, when the father returned home after being gone a few days, the son asked his dad if they could go and sit in the car for a while. This surprised his dad, who asked where he wanted to go.

"No where," the son answered. "I just wanted to sit in the car with you."

The son's preferred form of showing love was to spend time together, and it didn't matter to him if he had sweat dripping from him the whole time. He was with his daddy and that was what mattered to him. Ten years later that man's son still talks about that time he and his dad spent sitting in the car that day. The son remembers it fondly, while the father remembers it as a major inconvenience.

When children don't get the LOVE they crave, they find ways to get it. When a child does something and gets the attention they long for, and that is the only time they get the attention, their unconscious mind picks up that the way to get their NEED for LOVE met is to do things.

The things could be anything. Sometimes they're good and sometimes they're bad. A child's unconscious mind's first priority is to get their psychological NEEDS met. When the link is formed between getting their NEED for LOVE and CONNECTION met through doing things, a pattern is created. Doing good things usually rewards the child with their NEED for LOVE being met. Doing bad things always meets their NEED at the level of CONNECTION, but never at the level of LOVE.

"If I do things, I get LOVE. The more significant my accomplishments, the more LOVE I will receive." Add to this the cause and effect perspective regarding getting their NEED for LOVE met and the fact that in today's world success is measured by what you accomplish, and you have the makings of an almost inescapable trap.

Models and strategies are major players in forming and reinforcing a person's inner identity, which we will examine in the next section.

Humans are unique in that it is possible for them to lose respect for themselves. This is something that separates mankind from every other living thing. SIGNIFICANCE and self-respect are closely linked to each other and how they affect a person's self-perceptions.

Most people rarely consider themselves as significant in their own eyes. There are many reasons for this. Many people come to believe that they are somehow, in some way, less valuable as a result of the meanings they have given events that have taken place in their lives.

When they look back over their life, it is likely that they have not learned that they give events meanings and that those meanings alter them. Rather, it is highly possible that they look back over their lives and attribute the way they are to what has happened in their life, rather than the meanings they have given what has happened.

Remember, it is not what happens to you, but what you do with what happens to you that matters. What you do with what happens to you affects your self-perceptions and your inner identity, which we will explore in greater detail later.

When a person sees themselves as insignificant, they are restricting themselves to a small percentage of who they can be and what they can do.

VARIETY

CERTAINTY is important to each of us, but too much CERTAINTY can drive a person crazy. VARIETY is a need that each of us has in varying degrees. Too much of the same kind of food and we can get to the point that we dread eating. So it can be with work and other tasks, also.

The amount of VARIETY needed changes from one personality temperament to another. Some people love surprises while other don't. Roller coasters are a good example of excitement, which is another form of VARIETY. Whatever your temperament, you have a certain amount of VARIETY that fits you just right. Too much and you begin to lose your CERTAINTY, too little and you start to go stir crazy.

When an event contains too much variety for their temperament, the person experiences a rising level of uncertainty. The reason for this is simply that when variety and excitement cross the line for an individual, it can become very unsettling and can turn to fear. The intensity of the emotions an individual experiences will be determined by the meanings and words that person uses to describe the event.

The Greater the Emotional Intensity of an Event the Stronger the Memory

When the situation turns fearful, the meanings and emotions that ensue can be intense enough to leave strong memories. Once the event is labeled, the label becomes the event. From that point on, the label and everything that reinforces it are remembered. Anything that is contrary to the label is filtered out and forgotten as a result of the label that was assigned to the event.

Only the emotions that are in alignment with the label will be remembered. For instance, a boy loved dogs as a child. When he was a young man, he was attacked by a mad dog. After experiencing the attack, if he simply saw a dog, he became fearful.

SIGNIFICANCE

The psychological NEED for SIGNIFICANCE has driven people to do some pretty wild things throughout the years. *SIGNIFICANCE* has been referred to many times throughout this section on NEEDS, and we have already learned a great deal about it. The things that make a person significant are the things that set that person apart from others. This has a catch to it. The more significant a person is, the more isolated they are. This is because people can relate to them less because they are so different.

There is an aspect of SIGNIFICANCE closely linked to LOVE and CONNECTION. When someone is in love with someone else, it is common to refer to the other person as their "significant other" and there is good reason for this. The other person is significant to them, and they communicate it in many ways. If the other person begins to *feel* that they are no longer SIGNIFICANT in the eyes of the one they love, the *feelings* of LOVE they experience will drop proportionality. In reality, the five love languages are all different ways of communicating significance.

An individual's personality temperament and whether they have an internal or external frame of reference, coupled with their beliefs and models, will be key elements in how they seek to fill their psychological NEEDS that are unmet as a result of higher than average significance.

Each individual temperament has its own unique NEEDS hierarchy. The following list is for a single personality temperament makeup. It does not reflect the NEEDS hierarchy blends.

Sanguine
(Sang)

1. Significance
2. Love & Connection
3. Variety
4. Certainty

Choleric
(Chol)

1. Significance
2. Variety
3. Certainty
4. Love & Connection

Melancholy
(Mel)

1. Certainty
2. Significance
3. Love & Connection
4. Variety

Phlegmatic
(Phleg)

1. Love & Connection
2. Certainty
3. Significance
4. Variety

No one is strictly one personality temperament.

Each of us is a blend of two or more temperaments and each temperament blend has a general NEEDS hierarchy that is common to that blend. The list of the twelve blends and the NEEDS hierarchy list for each is on page 117. This NEEDS hierarchy is based on a 60/40 to 65/35 temperament mix. These are not hard and fast, but they do give some insights into what drives people.

The list on the next page is helpful in that it gives insights. Temperament blends vary in their make up. One person might be 50/50 while another is 70/30 or 80/20. Everyone is different. When you go through this list, you may notice some minor differences between the list and yourself. That is not unusual. You are simply a different ratio.

It is important to understand that your NEEDS hierarchy drives you toward certain things. As an example of this, let's consider the Choleric/Sanguine as compared to the Phlegmatic/Melancholy.

The Choleric/Sanguine, who typically has SIGNIFICANCE and VARIETY as their two top NEEDS, will be outgoing and will thrive in an environment where there is a great deal of activity, change, and where they are in, or near, the center of attention. As long as they know the sun will shine and there is food in the refrigerator, they have their CERTAINTY.

The Choleric side will look to fill their NEED for SIGNIFICANCE through accomplishments, while their Sanguine side will smooth some of the Choleric's rough edges off when they are working with people. Don't misunderstand: the Choleric/Sanguine can be very forceful if they are not careful. This combination has a double dose of extrovert, making them extremely outgoing. They love to talk and it is usually loud.

In contrast to the Choleric/Sanguine, the Phlegmatic/Melancholy is not nearly as outgoing. They are driven to get along with people and their NEED for CERTAINTY is geared in the direction of relationships. CERTAINTY is important to the Phlegmatic/Melancholy in many areas of their life, but it is especially important to them in their relationships with others. Phlegmatics do not like confrontation.

Listed out on the next page is the NEEDS hierarchy for the temperament blends.

Needs Hierarchy list for Temperament Blends

Sang/Chol

1. Significance
2. Variety
3. Love & Connection
4. Certainty

Sang/Mel

1. Significance
2. Love & Connection
3. Certainty
4. Variety

Sang/Phleg

1. Love & Connection
2. Significance
3. Certainty
4. Variety

Mel/Sang

1. Certainty
2. Significance
3. Variety
4. Love & Connection

Mel/Chol

1. Certainty
2. Significance
3. Love & Connection
4. Variety

Mel/Phleg

1. Certainty
2. Love & Connection
3. Significance
4. Variety

Chol/Sang

1. Significance
2. Variety
3. Love & Connection
4. Certainty

Chol/Mel

1. Significance
2. Love & Connection
3. Certainty
4. Variety

Chol/Phleg

1. Love & Connection
2. Significance
3. Certainty
4. Variety

Phleg/Sang

1. Love & Connection
2. Significance
3. Variety
4. Certainty

Phleg/Chol

1. Love & Connection
2. Significance
3. Certainty
4. Variety

Phleg/Mel

1. Love & Connection
2. Certainty
3. Significance
4. Variety

The Phlegmatic/Melancholy has a double dose of introvert, and as a result, they are comfortable around a few people, but uncomfortable around large groups. They like to be with people they know and aren't comfortable meeting people for the first time. When they do meet someone, they like the other person to come up to them, rather than going up to a stranger and introducing themselves.

The Choleric/Sanguine and the Phlegmatic/Melancholy will meet their NEEDS in totally different ways. If each were forced into the other's way of doing things, they would both be very uncomfortable. If these two were to meet, it is possible that they would not hit it off right away, though they would be able to get along and work together. The Choleric/Sanguine would typically be in the lead with the Phlegmatic/Melancholy taking up a support role, which they would be comfortable with and even enjoy. But as you can see, their approaches to every aspect of life would be from totally different directions.

As a rule of thumb, each personality temperament blend has a NEEDS hierarchy that is common to that blend. *This is not to say that they have to have this order to their NEEDS. Remember, if your top NEEDS are being met and your lowest NEED is unmet, it moves to the top of the list until it is met, then it returns to its normal position.* In reality, **a person's NEEDS hierarchy list is somewhat fluid.**

Too much CERTAINTY will drive you crazy. Have you ever become stir crazy, bored and feeling like you were about to go out of your mind? You may not have known what you wanted to do, but you knew you had to do something different. If you have experienced this, you have had an overdose of CERTAINTY.

In relationships, if there is too much CERTAINTY, one of the two will create some VARIETY, often in the form of a fight. In a fight there is VARIETY because you don't know how or what is actually going to happen, and it can be exciting. For some couples, the making up is worth the fight, which covers VARIETY and CERTAINTY.

When it comes to physical things, it is easy to confuse our wants with our needs. The American public has been bombarded for generations with the teaching that we need things to be bigger, better, and different. While watching what is being advertised, it is easy to feel we need to get it, and that is exactly what the advertisers are trying to achieve.

The reason people feel they need whatever is being advertised is a result of the way it is being presented. In reality, the most convincing and effective advertising is directed at the unconscious mind, with the intent of creating the feeling that an individual's psychological NEEDS will be met as a result of purchasing a product.

Any short-term advertising has caught your attention because it has appealed to your psychological NEEDS while being in line with your models. With long-term advertising, it is possible to shift people's perceptions about how their NEEDS can be met. This has been used very effectively by many of the larger businesses in their advertising.

In long-term advertising, the ultimate goal is to build its name into a brand name. This strategy appeals to a person's NEED for SIGNIFICANCE, CERTAINTY and VARIETY depending on the way their product is advertised. Short-term advertising is geared more for the quick decision: the sale. Each of these styles of advertising have their own unique approach, although there can be some overlapping of the two.

What takes place is the transfer of meanings and beliefs that the seller wants the buyer to embrace, as a result of certain psychological laws. An example is the law of association. If people are shown having a great time while using the product, if the product and the way it is being presented fits in with a person's models, it is possible to make an unconscious link that if they buy that product, they will experience a great time as well.

It is easy for people to unconsciously link things and lifestyle as a necessity for their psychological NEEDS to be met. Depending on the lifestyle you are accustomed to, you may think you require a great deal before you experience CERTAINTY. Someone else may find their psychological NEEDS met when they have much less. People who have a lower standard of living can have their psychological NEEDS met at high levels despite their economic situation.

If you were to visit a third world country, you would see families that have nothing compared to most Americans, yet they are happy, well balanced and having a great time. I have looked at the homes and situations that many people in third world countries are facing each day, but to my surprise, they are not concerned or worried.

Our beliefs regarding what it takes to meet our physical needs are key to determining when we can relax our pursuit in the area of physical things.

This is something that has caused, and is causing, many Americans a great deal of stress these days. One thing that has been a driving force in our society is that of getting better homes and nicer cars. For some it has been a race with the Jones'.

When a person unconsciously makes a link between the acquiring of physical things and getting their psychological NEEDS met, the result is the feeling that they have to have certain physical things that, in reality, they would be fine without. This is largely a result of the way advertisers are packaging and the way they present their products. When people are depicted as significant when they have a certain product, the advertisers know that people are likely to unconsciously link getting their product with having SIGNIFICANCE.

As a result, people actually feel they need to buy physical things that they really do not need because they have unconsciously linked the acquiring of physical item to the meeting of their psychological NEEDS. They buy what they otherwise would not purchase and later they often wonder why they purchased it to begin with.

Why do people buy things if the physical object is not necessary for them to meet their psychological NEEDS? Because they have been convinced that it will give them the feelings they desire. Things only fill a person's psychological NEEDS for a very short period of time. The reason for this is simple. As the newness wears off and they see that someone else has the same thing, they change the meanings that they are giving to the item. In reality, the thing never met the person's psychological NEEDS. Once the person got the thing they believed they needed, in their mind, they actually let themselves meet their own NEED.

So what am I getting at? We have all adopted beliefs of what we need so we can meet our NEEDS. For some, any car will do, while for others it has to be a certain kind and the newest year out. For others it has to be a certain house in a certain neighborhood. In reality, this has more to do with trying to meet our need for SIGNIFICANCE. If you ask any one of these people, however, they would probably be very adamant that they must have this and that.

While I was on a trip to Ecuador, I met many people who had families to support and the only work that was available paid one dollar for a twelve-hour work day. These people considered themselves lucky. You might find yourself wondering, like I did, how these people can make it on that. Their living standard is different from ours and they are ingenious when it comes to making do with what they have.

When people don't have much and have to make do with what they have, the by-products are numerous. When people overcome many challenges, they naturally reward themselves with SIGNIFICANCE. They gain CERTAINTY in their abilities, which fosters inner confidence and affects how they perceive themselves.

It is easier to expand our models, rather than being picked up from one model and set down into another, totally different one. The same is true for living standards. Granted, it is never fun going down from the living standard we are accustomed to.

I was on another trip to Nairobi, Kenya. I had never been to Africa before and it was like I had seen in many movies, but the movies can't bring the smells, heat and poverty to you like the real thing. As we would drive up to a slum made out of anything the people could find to build some form of shelter, hundreds and hundreds of children would come running alongside the matatu (African taxi) we were in. They would be smiling and just as happy as they could be. I was constantly amazed at their cheer. It was genuine.

The Happiness that People Seek will NEVER be Found in Getting More

A Person Must find Thankfulness First Only Then are They on the Road to Discovering Happiness

Each of us on that trip was taught a great lesson by those we met. I met one man who was hunting for food for his family. We found him looking through a garbage pile on the side of the road. Several trucks had just emptied their garbage and he was thrilled to be there when they unloaded. We have a hard time hearing about people in those situations. You may even have found reading this to be difficult and might be wondering why I have included it.

The reality is, those people who we looked at and felt sorry for, don't feel sorry for themselves. According to our standards, they are barely surviving. They don't have much, but everything they did have they are thankful for.

I said earlier that a person's psychological NEEDS could not be met until their physical needs had been met, and that is true. The point is, ***sometimes we are not happy because we are not thankful for what we do have.*** Happiness will never be found in getting more. Getting more by itself doesn't do it; being thankful for what we do have will open the door for happiness.

It can seem as though happiness and love are linked together when a person is on the positive side of the love equation. When a person is not feeling loved, that person will try to earn LOVE from the one they admire and look up to. They will often try to get the attention of the one they long to be close to by doing something. Usually they will do something that they think the other person will like with the hope that they will be recognized (SIGNIFICANCE) and be rewarded with the LOVE they so desire.

If that doesn't work, they can always get CONNECTION with the other person by doing things they know will get them in trouble with the one whom they are longing to receive LOVE from.

If you have ever wondered why a child will deliberately do something that they know they will be in trouble over, now you have new insights. Yes, it is true they will not get the LOVE they prefer, but CONNECTION will do. After all, it's better than nothing at all. When someone does something they should not, they get the undivided attention of the other person. One action can meet their psychological NEEDS for CONNECTION, VARIETY, and SIGNIFICANCE, all at high levels.

Their NEEDS are not only met through the CONNECTION that is forced in relation to the one whose love they have not been able to earn, but, if their peers are around and praise them for their actions, they are receiving praise, SIGNIFICANCE, LOVE, acceptance, VARIETY and CERTAINTY at very high levels. Add that to the rewards of CONNECTION, VARIETY and CERTAINTY they received from the behavior that got them into trouble. The strategy that was employed has the potential to become a major part of their routine and they rarely have any conscious idea of why!

Meeting Needs

The Why of Most Behaviors

Why do people do what they do? Why does a person start smoking when everyone knows that smoking can, and does, kill over the long term? At the very least, it will shorten their life by many years. So why do they do it?

I remember when I was a kid; several of the boys on our block were together when one of them pulled out a cigarette.

"Look what I got. Let's smoke it."

There were mixed murmurings within the group. The same one who had the cigarette had a match and he lit up the cigarette.

"Look, it's burning," someone said.

"Who's going first?"

"Not me," someone else said.

The guy who had the cigarette was the third one to go. I didn't want to try it. My dad smoked and he told me he wished he had never started. When the cigarette was handed to me, I puffed on it one time. It burned my throat and I started coughing. I had more than I wanted of cigarettes.

Some of the boys in our group that day went on to become smokers. Now, all of them would tell you they wished they had not started smoking when they were younger. So why did they? Was it because smoke did not burn their throats when they tried it, or that they liked the flavor of the smoke? The truth is, the smoke burned their throats and it did not taste good either.

What happened to them was that certain meanings were given to smoking that encouraged them to endure the pain of forcing their bodies to become accustomed to smoking. I remember hearing comments like "What's wrong, baby, can't you handle smoking? Grow up." That didn't bother me. My attitude was that I didn't care what they said, I was not going to smoke, and I am thankful that I didn't.

You may be wondering why some started smoking and others did not. I know that I have asked that question many times about smoking and many other things. There are actually two main factors that come into play regarding what people will and will not do. One is their NEEDS hierarchy and the other is their personality temperament makeup.

If a person has SIGNIFICANCE as their top NEED, they will be more apt to do things that are considered significant in the eyes of others. The higher the placement of SIGNIFICANCE in a person's hierarchy of NEEDS, the more they will be pulled to do things to gain the SIGNIFICANCE they crave. If someone were to ask them why they do all that stuff, they would likely be unable to explain it.

If you consider different groups that develop in high school students, there are the jocks and non-jocks. Those who are good at sports get their SIGNIFICANCE and popularity as a by-product of their ability to play sports well. This works the same way for the girls: you have the cheerleaders and the non-cheerleaders. So what do the non-jocks and non-cheerleaders do? Something else, of course. But what? Well, what did you do? Were you a jock or a cheerleader? The largest majority of students weren't, so chances are you were not. Typically, what happens is that something occurs that was not thought out or planned and your top NEED is met. If this is repeated, it becomes the method of meeting your NEED.

If a student gets praised for their ability in math or reading, it results in meeting their NEED for SIGNIFICANCE. SIGNIFICANCE is an important NEED in children and young people. If you don't stand out, you don't get noticed and you don't get the LOVE you need more than anything else. It doesn't matter if it is a large family or a classroom, each child will seek some way to get attention.

If a child, or even a teenager, is not feeling significant enough they will act up to get attention. It is not for the purpose of being bad or rebelling for the sake of rebelling: it is to get their NEED for SIGNIFICANCE and CONNECTION met. How much SIGNIFICANCE does a child get when he or she is taken out of class for disruptive behavior? What happens when they get with their friends?

I remember one day a friend of mine and I were in the alley behind my house. We were not really doing anything wrong, I remember we were throwing rocks down the alley to see who could throw the farthest. An old lady came out to put her garbage in her cans and started yelling at us.

My friend and I looked at each other, shocked at our treatment over a rock throwing contest. I didn't know what to say except sorry. My friend, on the other hand, had a great deal to say to the older lady. (As a kid everyone is old.) He let out a string of words that I had never heard before and from the look on the lady's face, I don't think that she had heard them, either. In fact, her mouth fell open and she said "Why, I never!" and she left in a hurry. I must say: I was somewhat impressed. I had never seen a kid have that kind of power over an adult before.

I remember I said to him, "Wow, Randy! I never heard anyone talk to anybody like that before." I still remember the look on his face. He *felt* SIGNIFICANT without doubt. I had no idea that I was encouraging a negative strategy for meeting his NEED for SIGNIFICANCE and CONNECTION. This happens every time a child or teen gets into trouble. They get their need for SIGNIFICANCE met, maybe not at that moment, but later when they are with their friends, they enjoy the fruits of their labors.

Each one of us can probably look back on our lives and see the same type of events. Knowing what I now know, I wish I had responded differently and not encouraged my friend to talk like that to people, but each of us does the best we can with the knowledge we have at the time.

Conclusion to the NEEDS section

A person's NEEDS for CERTAINTY, VARIETY, LOVE and CONNECTION, and SIGNIFICANCE are psychological in that each of these NEEDS are dependent on what an individual does in their mind. The direction of a person's focus and the meanings they give events will be the determining factor in whether a person's psychological NEEDS are met.

There are several challenges that people face. One is that the majority of people don't know that they have psychological NEEDS, let alone how to fill them. Another challenge is that often a tug of war is going on between their conscious and unconscious mind regarding what they are going to do. The conscious mind tries to guide them in one direction while their unconscious mind is steering them toward meeting their psychological NEEDS using auto-pilot programming that has been learned.

People have not been taught how this all works or how to make changes in how they meet their psychological NEEDS. As a result, many people find themselves stuck in a rut and have no idea of how to get out, or what is holding them back. ***What will keep people stuck is that they are meeting their psychological NEEDS in that rut.*** Until they begin meeting their psychological NEEDS through a different source, they will remain trapped in their rut. A key insight that frees people when they finally get it, is:

You as an Individual
Have the Ability to Meet Your
Own Psychological Needs
in a
Multitude of Ways

Once you realize this and learn how to do it, you can take your life to a whole new level. The quality of your life will be determined by whether you consciously chose how you are going to meet your NEEDS or if you simply let it happen to you. Beware, if you do not continually make the conscious decision to meet your psychological NEEDS in positive ways, you are placing yourself in a precarious position that will affect the quality of your life.

IDENTITY

Who are you?

Do you really know who you are or do you only know what others have told you? What is your identity? Yes, you have a name that someone else gave you, but is it a name you would have picked yourself?

How much of Your Identity Have You Decided & How Much Have Others Decided for You?

What makes up your identity? You have a face, a name and fingerprints, but is that the end of your identity or is it the beginning? What comes to your mind when you think of a person's identity?

Here is what Webster's Dictionary 2nd college edition has for a definition of Identity and Identity crisis.

Identity:

1. The condition or fact of being the same or exactly alike; sameness; oneness [group united by identity or interests]

2. The condition or fact of being a specific person or thing; individuality

3. The condition of being the same as a person or thing described or claimed.

Identity crisis:

The condition of being uncertain of one's feelings about oneself, especially with regard to character, goals, and origins, occurring especially in adolescence as a result of growing up under disruptive, fast-changing conditions.

The definition of identity crisis gives better insight into a person's identity than the definition of identity.

At birth you don't know your name, and everything about yourself you learn from others. Children have no idea of their intellectual capabilities until they are told by others. This reference, once established, is a major pillar in their beliefs about themselves.

There are some aspects of an individual's identity that a person does not get to choose. When babies are born, their personality temperament blend is already in place. Life does not give them an opportunity to choose the personality temperament blend that they would like to have. It is common for people to form a great number of conclusions about themselves as a result of their personality temperament, likes and dislikes.

There are many contributors to a person's identity. Have you ever been to a doctor's office and seen a skeleton hanging from a string? Well, imagine if you will that this skeleton represents the parts of your identity you don't have a choice in, such as your sex, the color of your skin and eyes, your face, personality temperament blend and fingerprints. These are unchangeable, although some of them can be altered to an extent through surgery.

It is on this skeleton that the balance of your inner identity is fashioned. Just as a sculptor works with clay to fashion an object of beauty, so you and I get to fashion our inner identity. This brings us to the question: if I fashion my inner identity, how and when do I do that?

When we look in the mirror, we see much more than others see when they look at us. We see everything about ourselves. From our perspective, little is hidden from our eyes and each of us sees the good, the bad and the ugly. No one else will see the inner identity that we see when we look in the mirror.

A Person's Models & Beliefs Reflect Back on How they See Themselves

Don't be discouraged. A great deal of what you see as your identity that others don't is a direct result of your models and beliefs. So, where do we start in getting an understanding of our identity?

It is important that we start with how models affect people's perceptions of themselves. The reason we must start with models is that models are people's understanding of the world in which they live. Their beliefs about their world will reflect back on themselves.

Remember, whether or not we agree with someone's model is irrelevant. The model is all he knows. Let's consider the model *poverty is life*. If a person has this as his understanding of the world, how will that reflect back on him?

It doesn't matter what the model is; it will affect the way people see themselves. If their model is small in size, the people who adopt that model will, by default, perceive themselves as being capable of only accomplishing that which is possible within their model of the world. If their model is small or big, what they believe they can do with their lives will be a reflection of their models.

I cannot overstate the importance models play in how people perceive themselves and what they believe is possible for them to accomplish. Models are constructed from beliefs, some of which have been tested, and some of which have never been tested. People's beliefs about their world affects their identity.

Beliefs are multi-faceted. For every belief you have about the world around you, there is an unspoken corresponding belief about yourself. This is often overlooked, but it is felt at many levels within an individual.

Let's look at a belief in the form of a line. The first part of this line represents what a person believes is possible.

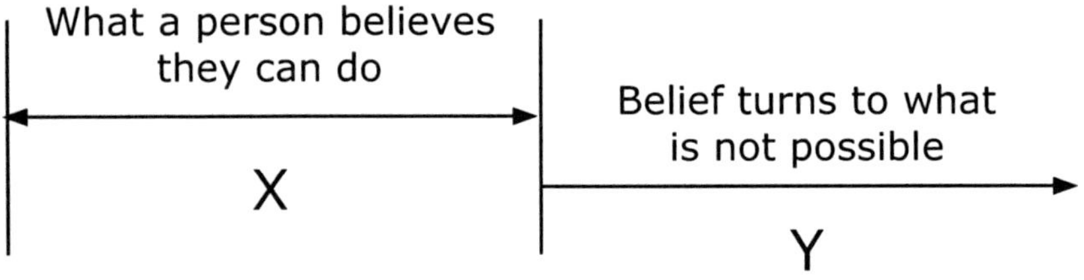

At the end of what we believe is possible, is the beginning of what we believe is *not* possible.

For the individual it goes like this: "I can do X" is what the conscious mind sees, and on the conscious level it stops there. The unconscious mind sees the bigger picture: "I can do X, but I cannot do Y." A person's unconscious mind is well aware of where a belief changes.

For the majority of readers, this may be the first time you have heard of this. If that is the case, you are now consciously aware of something that your unconscious mind has known all along.

The lack of understanding how a belief changes from positive to negative has confused more people than you can imagine. Remember, every time you consciously think through to yourself what you believe is possible for you, your unconscious mind acknowledges the positive side of the belief as well as the negative side.

What a person believes about themselves at the conscious and unconscious levels are incorporated into their inner identity. Until a person learns how this process operates, they will be extremely limited in what they can do to change it.

Typically a person's first conscious contact with unconscious beliefs is in the form of emotions that they don't understand and/or don't want to experience.

The effects of the unseen negative side of the belief will often show up in the form of uncomfortable feelings. So what happens when we experience this? Typically, we hesitate. We may want to proceed, but we are on shaky ground and we know it. Often the thought that we are somehow lacking crosses our minds, or the thought of "I don't have what it takes," or "I've got to be crazy." The farther a person goes beyond the point of where the belief changes, the more uncomfortable they are likely to become.

It is this uncertainty of what we are experiencing that can have an unsettling feeling that nobody likes and can be very fearsome for some. When all is said and done, we're not sure what happened except that we didn't like it and a boundary that has been felt before is reinforced in our minds.

How does this affect men who have grown up incongruent to their masculine core nature? Remember Keith, who was barely able to function when his mother passed away? His mother was always there for him to reassure him and encourage him in what he did. If something went wrong, she was there to support him and help him figure it out.

Keith, like all of us, had beliefs about what was possible for him, although Keith's situation was different from some people's. What Keith believed was possible for him was supported by a strong woman. During the first part of his life, his mother filled this spot, and after marriage his wife filled that spot until she had children. When Keith's wife was no longer the support he needed, he found that he could look to his mother again.

What happened with Keith was that he, like everyone else, believed in what he could do, but he had an additional twist to it; Keith's beliefs about what was possible for him at his unconscious level included his mother. At the conscious level, he was running his business and many other tasks in line with his beliefs of what he could do.

The drawing below shows how this played out for Keith. He had what he believed he could do just like everyone, but there was something more that Keith did not realize at first, but that he felt strongly after his mother died.

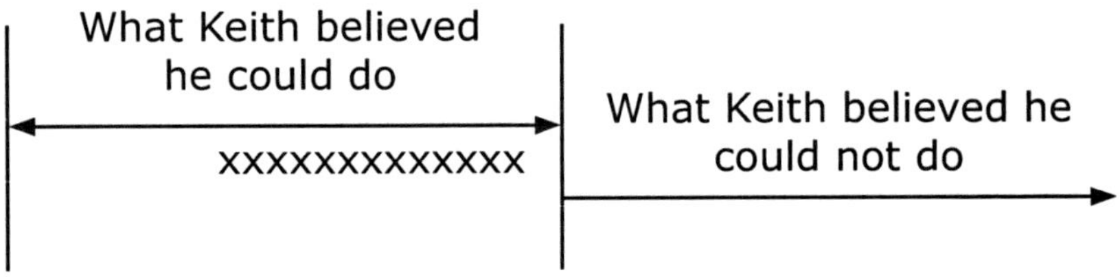

The XXXXXs between the lines represent the emotional support that Keith received from his mother. When his mother died and her support was removed, his world became very shaky. At the conscious level, Keith had been running his business by himself, but occasionally he would run things past his mother. At the unconscious level, it had been he and his mother who were running the business, not him by himself.

When Keith's mother died, he not only lost someone very dear to him, he lost his main emotional support. He had learned from experience that his wife would not take up the role his mother had played. Many of the things that Keith had been doing for years he now found unsettling.

What Keith didn't know was that he had lost his main source of CERTAINTY. His confidence was not completely in his abilities. Keith was skilled and capable of running his business, but at the unconscious level he lost his primary source of CERTAINTY when his mother died, and CERTAINTY was his top psychological NEED.

Keith did not lack anything in his abilities. The problem was that he had not learned to create the CERTAINTY he needed from within himself. Instead he had been trained, unintentionally, to draw his CERTAINTY from his mother.

When Keith got married, his wife, who was a strong woman, replaced his mother. When they had children and Keith's wife became congruent with her feminine core, Keith found himself leaning on his mother for support again. When she was no longer there for him, he faced challenges regarding what he had believed was possible before. Now that he was alone, on his own, he didn't have confidence in himself.

When the support that had steadied him in the past was gone, his world was shaky. Keith didn't know how to operate without the emotional support he had depended on all his life. He had no idea that his mother was his main source for CERTAINTY. When Keith's mother died, he not only lost his mother, he lost his source of CERTAINTY. As a result of not understanding the two different losses that he was experiencing, he became more confused and began doubting himself even more.

On the next page is a diagram that is found in the section on gender dynamics, illustrating what happens to a man, who has not developed his own internal support system but has learned to look to someone other than himself for support.

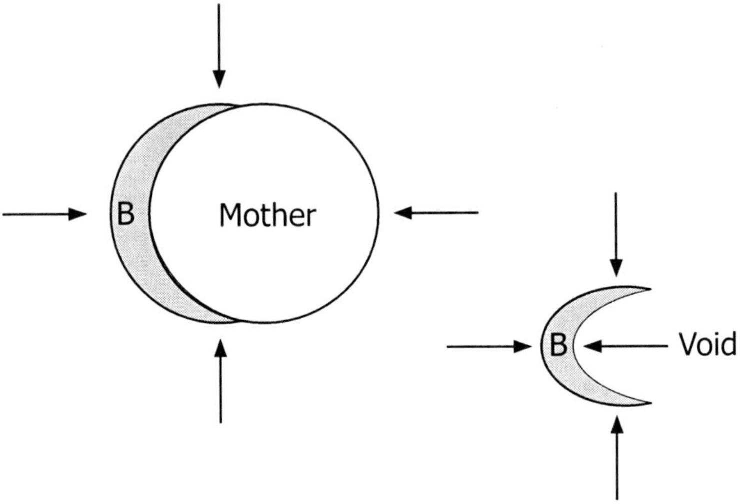

Keith felt he could not cope by himself. The feelings he was experiencing was a direct result of having become dependent on external support. Because his mother was involved in many of the decisions that were made, Keith unconsciously came to the conclusion that he was incapable of making decisions by himself.

In reality, he was completely capable, but unconsciously he knew he had never made important decisions without her, which resulted in a dependence on external support. Keith's emotions corresponded with his unconscious beliefs about himself.

The crippling thing for him was that he was unaware that he had unconsciously become dependent on his mother. He didn't consciously understand what he was feeling or why. Since his focus was on what he didn't understand, he began doubting himself even more which magnified the emotions he was experiencing.

From Keith's perspective, his wife was no help. She would tell him "You're the man; figure it out and take care of it." In reality, she was doing for him what his mother should have done many years earlier, but did not. No doubt, Keith's mother received SIGNIFICANCE from helping her son and always being there for him, but she inadvertently encouraged a relationship that was based on dependence.

The model that Keith grew up with and adopted into his life contained beliefs that were taught and caught: beliefs which, in the long term, were hindering him from becoming the man he needed to be for his own sake, as well as for his family.

Keith's perceptions of his role in life and his beliefs about himself were a direct result of the models he adopted while growing up. The beliefs a person embraces regarding what they can and can not do without external support operate at the unconscious level. A person's conscious and unconscious beliefs about themselves are incorporated into their inner identity. As you can see, it wasn't just his role in life as a man that was affected by his models, every aspect of his inner identity was touched as well.

Without the support that Keith's mother had provided, Keith's inner identity was not strong enough to support him to the point where he could comfortably stand by himself as a man. In time, Keith made the adjustments he needed to make years before. I never met Keith's mother, but I'm sure the last thing she wanted to do was to set her son up for problems later, after she was gone.

When individuals have developed a strong, balanced inner identity, they can stand strong no matter what happens. The ability to stand strong with an inner strength is not as common as everyone would like, but it can be learned, and once it is learned, it is easy to maintain.

There are many contributing factors to a person's inner identity. One of the four psychological NEEDS has a greater influence in the formation of someone's inner identity than the others, and that is the NEED for LOVE and CONNECTION. Meeting this NEED requires interaction with other people, which of course adds a great deal of uncertainty and haphazardness into the process of meeting this NEED.

The NEEDS of CERTAINTY, VARIETY, and SIGNIFICANCE can be met within a relationship, but they are not chained to people as is the NEED for LOVE and CONNECTION. The other three can be filled in many other ways, whereas LOVE and CONNECTION cannot be met in a healthy way without others.

We are social beings, whether we like it or not. Relationships are important to us. All children long to be loved by their parents. When there is a good relationship between child and parents, the child feels valuable and has a healthy self-value. Every person on earth has a NEED to be loved. When there is no relationship between the child and their parents, or a very poor relationship, the child often develops a very low self-esteem. They don't see themselves as valuable or important.

A Person's Conscious & Unconscious Beliefs About Themselves are Incorporated into Their Inner Identity

When a person adopts the belief that they are not loved and that they don't matter to anyone, it can have devastating effects. If they should hold onto that belief for a long enough time, they will begin to view themselves with contempt.

It is common for people to ask "why" questions when they don't understand something. This is true for children and adults. When people start asking themselves questions about why people don't like them, their brain automatically thinks about what they don't like. They start picking themselves apart, listing everything they believe is wrong with them.

A majority of people experience undesirable emotions when they feel they are rejected by others. These emotions can be intense at times. When people who are experiencing strong negative emotions turn their focus inward looking for reasons why they were rejected, there are two things that can happen.

They lose all touch with what is great about themselves, and they unconsciously link the strong negative emotions they were feeling to themselves.

As a person's emotional state rises, their ability to reason intellectually decreases. There is a point when people stop thinking with their intellect and simply respond to the emotions they are feeling.

I have heard some proclaim that it is possible to think with our emotions: the problem is that emotional thoughts are usually irrational thoughts. Emotions have a way of intensifying themselves the more someone focuses on them. Negative emotions are dangerous in that they have a way of gripping someone by their throat and getting their attention. Negative emotions are the easiest to remember because they can reach deep into the individual who is experiencing them.

Without realizing it, the person who feels unloved may start to build a case against themselves as to what is wrong with them and why people shouldn't like them. It is possible for individuals who are feeling unloved for a long period of time to conclude that there is something wrong with them and that they don't deserve to be loved. When this happens it is only a matter of time before their conclusions are incorporated into their beliefs about themselves.

I remember a friend of mine, (I'll call him Joe), was telling me about a girl he went to school with. She was beautiful: yet, in her own eyes, she was ugly. While we were talking several other guys overheard part of the conversation and asked if my friend was talking about "Cathy." Yes, my friend responded. Two other guys piped in and confirmed what Joe was telling me. Every guy in the school wanted to go out with this girl, but she would rarely go out. She didn't believe anyone would want to go out with someone as ugly as she believed she was.

Joe was wanting to go out with Cathy but she kept turning him down. A lot of girls wanted to go out with him, but he had gotten to know this gal and liked her.

After asking for several months, she finally asked him, "Why in the world do you want to go out with me? I'm ugly and there is nothing nice about me!" This floored my friend who said, "What are you talking about? You're a great gal who cares about people and I don't know where you get the ugly part from, because you're beautiful."

He told me that just made her more upset. Over the next several years this young lady went from bad to worse. She would only date losers that treated her poorly. Eventually my friend lost contact with her. He still shakes his head when he mentions her.

So what happened? I found out that this gal grew up in a home where they didn't show love. The home was torn apart by drugs and alcohol. She didn't feel love from her parents. She felt unwanted and shunned. She looked for anything that could be used as an excuse for someone not to love her, and she did not let go of what she found.

The more she focused on what she thought was wrong with her, the bigger it became, and the uglier she was in her own sight. She had built a case against herself, and it became part of her identity. In reality there was nothing wrong with her as a person. The model of the world and the beliefs she adopted reflected back on herself and she embraced them into her identity. She believed the case she built against herself so completely that it became her identity.

* * *

Another aspect that influences people's identity is their thinking loops. Thinking loops are comprised of reoccurring thoughts that are continually rethought silently in their mind, sometimes many times a day. Thinking loops consist of thoughts and/or beliefs.

Both thoughts and beliefs look/sound the same in a thinking loop. This can be beneficial or dangerous. Thoughts that are incorporated into thinking loops have the potential to be turned into beliefs as a result of repetition. A thinking loop is repeated many times over, per day or per hour. Over time, the person's unconscious mind will incorporate the repeated thought into a belief and accept it as truth and reality.

Some of our beliefs have come into existence through this very process. This does not, in itself, make them wrong, but it does explain how we can believe something to be a certain way, when in reality it is not as we may think. The dilemma is that many individuals have embraced beliefs that they run their lives by, and some of them are false.

Most new beliefs that are offered to us by others are thought through and weighed before being accepted as truth. Remember the young man and the special breed of cow? He was critically evaluating what I had told him before he was going to believe it himself. The personal conclusions we come to rarely go through the same critical evaluation process as do the things that other people tell us before we believe it.

How, and why, do negative conclusions, thought patterns and thinking loops become embraced as they are? Let's consider someone whose life is not going as he would like and who is not getting what he wants or needs. It is easy to feel sorry for ourselves when we are in these situations.

When a person is feeling unloved, unappreciated or alienated they can experience psychological NEEDS trauma. A person's unconscious mind is programmed to keep that person alive physically as well as psychologically. No person sits down and consciously concludes that they are going to feel sorry for themselves. It just happens.

The More a Person Focuses on Something the Bigger It Becomes in Their Perception

So what is the motivating factor that drives a person to feel sorry for themselves? Feeling sorry for oneself is actually a process through which the individual affirms, comforts and expresses love toward himself. This process is a valid, although negative, method through which a person can meet their own psychological NEEDS.

Even though they are unhappy, they are meeting their own psychological NEED for LOVE and CONNECTION at a deep level. They have no doubt as to whether they are right because they reassure themselves that they are right and everyone else is wrong. They are meeting their NEED for LOVE and CONNECTION, CERTAINTY, and possibly SIGNIFICANCE, depending on how they are explaining it to themselves.

Depending on how others respond to them feeling sorry for themselves, this method through which they are meeting their NEEDS could become addictive. It is never anyone's conscious intent to adopt behaviors that are personally harmful, but if a behavior meets psychological NEEDS at a high level, that behavior has the potential to become habitual.

If people are not getting their NEED for LOVE and CONNECTION met through others, they can, and will, meet that NEED themselves. This is when a thought can easily be transformed into a belief without evaluation. If they are starved for LOVE and CONNECTION, their hunger for filling that NEED will short circuit the conscious thought process that would normally evaluate the thinking loop.

Children invent make believe friends. People become attached to animals and treat them as though they were human. Why? To meet the NEED for LOVE and CONNECTION.

If a person's situation is that they don't have friends that are close, they can still meet their psychological NEED for LOVE and CONNECTION through a pet. The emotional attachment people have toward pets is a good example of how important LOVE and CONNECTION is. People can become as attached to their pets as they would another human. If pets are not available, people can find CONNECTION talking to their plants. People can and do use anything to fill their NEED for LOVE and CONNECTION.

Thinking loops can, and do, influence a person's beliefs about themselves and their models. Something has to happen to create a thinking loop. It could be almost anything. There are two types of thinking loops. They are either in the form of statements or WHY questions that have no direct answer.

The first type has to do with beliefs that make up models or simply just thoughts that keep running through a person's mind. This type is easier to change. I will cover the way to change the thinking loop later.

The second type of thinking loop is similar in that it, too, is run again and again. Instead of simply repeating a thought or belief, the loop consists of a WHY question that really can't be answered. Because there is no real answer to the *why* of the question, it can easily become a thinking loop.

"Why" Questions that Don't have an Answer Can be Dangerous

Thinking loops that contain a WHY that cannot be answered are dangerous because they continually result in an answer of "I don't know, I can't figure it out," etc. Each time a person rethinks the *why* question and comes to the conclusion that they are inadequate or lacking, that conclusion is incorporated a little more into their inner identity.

When a WHY question is asked that cannot be answered, that why question can become habitual if one of the following things happen:

One, the individual accepts the "I don't know, or I can't figure it out" as reality and begins feeling sorry for himself, resulting in self pity which is a form of self-love. Since this behavior meets the individual's NEEDS for LOVE and CONNECTION, CERTAINTY, and in some ways SIGNIFICANCE, it can become habitual. Two, while verbalizing their unanswerable WHY question, other people around them respond in certain ways which results in their psychological NEEDS being met.

When either of these two things happen, the unconscious mind latches onto the behavior as a viable way to meet that person's psychological NEEDS. Without realizing what has happened at the unconscious level, a person is often confused and perplexed when they find themselves doing something they may have consciously decided not to do.

The challenge in either one of the above situations is that the individual is actually getting some or all of their NEEDS met as a result of negative thinking loops. A thinking loop that is meeting a person's psychological NEEDS at a high level will be impossible to break until those NEEDS are met at the same or higher level through another avenue.

It is important to note that ***unanswerable why questions always move the individual into a weak position.*** As this type of thinking loop is rerun continually over time, it will alter how that person sees themselves.

Thinking loops do not exist by themselves. Every time a person reruns these thinking loops, they convince themselves all the more of their validity and truth. This does not happen in a vacuum. Thoughts do not exist by themselves. Thoughts contain meanings which create emotions. With every thinking loop there is a corresponding emotional loop that accompanies it.

It is because of this close relationship between thoughts and emotions that thinking loops have the ability to alter the emotions a person feels on a regular basis in either positive or negative ways. As you can see, the quality of the emotions that are experienced are linked to the quality of the thinking loops themselves. Thinking loops are not all harmful. There are positive and negative thinking loops.

Each of us has what I call an emotional identity. This is simply based on the overall flavor of the emotions that a person feels in a given day. In order to find out your emotional identity, make notes throughout the day, jotting down the emotions that you feel. Keep track of this for several days. We will be referring back to this later. There are no right or wrong answers, and this is for your eyes only.

NEEDS play an important part in our lives, but not directly in a person's identity. Let me explain. Everyone has NEEDS, but what sticks out in relation to a person is how they meet their NEEDS. For some reason, people make a link between what they do and who they are. Although this is not truly the case, it is the most common approach people use in trying to understand and explain their identity.

In reality, many people took whatever job they came across, and it met their needs, both physically and psychologically, for a time. The problem a lot of people are faced with is that the job that once met both their physical and psychological NEEDS no longer meets them, and they are dissatisfied with what they do and their lives. This dissatisfaction occurs because either their physical and/or psychological NEEDS are no longer being met through their job.

To the surprise of many, much of what people do is directly related to meeting their psychological NEEDS. The only ones I know who intentionally think through how they want to meet their psychological NEEDS are those who have learned about them and know how to meet their psychological NEEDS in positive ways.

Most often when you ask a person about themselves, they will tell you their name and what they do. In reality, what we do is not our identity, but if we believe it to be our identity, we are dependent on it.

Over time, a link of dependency is made at the unconscious level between the individual and their job. This is a direct result of their psychological NEEDS being met through what they do. This is why many people are devastated when they lose their job. They literally become psychologically attached to their job because the majority of their NEEDS are met through it.

Consider all the psychological NEEDS that can be met through a job. CERTAINTY is a big one, knowing that you will have money coming in to take care of your family. VARIETY -- some people's jobs have a built in guarantee of VARIETY. CONNECTION with your fellow workers and then the SIGNIFICANCE you get from doing a job well and of providing for your family are also NEED-fillers.

When a Person Loses Their Job Often the Job is only a Small Part of What They have Lost

Is it any wonder that people feel a terrific loss when they no longer have a job, whether it is a result of a lay-off or even retirement? If a person who is retiring doesn't have things planned to meet the psychological NEEDS that their job met, they, too, will be feeling a sense of loss and wondering why they aren't happier.

The activities through which a person learns to meet their psychological NEEDS are typically incorporated into their identity. From a young age, how your NEEDS are met will influence your beliefs about your identity. For instance, if your NEED for SIGNIFICANCE is being met through accomplishments, your identity is going to be formed around, and intertwined with, accomplishments. If on the other hand your NEED for SIGNIFICANCE is being met through relationships, then relationships with others are going to play a large role in your identity.

Self-value is connected to SIGNIFICANCE through false logic. If someone spends time with us and cares for us, then we must be special. It is common for people to base how valuable they see themselves by how others treat them.

When people perceive themselves as special to others, they think more of themselves than if someone doesn't treat them nicely. This also affects how worthy they feel they are of love, and how much they allow themselves to feel loved.

There are two aspects of SIGNIFICANCE. One is through accomplishments and the other is through relationships. Both are incorporated in the lives of children from an early age and do not need to be taught.

When a female is young, it is common for her to hear things like "Daddy's little girl." That is an expression of SIGNIFICANCE between a father and his daughter: she is special and she understands it that way.

A boy, on the other hand, might be referred to as "Dad's little helper" or "Daddy's sidekick." The boy who is introduced this way is being conditioned in several ways. One is that he is special (which he is) but the other, which is caught rather than taught, is that he is special because of what he is doing. In reality, he is special for who he is, and what he is doing--helping his dad--is appreciated most of the time. But if children who find themselves in that position unconsciously conclude that they are special because of what they are doing, this can be a real challenge for them later in life.

To be in a relationship and to be special in the eyes of another is, without doubt, an elevated position. Children beam when they understand that they are special to someone else. So do adults. However, adults are more discriminating with whom they want to be special.

Children, as well as adults, will adjust their behavior (and ultimately their identity over time) to achieve the level of SIGNIFICANCE they need. All children long to be accepted and loved by their parents. When a girl is accepted more for acting like a boy, it can, with repetition, set her course toward becoming a tomboy without anyone realizing what has happened.

When a girl learns her dad has always wanted a son and does not have one, she unconsciously may adjust her behavior to fill the role of a boy. This makes her father happy since he now has the boy he has always longed for. Instead of being a disappointment, she is now significant because she is getting the love and attention that she longs for from her dad.

When a tomboy is young, the only way to tell she is a girl is if she has longer hair. This young lady might even take offense at being called a girl. I have known several tomboys who would hit you for saying they were girls. I have seen where the tomboy of a group was the roughest and toughest of them all, and proud of it. This naturally will vary from girl to girl, and her personality temperament will be the determining factor in whether she is a hard tomboy or a soft tomboy.

When a daughter gets showered with attention and praise for being a tomboy, this in turn encourages her to become even more so. What is really happening is she is being conditioned, at the unconscious level, that the way to get her NEEDS met is to wear her masculine hat. As a result, she is getting her NEEDS for LOVE and CONNECTION, VARIETY, CERTAINTY, and SIGNIFICANCE all met through being a tomboy. This is not life threatening, but it can, and often does, lead to challenges later.

It is important to remember that people are not aware of what is going on in the area of gender dynamics in the situation listed above. They are simply living their lives. Chances are, she will meet a soft and understanding man who has grown up wearing his feminine hat, and they will hit it off and get married. Later she will wonder why she has a hard time respecting him. He will wonder what happened because she use to be happy with him and now he can't please her. Both of them will be looking at the other, not understanding their spouse or themselves.

The personality temperament make-up of the girl will have a limiting effect on how hardened a tomboy she will become. A girl whose primary personality temperament is choleric could easily become a much tougher tomboy than a girl who has phlegmatic as her primary personality temperament. The stronger the girl's temperament, the harder the time she will have letting go of being a tomboy. This could cause some challenges for her and her spouse that they will have to work out in some way. This is not to say that they can't work through the challenges; it will just require more effort.

The components that contribute to our inner identity are major influences that determine what we believe about ourselves. People aren't born with an understanding of their personality temperament makeup or models, but they feel the impact in many ways. In school, an individual's temperament makeup and the models they are taught can have far reaching affects on the child.

Let's look at what often happens in a classroom. The students are given a reading assignment, and they are to write a short report on what they have read. Some of the children are happy and some are not. What do you suppose is behind some of their different reactions?

Let's take a look at how two different personality temperaments are likely to respond to this assignment and why. As the melancholy child reads through the assignment different details jump out at them. They are fascinated by the many new and interesting facts they are learning. A melancholy child who loves details is more likely to enjoy this assignment and find it easy to write about the new things he has learned.

The choleric child on the other hand is not interested in details. They are more interested in making things happen. Reading is boring and details are just as bad. One thing a choleric child likes less than reading, is writing. From his perspective simply telling the teacher what he has learned is quicker. For the choleric child to do this assignment will take more effort because it does not flow with his temperament leanings. This does not remove the fact that it is good for every child to learn to do these assignments well, regardless of their temperament leanings.

Who do you think will do better on that particular assignment? Who do you think could be in a position to mis-evaluate their intellectual capabilities if this same thing continued over a period of time? One personality temperament, in reality, is not smarter than another personality temperament.

In this situation it would be easy to come to the wrong conclusion that there is an intellectual difference. In reality, their preferred areas of study are simply different. One temperament will do better in one subject because it fits their temperament style while having difficulties in another area of study. This difficulty is more a reflection of a preference rather than a lack of intellectual capabilities.

Whatever situation people find themselves, it is common for them to judge their intellectual capabilities on surface information that is not necessarily correct in light of the big picture. Once they embrace beliefs about what is possible for them at an intellectual level, those beliefs are incorporated into their inner identity.

I once met a very accomplished woman who told me of an event that shaped the majority of her life. When this woman, Betty, was eight years old, she had a teacher that she adored and wanted to grow up to be just like. One day, Betty handed in an assignment of which she was very proud. As it turned out, she had misunderstood the instructions and had done the whole assignment wrong. When her teacher looked at it, she started yelling at Betty and told her she was stupid and would never amount to anything. As you can imagine, this devastated Betty. She told me that from that day on she believed she was stupid. Being stupid became a major part of her identity.

As she told the story of her life, it was clear that she had never tried to do what she wanted. After all, why bother? She wasn't smart enough. She had married the first man that would have her. That marriage didn't work out, which, to her, confirmed all the more what she had thought of herself all along.

Thankfully, someone came along and confronted Betty about her lack of belief in herself. She would not let Betty off the hook until she realized what had started her self-bashing line of thinking. When Betty realized what had happened and how she had embraced what the teacher said as reality, it was the key to unlocking her prison cell. It took time and persistence, but Betty was able to totally change her life. She is doing extremely well and enjoying life as never before.

Everyone is significant in his or her own right. In reality, no one is just like you; you are unique and special. When people do not feel special for being themselves, they soon discover that if they do certain things, they are rewarded and considered special. They are meeting their NEED for SIGNIFICANCE through doing something.

Once again, if the same response continues to occur, they are conditioned that if they want their NEEDS met, they have to achieve and accomplish certain things. This is a conclusion that is come to at the unconscious level. Rarely do people consciously think about getting their psychological NEEDS of SIGNIFICANCE, CERTAINTY and CONNECTION met through accomplishments.

People's personality temperament blend will affect their self-perceptions. Their temperament will initially be their default approach to events. For example, people who prefer to stay out of the limelight often compare themselves to others who are comfortable getting up in front of people. Many times they come to the conclusion that they just aren't that way, and are not cut out for that type of thing.

Melancholies like details whereas Cholerics dislike details. Phlegmatics get along with people but Cholerics don't much care about people. Sanguines love people and people love Sanguines. Just from those simple observations it would be very easy for each of the different temperaments to come to conclusions about themselves, and others, that would be incorrect and self-limiting. Those conclusions would alter their beliefs about themselves, which would affect their inner identity and would alter who they would become.

* * *

Each of us has an identity framework composed of the beliefs we have embraced about ourselves. When people think about themselves, in reality it is this framework of beliefs that they think about. These beliefs can be true or false. It is from this framework of beliefs that a great deal of our recurring thoughts and emotions originate. An individual's models will flavor many beliefs about themselves.

In reality, a person's identity is simply what a person believes about himself or herself. Some of their beliefs are related to strategies they have stumbled onto and have used as a means of meeting the psychological NEEDS critical to their psychological survival.

The reason I point this out is to show how much about a person's identity is not normally thought about, or addressed, on a normal basis. There are many aspects to a person's identity and to illustrate what I am saying, let's consider the following scenario.

A man is involved in an accident in which he receives a head injury that leaves him with total amnesia. When he wakes up, he realizes that he doesn't have any idea of who he is, or where he is. After a little bit, he is finally able to get someone's attention. In the hospital room where he has found himself, the nurse smiles and is excited to see him awake and greets him.

The man returns the greeting and asks what is going on. The nurse tells him he was found at the scene of an accident. "Nobody knows who you are. You didn't have any identification on you, and we are in the process of trying to identify you through your fingerprints."

He looks down at his fingers and they are colored from the ink.

"In the meantime, we are referring to you as John Doe," he is told.

A doctor comes in to see him and they discus his case. The doctor tells him he should be fine. "Hopefully your memory will return soon. Until then, try to relax and take it easy."

Later that day when some nurses are talking outside his door, he overhears them talking about the bum who came in not knowing who he was.

"Can you believe that guy? He had no sense at all."

One of them commented that she didn't think he had made it to high school. Someone else is heard coming down the hall and the nurses leave.

At this point, anyone could go in to this man's room and tell him anything they wanted and he would have no references from which to evaluate what they told him. Someone could tell him he was a bum and a drunk. They could say, "Look at yourself, you haven't shaved and you were driving around drunk. It's a wonder you're not dead."

What if the man believed that he was the bum that was brought in and that he is the one the nurses were talking about in the hallway? What beliefs would he be embracing about himself?

This man would be in a spot and wouldn't know who or what to believe. But if his memory didn't come back, he would have to believe someone, at the very least, about his name.

If he were to embrace what people were telling him about the type of person he was, what would actually be taking place? This man would have to believe what he was being told about himself. This happens every day. Someone says something to another person and it is taken personally. In this case, he would be accepting what others were telling him as truth. In reality, they could be totally lying to him and yet he could actually believe them and conform his life to what others said he was like.

There is something I call internalization and externalization. We saw an example of this when we read about Betty and what happened when the teacher she looked up to told her that she was stupid. Betty internalized what the teacher told her and it became part of her inner identity. It is sobering when we realize this happens every day, with individuals feeling the impact for many years.

The man with total amnesia could find himself internalizing a great deal of what he is being told. Internalization happens all the time without people realizing it. I explore internalization and externalization in greater detail in another book, *Building Blocks to Change.*

When a person internalizes an event, the normal filters that they would use to evaluate the situation are bypassed. As a result, their unconscious mind begins incorporating the meanings that the person has given to the event into their inner identity much quicker than it would have otherwise.

There are varying levels and speeds of internalization. What happened with Betty is an example of internalization at a deep level that was life altering. The majority of internalization that takes place is not at that level, although it does affect the one who is internalizing the event, often in negative ways.

Internalization is when a person grabs what has happened and pulls it into their identity. Or, on the lighter side, it could be incorporated into one of their thinking loops first, then settle in over time. On a deeper level it could be pulled into and incorporated very quickly into their identity, as was the case with Betty. Fast, life altering internalization rarely happens unless triggered by some sort of physical and or emotional shock.

Normally your thoughts are thought through your conscious mind. Once repetition has been detected by your unconscious mind, the thought is soon turned into an automatic response. In this process, the unconscious mind finds a common thread or point in each of the times that these thoughts, meanings and emotions are given.

Once the trigger point is detected, your unconscious mind has everything it needs and programs in an automatic bypass of the conscious mind. This shortens the process and delivers the end product to you, without thought or request. This end product shows up instantly as a thought or an emotion.

Your conscious mind can only focus on a few things at time. Your unconscious mind is always on patrol for how and what it can streamline with short cuts to free up your conscious mind. A good analogy of this is the way a computer works, in that it has an operating memory and the hard drive. The conscious mind is similar to the RAM in a computer which is limited, as compared to the hard drive which can have thousands of times greater capacity.

Your unconscious mind determines the trigger points that are employed. This is not up for discussion with the conscious mind. When something happens that has been chosen as a trigger point, presto! Your unconscious mind says, "I know what this means!" and you have the corresponding emotions. Your conscious mind was not involved in the decision because your unconscious mind bypassed it. This can work to our benefit as well as to our harm.

When people learn how these different parts operate, they can begin to understand what is happening and why they are feeling an emotion.

Your unconscious mind monitors everything that is happening throughout your day. When it notices what it has determined to be a trigger point, it will engage a thinking loop, or hand you an emotion instantly.

To get some insights into how your unconscious mind is directing your thinking loops throughout the day, make some notes about what keeps popping up in your mind. This will give insights into some of the thinking loops that your unconscious mind is running.

When you do this exercise, the results will get your attention. It is amazing and sobering to discover how much of what we think about are reruns and how little is actually new thoughts.

Your unconscious mind knows more about you than you do. It knows your models and emotions in great detail, and monitors your self in relation to your inner identity or self portrait (which we will examine later).

Your unconscious mind is your command center. It operates behind the scenes, hidden to those who are unaware of it and how it operates. It monitors and operates your life support systems that, literally, keep you alive. The unconscious mind monitors all the necessary chemical balances in your body, as well as all organ functions. Your unconscious mind never sleeps. It is always on patrol. It has its fingers on everything that has to do with who you are. It also monitors your thoughts, the models you have adopted as your own, and your actions. Your unconscious mind monitors not only the physical systems that keep your body alive; it has a detailed understanding and list of who you believe yourself to be as a person.

The mass of information your unconscious mind pulls from includes the following: models you have adopted as your own, beliefs, meanings, emotions, information that has been taught to you and accepted, and conclusions you have come to yourself and accepted as reality. Your unconscious mind uses this information as its guidelines, which it works from to guide you and to keep you consistent with who it understands you to be.

You may be wondering how all this plays out in our lives. Initially, your conscious mind thinks things through, and your unconscious mind is listening and taking notes. As your unconscious mind recognizes patterns, it starts to create short cuts. This is how habits are formed, and after a while you can do complex tasks without thinking about them.

The way the unconscious mind monitors everything is beneficial in that the individual doesn't have to worry about it. The challenge comes into play when the unconscious mind engages outdated or negative strategies to meet the individual's psychological NEEDS. How does this work? Most people don't know about the psychological NEEDS that they have. Yes, they may feel something is missing, but they don't think through how they are going to meet their psychological NEEDS with positive methods.

As people go through their day, their unconscious mind is monitoring everything they are doing and at what level these different things are meeting their NEEDS. Whatever the unconscious mind concludes will meet their NEEDS at the highest level has the potential to become an automatically engaged behavior.

Not only does your unconscious mind watch behaviors, it records your thoughts and the meanings that you give events and conversations. It looks for patterns in everything for the purpose of creating short cuts to minimize conscious thought.

Once your unconscious mind has marked a particular behavior as meeting certain NEEDS, then that strategy becomes one of its many available methods for meeting that NEED. Your unconscious mind knows through watching that certain behaviors are more effective at meeting psychological NEEDS than others. The behaviors that meet their psychological NEEDS at high levels are set as the default approach for meeting their NEEDS.

Have you ever seen a person who was acting several years below their current age and thought that they need to grow up? What is happening is that their unconscious mind has put into play an old behavior or strategy that it had learned years before. This action is often implemented in the unconscious mind while their conscious mind hasn't really given it much thought and is simply going along for the ride.

As people grow, they learn strategies for doing things and dealing with others. As they grow older, their strategies from when they were younger often become inappropriate and outdated.

People form habits that they outgrow. Just because a person has aged doesn't change the habit; it has to be replaced. Until it is replaced with a better habit, the old way of doing things remains, even though it is inappropriate.

Have you ever asked a child "Why did you do that?" and had him just look at you and say he didn't know? If you ask him what he was thinking, often times the response will be that he didn't think about anything. He just did it. This is a good example of his unconscious mind engaging what might seem to be an inappropriate behavior. The unconscious mind seeks to fill psychological NEEDS through the behavior. In reality it is not the behavior itself that meets their psychological NEEDS, but rather the meanings that are given the events or the reactions of others that result in a person's psychological NEEDS being met. This does not justify the behavior, but it does explain the motive behind it.

On a more personal note, have you ever purposed in your mind something you were going to do and what you were not going to do, and then found yourself doing opposite of what you wanted to do? I know I have, on more than one occasion, and almost always it was to my regret. I was confused as to why I did what I did. I had consciously decided what I was going to do, and without thinking, I did the very thing I consciously did not want to do.

This was not only confusing and irritating, but it made a mess of things and it usually took me a long time to correct the situation. If you can relate to this, you remember times when your conscious and unconscious minds were not in agreement, and you notice which prevailed: your unconscious mind.

Have you ever gotten in your car to go somewhere, started driving and the next thing you knew, you were there? For some strange reason you couldn't remember anything in between a certain point and when you found yourself at your destination.

What happened? Your conscious mind became so engrossed in what you were thinking about that your unconscious mind took over and got you to where you were going. There are times when your unconscious takes over but this does not remove our responsibility for our actions. If you are not paying attention while driving chances are you will have an accident. Don't day dream, read or text while driving. Someone could get killed if you do.

Your unconscious mind is your best friend. It never leaves you. So how do you keep your best friend on your side, so that you don't find yourself doing the things you don't want to?

The first thing is to understand that your unconscious mind has some non-negotiables that it must take care of. They include keeping you alive physically and psychologically. If you doubt this, how do you explain how in emergencies people are able to do things that are normally impossible? When we understand how our unconscious mind works and what it does for us, it is much easier to give it what it needs so that it helps us rather than hurts us.

When the models people have adopted cause them to look to others and they are dependent on outside events or sources to meet their psychological NEEDS, their inner identity shifts to that of perceived neediness and lacking in abilities. Once a person understands how their models and beliefs are affecting them, they are in a position to make some changes that will be in their favor rather than to their hurt.

Models will have an influencing factor in the strategies through which a person meets the majority of their psychological NEEDS. In turn those strategies are going to reflect back on that individual's self perceptions, which in time will affect their inner identity. Typically strategies, like models, fall into four different classifications which we will examine in MFD-R.

If a person learns to consciously choose how they will meet their psychological NEEDS through the meanings they give things and events, their choice and follow through will affect that person's emotional life and self-perceptions in very positive ways.

On the other hand, if a person looks to outside sources for meeting their psychological NEEDS, they are at the mercy of what ever comes their way. This, unfortunately, is what most people do on a daily basis. Looking to outside events for the meeting of your NEEDS can result in a person experiencing many undesirable emotions.

In reality, people meet their own psychological NEEDS from within themselves. The problem comes about as a result of a person believing that an external event is required in order for them to meet their psychological NEEDS.

How does this play out in real life? Let's consider what happens when a person receives a gift. As was mentioned earlier, they give receiving the gift meaning. The meaning they give the event will determine what NEEDS are met and at what level. There is nothing wrong with giving meaning to receiving a gift. Remember people are hard wired so they have to give a meaning to everything. When a person is not in conscious control of the meanings they are giving events, that is when it is a roll of the dice as to what emotions you get.

Earlier I mentioned an example of a gift, and in that example their unconscious mind took notes from watching what their conscious mind did when they received the gift. SIGNIFICANCE was met at a level eight, VARIETY was met at a level six, and LOVE and CONNECTION was met at level nine. Whatever meanings an individual gives will determine how high or how low the numbers would be for each psychological NEED.

I have a friend who told me of his mother who was a little girl during the depression. She had ten brothers and sisters and her parents were barely able to keep food on the table. One year no one received any presents for Christmas. The following year, this little girl's sister woke her up saying Santa had come during the night. She and her sister went out to see what he left.

In an old sock was something that she thought might be an orange. With anticipation she opened the sock and pulled out what was in it. It wasn't an orange. She discovered that she and the rest of the children had each received a lump of coal.

This girl wished she had received nothing for Christmas that year. Fifty years later she still spoke of it with pain in her voice. So what happened? She was excited that she had received a gift from Santa, which filled her SIGNIFICANCE NEED in a big way. When she discovered it was a lump of coal, the coal was a large withdrawal from her SIGNIFICANCE account.

If her level of SIGNIFICANCE was at a 2 before she knew there was a gift from Santa, it might have jumped 10 points to 12 when she heard there was a gift from Santa. When she discovered the coal, it probably lost 20 points and ended at -8 for the SIGNIFICANCE she felt.

Before she knew what was in the sock, she was excited. Santa (somebody) cared enough to give her a gift. It also met the NEEDS for VARIETY (she didn't know what it was), SIGNIFICANCE (she was valuable enough to give a gift to) and LOVE and CONNECTION (someone loved her enough to give her a gift).

What happened when she saw the lump of coal? In order to understand this, we must first consider that each of us has a model of what a gift is, and this model contains many beliefs about gifts. When she discovered the lump of coal, her conscious mind searched all her beliefs about gifts and found nothing regarding coal as a gift. In fact, the coal was so far away from her understanding of what a gift should be that instead of experiencing positive emotions, she experienced negative emotions, and at very high levels.

It didn't matter that everyone received a lump of coal. That fact was on the outer, blurry edges of her focus. She didn't realize her parents felt badly about not having money to purchase gifts for the second year in a row. Her parents thought that to receive something would be better than to receive nothing at all again.

Fifty years later one daughter was still saying that she would have rather not received anything at all that year. So, is it the gift or the meanings? For those who see the meanings, the answer is the meanings. For those who have not yet been able to see that they give meanings and how the meanings create their emotions, they would say it is the gift. In both cases the individuals would be telling the truth as they understand it.

There are things that happen in each of our lives, and the meanings we give these events will have an enormous impact on our lives, either toward the positive or the negative.

In life, the label we put on an event becomes the event in our memory. Labels are representative of the meanings we give events. In turn, the meanings we give events are directed through the beliefs that make up our models.

Remember that our beliefs about the world have corresponding beliefs about ourselves linked to them. So too, the meanings and labels we give events have an immense amount of power to shift a person's position in relation to the event. The meanings and corresponding labels that are given an event will determine how a person's inner identity will be affected.

If a person gives meanings that make him bigger than the event, he is literally putting himself in a powerful position. If, on the other hand, he gives meanings that make the event bigger than he is, he is literally putting himself in a much weaker position. In each case one person's emotional state is going to be radically different from the other's.

Where a person consistently places himself over time will have a big impact on his inner identity and beliefs about himself.

This is a good example of how each area affects and reinforces each other.

A person's beliefs and models of the world will initially play a part in directing the meanings they give an event. The meanings that are given reflect on and affect the inner identity or self-perceptions. The inner identity will, on the next go-round, reinforce the beliefs of that model. Over time there is a synergy that develops where models, meanings, beliefs, inner identity and the method through which the person meets their psychological NEEDS all strengthen each other. This synergistic affect is almost impossible to break if a person does not understand how to change the individual components that contribute to the whole.

People Don't Remember the Event They Remember the Label They Put on the Event

I give the coal gift example because it shows clearly how our models, the meanings we give the event, and whether we internalize or externalize the event all contribute to how we are affected by the event more than the event itself. What we choose to do with an event will/can have long lasting consequences.

This is a major hurdle for men who have been taught to look to women for leadership. Not only does looking to someone else presuppose dependence, but looking to the opposite sex carries with it the inferred hurdle of never being able to fill that role because he is the wrong sex. This is a conclusion that is made at the unconscious level and surfaces in the form of emotions that are rarely understood.

Dependency is relationship orientation at its worst. Once the unconscious mind has accepted the position of dependency, that person's meanings, emotions and reactions will be heavily influenced by their unconsciously accepted conclusion of being dependent on someone else. Regardless of what sex a person is, dependency is unhealthy for everyone involved.

If that individual enters a leadership position, which is in opposition to what the unconscious mind has accepted and has interwoven into his internal identity, the result will be their unconscious mind will make it clear through emotions that they are beyond their abilities, and that they should give up. At this point the natural tendency is for the person to return to their comfort zone. The reason for this is simple. One of the main tasks of the unconscious mind is to keep the person consistent with the inner identity that has been accepted.

This happened to Betty who believed a lie when she was young and her unconscious mind kept her consistent with the inner identity that was embraced. It didn't matter that all of a sudden she discovered she had believed a lie all of those years. Her unconscious mind would not change her inner identity simply because her conscious mind said, "Look, we were told a lie!"

Your unconscious mind is the gatekeeper. One if its jobs is to produce stability within your identity. Remember that once a model is accepted, anything that reinforces that model will be accepted, but anything that goes against it will be either discarded, or if it is considered, the new information will be set aside and evaluated for a time with the intent of discovering whether it is correct or incorrect.

Each person's inner identity took time to form in the beginning, and will take some time to change. ***The good news is that you can shift your inner identity which will allow many of the other changes you want to make become much easier.***

Hopefully, you have a greater appreciation for your own identity and the complexities that exist within you. Now, let's take another look at the dictionary definitions of identity.

Identity:

1. The condition or fact of being the same or exactly alike; sameness; oneness [group united by identity or interests]

2. The condition or fact of being a specific person or thing; individuality

3. The condition of being the same as a person or thing described or claimed.

Identity crisis:

The condition of being uncertain of one's feelings about oneself, especially with regard to character, goals, and origins, occurring especially in adolescence as a result of growing up under disruptive, fast-changing conditions

As long as a person is alive, their inner identity has the potential to expand and grow just like their models of the world. In these days where things are changing faster than people would have thought possible, many people are experiencing an identity crisis that has nothing to do with adolescence.

In life you have two choices. You can say, "this is who I am, and this is how I will remain," or you can grow in your understanding and knowledge and in who you are as an individual. Often the second option is the path taken, but not by choice. People find themselves forced into learning and growing, and they kick and scream the whole time. Yes, they may learn. But do they really learn as much as they could if they would embrace personal growth and learning?

Life is a constant process of change. If you will make growth and learning a consistent part of your life, you will find that your inner identity will be easier to work with because it is use to change and growth.

We, as people, are susceptible to hanging onto beliefs that were true for us at one time but that aren't necessarily true any longer. Many of the old beliefs we embraced at one time may have fit then, but are they fitting for us now?

It is well known that an elephant is one of the strongest animals alive. That is clearly understood by everyone except the elephant itself. When an elephant baby is domesticated, the trainers tie it up to a rope and a stake. The baby elephant tries for hours, and then days, to break the rope or pull up the stake. Finally it gives up, realizing that the rope and stake are much stronger than it is.

As time passes, the baby elephant grows up and is taught to do the work of many men. It lifts objects that weigh hundreds of pounds and pulls tons of weight with ease. At the end of each day the elephant is tied to a stake that is in the ground. It will return day after day to that same stake, until a man comes over and pulls it up and drives the stake into the ground in another location.

The baby elephant is no longer a baby, but it still thinks that the rope and stake are stronger than it is, and it does not even try to break free. It knows it can't do it, so why bother? In the elephant's inner identity, it is incapable of pulling the stake out of the ground; the stake is bigger and stronger than the elephant.

What is your stake?

MFD-R

Gender Dynamics Gives insights into the interactions Between Couples and People in General.

Masculine/Feminine Dynamics (MFD) Operates at two levels.

MFD operates at the Big Picture Level which we saw in Gender Dynamics but it also Works at Another Level: **Within Each Individual**

All emotions fall into One of Two Categories: They are Either Masculine or Feminine in Orientation.

We touched on this in the section on models and meanings. All of the emotions that a person is capable of feeling are distinctly masculine/self oriented or they are feminine/relationship oriented. Breaking the emotions down further, both masculine and feminine emotions are either positive or negative in their composition.

Let's consider different emotions and where those emotions fall in masculine/feminine dynamics. Look through these four groups on the next page and see if you can tell which section they would fall into. The positive or negative of the masculine side or the positive or negative side of the feminine side.

The emotional groups that comprise the different quadrants within the Masculine Feminine Dynamics Rectangle

Rage	Love	Overwhelm	Confidence
Anger	Compassion	Fear	Self-assurance
Hatred	Tenderness	Depression	Determination
Selfishness	Mercy	Helplessness	Optimistic
		Pessimism	

Everyone is capable of experiencing each of these emotions in their life. The first group include very powerful emotions. The problem is they are also very destructive if allowed to run rampant. They are the negative masculine emotions. The second group--the emotions that are relationship oriented--are the positive feminine emotions. These are followed by the negative feminine emotions and finally the positive masculine emotions.

Can you see how the masculine emotions are self-oriented and the feminine are other-oriented? If you have emotions other than those listed, you will be able to tell what section to place them in from the examples above. In order to help make sense of how all of these different parts work in conjunction with each other, I have developed what I call the Masculine/Feminine Dynamics Rectangle.

As mentioned earlier, both men and women have masculine and feminine energies within them. This allows both to be strong when needed and still have the ability to feel compassion toward someone else. If men were strictly masculine, they would be incapable of feeling love and compassion. If women were strictly feminine, they would not be able to stand up for themselves or defend the ones they love.

On the following page is the MFD-R, Masculine-Feminine Dynamics Rectangle. This diagram demonstrates how the emotions relate to each other.

This diagram shows the basic emotions that make up the four emotional quadrants and how they relate to each other.
(Both men and women are capable of experiencing all of these emotions.)

Masculine-Feminine-Dynamics-Rectangle

Confident
Determined
Self-assurance
Optimistic

Love
Compassion
Tenderness
Mercy

Strong & Powerful

Positive

Soft

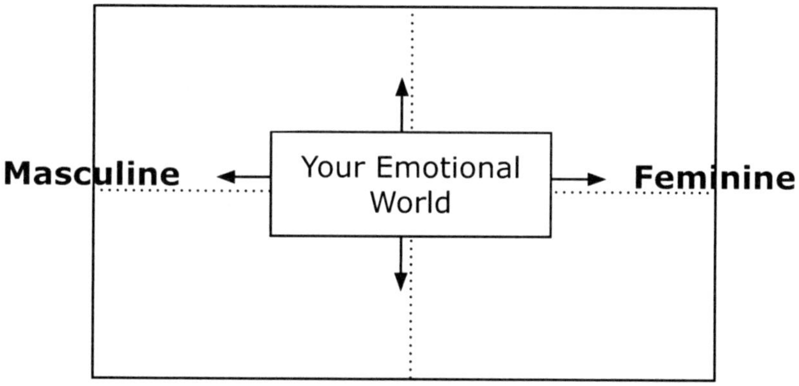

Hard

Negative

Weak & Vulnerable

Anger
Selfishness
Rage
Heartlessness

Overwhelmed
Helplessness
Fear
Pessimism
Depression

As you can see in the diagram on the previous page, each group has its own flavor even though it is comprised of individual components (emotions). Each of the emotions can be experienced separately, or in any combination. This is true for each of the four quadrants.

Remember the section on personality temperaments? I included this diagram below, which shows how the four temperaments place in regard to accomplishment as compared to relationship in their natural tendencies. This does not mean that the Choleric cannot learn to be skilled in the area of relationships, or that the Phlegmatic cannot learn to excel in accomplishing a great deal.

Accomplishment Orientated			Relationship Orientated
*	*	*	*
Choleric	Melancholy	Sanguine	Phlegmatic

Thankfully, each of us is a combination of two or more of the temperaments. It is important to note wherever a person's temperament shows up, in no way does it mean that he is stuck there. This line shows the strong points of the temperaments. If these strong points are not overdone, but rather understood and controlled, they will not be a weakness but an asset.

As I mentioned in the personality temperaments section, people are often misinformed about the category of the weaknesses. This is often seen as something that is terrible or an area that they cannot master. Quite the contrary. Unlike strengths that can be overdone and be devastating in their effects on others,

weak areas can be strengthened to a point that they are no longer weaknesses, but rather finely honed skills that are of great value. When a person strengthens their weaknesses to the point they are strengths, the advantage is that what is now a strength is rarely, if ever, overdone to the point of doing harm to anyone.

Each personality temperament will respond differently when they first learn that they have masculine and feminine energies. The individual beliefs that make up their models of the world will have a large impact on them and their reactions.

For the most part, women have the easiest time accepting that they have a masculine side, as compared to the men who might find the idea of having a feminine side harder to swallow.

Most men have grown up with the model of manhood that if someone says something about him that is of the feminine nature, it takes away from the man's masculinity. It comes across as saying that he is not a man; this is an insult to many men. It disagrees with their model of what it is to be a man.

Some models contain the idea that to show, or be referred to as, anything less than strong and tough is to be less than manly. Remember, if someone gives something a certain meaning, they will experience the corresponding emotions that go with their meaning.

When some women hear they have a masculine side they say "Hey look! I'm a new and improved model." Many women see it as a plus.

Many men, on the other hand, see having a feminine side as being less than a man. This is not the case at all, but that is what he has lived with throughout childhood. The feelings that get linked to certain comments or names are powerful emotions.

It may not sound as if it would be very hard to change hats from feminine to masculine, in and of itself, but when we examine different personality types, we see that it can truly be a huge undertaking for few to even consider doing it.

Different temperaments will have different responses to the idea of having a masculine and feminine side. The models that a person adopts are going to have an impact on how a person feels about it also.

When Miss Sanguine discovers that she has a masculine side also, she would probably come up to a man and say, "See darling, I knew we really were related somehow," and give him a peck on the cheek. "Not a big deal! Nice to know and by the way how do I get to what's his name's house? He is having a party tonight."

When Mr. Sanguine is informed that he has a feminine side he might look at you strangely for a moment and ask if you are kidding. Once he finds you are serious and it is explained, it won't be all that big of a deal.

Mr. Melancholy's response to having a feminine side might be one of disbelief at first, but if you give him some examples and a little explanation he will do some in-depth thinking on the subject. He will want as many details as you can give him. This will be something that he will mull around in his mind and analyze from every angle until he has it figured out to his satisfaction. Once all of the facts settle into place, he will come to grips with it and do all right, if he doesn't analyze himself and others to death over it.

Miss Melancholy, like her counterpart, will give it some deep thought and find it interesting. She will not, however, have to analyze it as much as Mr. Melancholy will. And life will continue as usual.

Let's take a look at the Choleric. Mr. Choleric is strong and he knows what he does and doesn't want. He wants answers: straightforward and no beating around the bush. Give him the facts so he can make a decision. Emotions are something that other people have problems with, but not him. With Mr. Choleric it is his way or the highway, nothing to get emotional about, just do it (now).

Have you guessed what hat Mr. Choleric wears all the time? You have it, his masculine hat. Why, he is not even aware that he has another hat that he can wear. Mr. Choleric sees himself as 100% masculine to his core, and he would probably say that men are masculine and women are feminine. Period. Cholerics aren't known for their love of details. In fact, when you start to give a Choleric a lot of details he will get annoyed with them, and you, in short order.

Mr. Choleric will most likely have a challenging time accepting the fact that he has a feminine side to himself. That is not to say that he cannot. The question is, will he? This will be dependent on his models. Typically, a Choleric will adopt a real man's model of what it is to be a man and it could very well include no soft or fuzzy stuff.

Cholerics can be open to learning and accepting new things. As with most people, "it's not only what you say, it's how you say it" that makes something acceptable or intolerable. This is true for all people. Most Cholerics are not in touch with their softer emotions. Thankfully, no one is totally Choleric and their secondary temperament will help the predominantly Choleric make the connections he needs to make with his emotional, feminine side.

One thing that Mr. Choleric has going for him is that he sees the big picture easily. This is one of the strengths that paves the way for him to lead himself and others. If this is a brand new idea that he has never heard before, his natural process is to check his internal references. If it is nowhere in his internal references, he will likely set it aside or dismiss it.

A major factor in whether the Choleric totally dismisses it or sets it aside for consideration will be dependent on the direction of his models. If his models contain beliefs that any tenderness or compassion is a sign of a lack of manhood, then he is likely to totally dismiss it and the one who told him about it.

If he has heard of it before and the idea is not totally against his models and beliefs, he will likely set it on the shelf and consider it over time. Once he sees how it does not take away from him as a man, and he sees how life is enhanced by it, he will soon be experiencing a more enjoyable life.

If you are a Choleric man and you are hearing about the masculine and feminine aspects for the first time and you are concerned, I understand. It is helpful to see clearly what is causing that concern. No man wants to be anything less than a man. What we understand makes a man a man is found in our models and beliefs. If this is outside your model of manhood, it can be a stretch.

When a man constructs his models so that they allow him to be strong and courageous and still be able to show compassion and tenderness when that is appropriate, it allows him to enjoy all aspects of life, without feeling like he is less manly.

As with everything, once the shock has worn off and he has had time to think about it and mull it over in his mind, Mr. Choleric may accept the fact that he has a feminine side, if all of the facts are there for clear inspection (or should I say summary sheet of the facts?).

Cholerics are about power. It is that simple. They want to make things happen; don't get in their way or you may get swept up with the trash. For the Choleric man, this is news that could be perceived as taking away some of his strength and power. So, for the men, it could be misunderstood as a big minus.

Miss Choleric would have a different reaction to the news that she has a masculine side. She, too, likes and feels comfortable in a powerful position. This being the case, Miss Choleric's reaction might be something like "Bring it on, I'll really go kick those guys' butts," and she will mean it. Miss Choleric will eat everybody else's lunch and be proud of it. You may be wondering, why the different response between Mr. Choleric and Miss Choleric? The difference is in the meanings that they give it.

Michelle was a young lady who had been raised in an average home. When I met Michelle she was about nineteen. We were introduced by a mutual friend who had known her for some time. I remember I was surprised at what she did for a living. During one of our conversations she mentioned that she had started a new job and I asked what kind of work she was doing.

"Moving," she said.

I was sure I had heard wrong and asked again, only to get the same answer.

"Surprised?" She beamed!

"Yes!" I responded and asked her what aspect of moving she did.

"Moving," she told me. "You know: packing the boxes and furniture into the truck, that kind of moving."

That was one occupation that I would have never guessed. She told me how she got started as a mover. Some friends needed help and she decided to give them a hand. She confided in me that at the end of the day she felt like she was going to die. She was so sore, it hurt everywhere. It was a day or two before she could really move much.

"But it was worth it," she proudly told me.

"Did they pay you that much?" I asked.

"No, they didn't pay much, but you should have heard them talk about how I carried all that stuff and how good a worker I was." She was beaming the entire time she was telling me about her moving job.

As I got to know Michelle, I learned that she loved to outwork guys. She got the greatest glee when a man had to stop and take a break while she kept going.

Some Choleric women have a very different response than Michelle did when it comes to moving, but you put before them a challenge and they will give you a run for your money. They won't intentionally let you win. They will leave you in their dust if they can, and it will make their day.

When it comes to wearing the masculine and feminine hats, the Phlegmatic and Choleric are polar opposites. The Phlegmatic male and female will find their feminine hat the easiest hat to wear.

Due to the nature of Miss Phlegmatic's personality type, it will not really make much difference to her. She might ask a question and then respond with a "That's interesting" and carry on as if nothing has happened at all and things are as they always have been. In reality, nothing would have changed, except for knowing something that has always been.

Mr. Phlegmatic will be similar to Miss Phlegmatic, once he gets over his surprise and possible disbelief. Being the diplomat that he is, he will not argue with someone over this. Once he finds out the other person is serous, he'll think about it and realize that either way there's not much you can do about it, and that is that.

For the Phlegmatic man to wear the masculine hat is to invite the possibility of confrontation. It is not at all impossible for the Phlegmatic to wear the masculine hat; it is just that it will undoubtedly cause more stress than for the other temperaments.

Phlegmatic women initially will expend more energy when they take up the masculine role. A Phlegmatic woman has to become incongruent with her feminine core and go against her Phlegmatic desires to avoid confrontation at almost any cost. A woman who has a strong primary Phlegmatic temperament will have her hands full going into her masculine energy. She, of all of the different temperament blends, will expend the most effort in the masculine role. She can do it, but she will shed the masculine role as quickly as possible because it will drain her emotionally and physically as well.

When the Phlegmatic woman learns how all of these different aspects work together and why some things are more challenging, she can make adjustments and access her masculine side with less difficulty.

Even though the Phlegmatic male would also like to avoid confrontation at almost any cost, he has a masculine core nature. He will not have to expend near the energy that the Phlegmatic woman will because he has a masculine core. He is congruent when he is in his masculine role.

The Phlegmatic male who was raised wearing his feminine hat and who is not accustomed to wearing his masculine hat will find it a real challenge to put it on. It is outside his identity and will feel foreign to him at first. It is not that he cannot wear it. It will simply require much more effort for him to continue to wear it until he becomes accustomed to it.

If a Phlegmatic man's wife is wearing her masculine hat, it would be a great help to him if she would voluntarily diminish her masculine side while her husband is building his masculine hat muscles, so to speak. It is important to note that a woman might not feel safe to totally let go of her masculine role because that is where she gains her security (feeling safe). This is where honesty and openness (accompanied with diplomacy) is critical between the husband and wife.

It is not uncommon for a Phlegmatic man and a Choleric woman to marry. In this combination, the wife will naturally be more outspoken than her husband. This, though, does not remove his ability to lead in their relationship. If the couple is incongruent when they marry and she is overly domineering, her Phlegmatic husband may never put on his masculine hat because to do so will result in extreme and intense conflict, something Phlegmatics try to avoid.

I have seen couples where the man could no longer take it and simply left the relationship without a word. This need not happen. Some couples are quite content for the woman to be the masculine force. The problem with this arrangement is that the woman will never totally respect and love her husband as long as she wears a hat that is incongruent with her core. And the husband will feel like he is not really measuring up, because he is not living life as a man.

Personality temperaments will have a major effect on how uncomfortable incongruence will be for an individual. For the Phlegmatic man, incongruence is not as uncomfortable as it would be for a Choleric man because each of the different personality temperaments has different leanings. The Phlegmatic is more relationship oriented while the Choleric is more self-oriented.

When a man's primary personality temperament is Phlegmatic, it does not alter his core nature of masculinity. Likewise when a woman has a Choleric primary personality temperament, it does not alter her feminine core nature, although ***a person's personality temperament make-up will alter and effect how congruence or incongruence will show up in life. This is true for both men and women.***

A Choleric woman, as we examined earlier, will experience less discomfort when she is incongruent, as compared to a Phlegmatic woman who will be very uncomfortable while she is incongruent from her core nature. A woman who has a very heavy Phlegmatic primary temperament will want to dump the masculine role as fast as she can.

When you add that we each have our own unique models and beliefs, it can get very interesting. Personality temperaments are a major influence on people and how they will tend to respond to things. It is the models, and the wide variety of beliefs that make them up, that cause a person to become incongruent from their core nature.

Add to this a person's NEEDS hierarchy and their current unmet NEEDS, and it does become more interesting. However, this is not beyond our ability to grasp what is going on and taking control. First, let's look at the contributing factors that go into the emotions that we don't always understand.

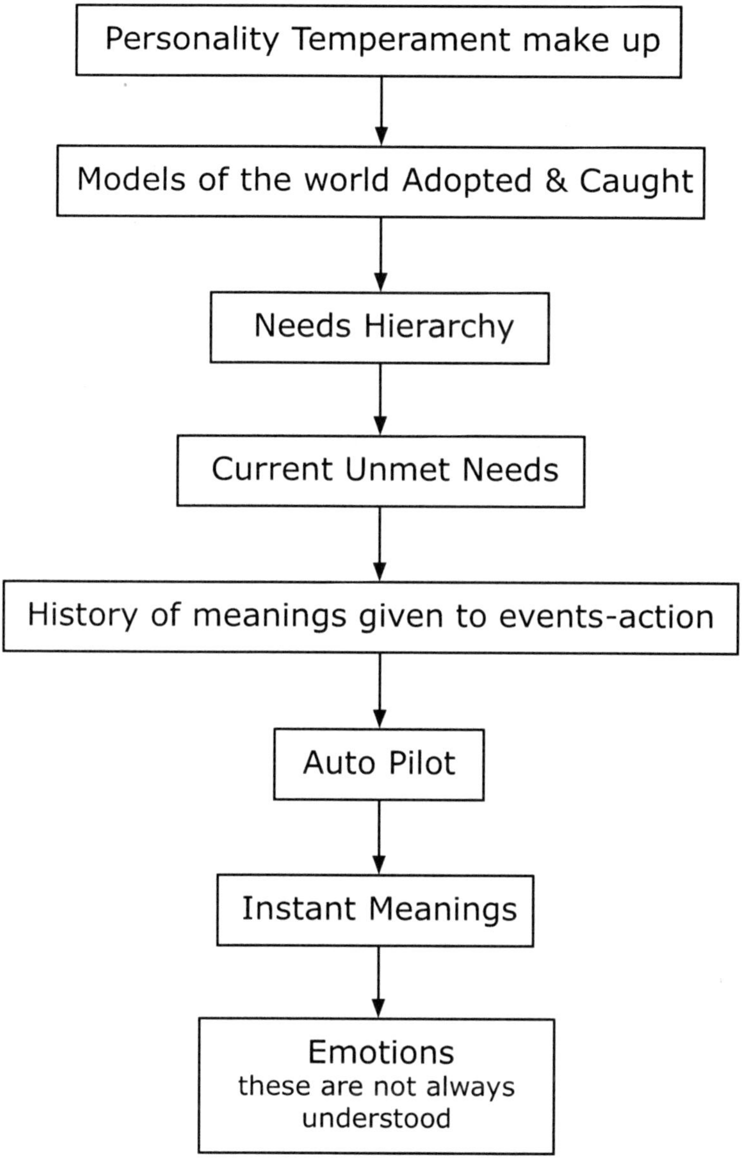
Personality Temperament make up
Models of the world Adopted & Caught
Needs Hierarchy
Current Unmet Needs
History of meanings given to events-action
Auto Pilot
Instant Meanings
Emotions
these are not always understood

In the NEEDS section we examined the typical NEEDS hierarchy for each of the different personality temperament blends. This is a general rule of thumb to go by: it is not a hard and fast rule of a person's hierarchy and there are exceptions.

Remember, a person's NEEDS hierarchy can be shifted temporarily as a result of a NEED that is lower on the list not being met. When this happens, it is elevated up on the list until it is met to a satisfactory level. At that point, the person's hierarchy will return to the normal order that they have established.

There are times when a person may find themselves experiencing emotions they do not understand. This is never a fun place to be; in fact, it can be unsettling, to say the least. I found it most helpful when I learned what had caused the emotions that were in question.

The majority of what we have considered so far operates primarily at the unconscious level. What we are going to look at in the next few paragraphs operates completely at the unconscious level, which is why we can find ourselves feeling emotions that we don't understand at all.

When an event happens, in a flash your unconscious mind scans your memories and instantly has a list of meanings from your past. Attached to the list of meanings are the corresponding emotions from the past, also. The unconscious mind operates this whole procedure from an autopilot mode, which operates without the conscious mind being aware of what is happening.

At the end of this process the conscious mind is handed an emotion. If the emotion is considered appropriate, it is not noticed and all is well. But if the emotion is not what is desired or not understood, the conscious mind notices it and has no idea of why the emotion is being experienced.

These feelings are not always appropriate for the situation, or even what we would choose to feel, yet we find ourselves feeling them. This process reinforces the idea that emotions happen to us and there is nothing we can do to avoid them. This conclusion, which is internal and not filtered for accuracy, is accepted as fact when it is far from the truth. There is a way to make corrections in the process, if you are willing to work at it. What you will need to do is not complicated or hard, it simply requires you to take charge of your focus.

For each of us, it is the meanings that we give things that create our emotions. Meanings are given on two different levels. The emotions you experience are a direct result of a conscious meaning that is given or it is the end result of a meaning that the unconscious mind gave to it automatically. Your unconscious mind learned to give certain meanings to events/things through conscious repetition. It monitored what you were thinking and found patterns and copied those patterns, making shortcuts from them. Let's look at how to start changing your meanings and the emotions they create.

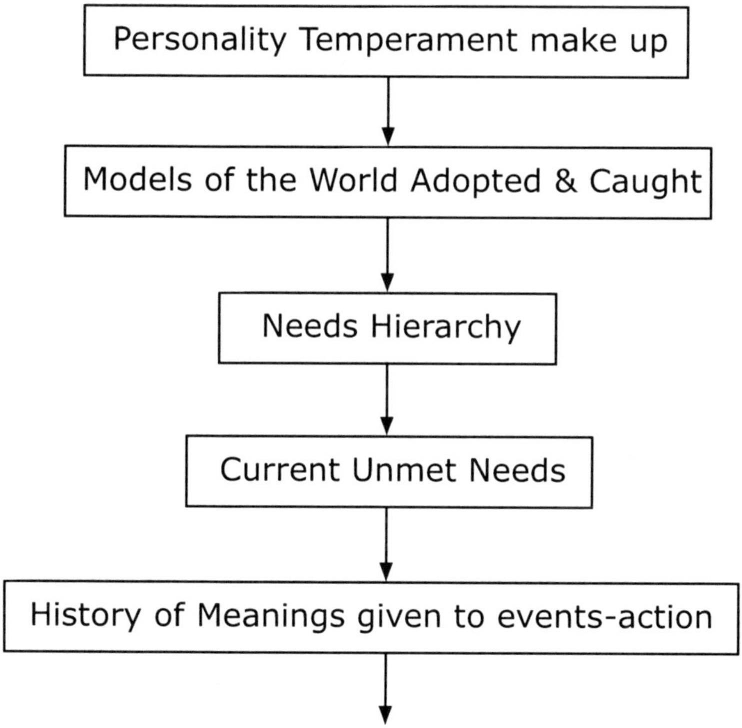

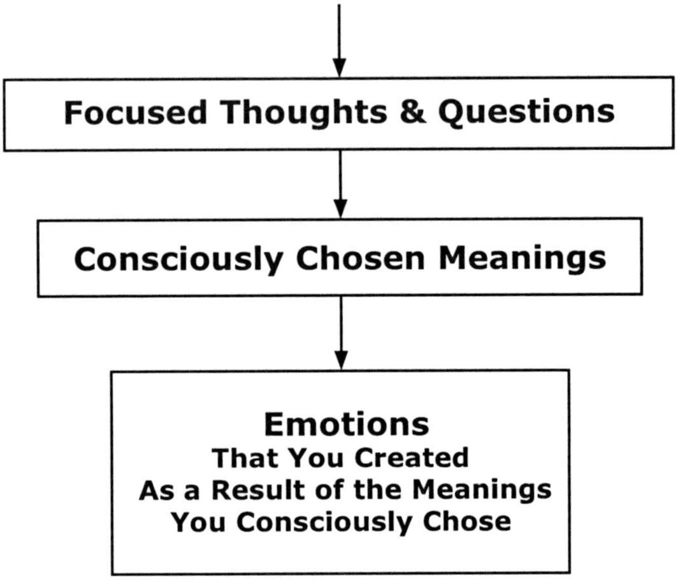

As you look at the first part of the chart on page 181, it is the same as the previous chart on page 179 until we get past the history of meanings given to events-actions. When people consciously become aware of the meanings they have been giving events on a regular basis, they will start to catch themselves in the process. It is at this point that they can begin the process of gaining more control of their emotions.

When you consciously focus your questions and thoughts, you have begun the steps to change the meanings you give things. You begin to take control of the emotions that you create in your own life.

The part of the chart on this page that says "Focused Thoughts & Questions" is where each of us can redirect our thinking. The questions we ask ourselves will direct our thoughts. Many people have a habit of asking the question "Why does this always happen to me?" A better question is "What can I learn from this and how can I turn this around to serve me?" This serves two purposes. First, it changes the position of the person from under it (it happening to them) to being larger than the event. Secondly, it redirects his thoughts to how he can benefit from it. This also predisposes him toward action.

The Questions You Ask Yourself Will Move You in Either a Positive or Negative Direction

When people use focused thoughts and questions, they can literally begin the process of shifting themselves from the negative quadrants into the positive quadrants. This is a very powerful and valuable skill to learn and to use on a daily basis. Remember, ***your brain will seek to answer any question you put before it.***

It is this area of focused thoughts and questions that will lead you to errors in your models and the beliefs that make them up. As you realize that you have been holding onto beliefs that once served you, but now hinder you, you can let go of them and embrace a new belief that serves you rather than hinders you.

This takes some time and persistence. Remember, your unconscious mind was not programmed in a day, and it is not going to be reprogrammed in a day, either. If you are consistent in applying this process, you will make progress.

As you are doing this reprogramming, you need to be conscious about the beliefs you are holding onto. If you have a conflicting belief, it will start to surface in the form of doubts about what you are saying to yourself. If you find yourself experiencing doubts, investigate your beliefs. Write them down on paper. This act actually allows you to step back from them so you can consider them more objectively. Once a belief is written down, it is easy to consider where it came from and if it is really applicable in your life. Sometimes a belief was proper earlier in our lives, but it is now outdated and needs to be set aside.

It is a liberating moment when you consciously choose the meanings you give an event and experience the emotions you have created. It is at that moment that you realize you can be in control of your emotions instead of your emotions being in control of you.

Ask Questions That Serve you

One of the best questions to ask is "What is the good in this?" (Especially if it is bad news.) Always ask questions that take you in a positive direction. An example of this is: "How can we make this work?" Instead of "Why won't this work?" The quality of the question will determine the quality of your answer. This is true in business and relationships.

When you ask the question "How can we make this work?" it will take your brain in that direction. When you ask the question "Why won't this work?" Your brain will give you all the answers as to why it won't work. This path takes your focus in the opposite direction from where you want to go. You can also ask the question "Do I have to make this work, or is there another option?" Different questions direct you to see opportunity or obstacle in the same circumstances.

When you want to make a turn in your car, you turn your steering wheel and your car goes in the direction that you want. So too, if you want your mind to go in the direction you desire, you must take hold of the steering wheel of your mind, which is your thoughts and questions. By doing this, you will be able to direct your mind and make greater progress with less effort.

Do you steer your mind currently or does it just go where it wants, wandering aimlessly? I know that if I don't take my mind where I want it to go, it does its own thing, running old thought patterns and thinking about things that really don't matter at all. There is nothing wrong with letting your mind wander, but not all the time. Each of us needs to learn to take control of our thinking and the meanings we give events. If we don't, we will constantly find ourselves and our emotions in places we would rather not be.

When we get into a car, we take hold of the steering wheel and we don't let go until we get to where we want to go. Unlike the car, some of us have not taken hold of the very things that control our minds. Who directs your thinking? If you are always listening to the radio or the TV, your thinking is being directed by what you are listening to.

It is possible to disagree with what is being said, but your choices are limited: you agree with it or not. As long as it is on, your thoughts are going to be continually guided by what you are listening to. **When a person turns off the outside things that are constantly grabbing at their focus they will be able to begin steering their thoughts with more accuracy.**

Once you turn off those outside things that constantly try to steer your thoughts, there are several factors that influence your thinking. The first is your models and the beliefs that make up those models. Your models are the maps that tell you where you can go and where you cannot go. You may have some sections blocked off with a big red X because, according to your map, it is unsafe. This first affects your thinking and then your actions.

I know some people (in a wide age range) who will not drive in snow or ice. They tell me it is too dangerous and unsafe. Their model or map of the world has a big red X through any place where snow is on the pavement. I look at them and I understand what they are saying, but my model of the world doesn't have a red X through that area.

What is the difference between my model and theirs? Yes, beliefs are a big one. There are several more things. I grew up in the city of Chicago. We would get upwards of 115 inches of snow a year. Now, we didn't have all that snow at one time. It would snow and melt repeatedly throughout the winter. When I was learning to drive, I had no choice: I had to learn how to drive on slippery roads.

There is much we can learn from this example. It is important to learn the skill of seeing someone else's model. I did not like driving on snow either when I first started, but I didn't have a choice. Life had to go on and if I wanted to eat and live, I had to drive in the snow. It helped a great deal when I began seeing it as an adventure and not something that was to be dreaded.

> **A**
> **Person's**
> **Beliefs**
> **Will be the Walls**
> **That confine them**
> **or**
> **Highways**
> **That free them**

It is obvious that the others made a decision not to drive on snow. They gave a meaning to driving on the snow that created some intense emotions within them. We need to play detective here. Remember that emotions are created as a result of the meanings we give things. Those meanings are going to agree with, and have the same flavor as, our models and the beliefs that make them.

A person's inner identity is going to have a key role here also. This person's beliefs about the snow are going to reflect back. For a man, incongruence could be involved. For a woman, it could be that she has not learned to access her masculine side when she needs to.

Their decisions were based on several things. At first their beliefs about the snow and themselves are what prompted them to not drive on snow. Their beliefs about the roads being so bad, that it was unsafe to drive, reflected something back to them that their unconscious mind picked up on. Remember, all models reflect back on those who hold them. What their unconscious mind picked up on was that their model portrayed them as lacking the skills and the abilities that are required to drive on those roads.

As this happened a time or two, their unconscious minds picked up on how this worked for meeting some of their psychological NEEDS and, over time, incorporated this behavior as a strategy for meeting those psychological NEEDS.

This leads us to another point. Do you think that *CERTAINTY* has a very high placement in this person's NEEDS hierarchy? I would say yes, and the counterpart to that is that VARIETY is probably very low in their hierarchy. Or is it? Could it be that they had an event happen in their life and they gave it extreme meanings which altered their models and beliefs? When this happens, it changes a person's approach to life.

At the very least, we know that when it comes to driving, they want much more CERTAINTY than they believe they can have while driving on the snow. How can a person's models affect them in this area? Their model contains beliefs about how safe or unsafe it is to drive on the snow and ice. This tells us about their beliefs. They don't believe they can drive safely on the snow and ice.

In what direction do you perceive their thoughts are taking them? Is it toward the positive or the negative? What insight might this give in regard to their overall model of the world? In and of itself, this information is simply information: a dot. If enough of the dots line up, a picture begins to take shape that is quite revealing and helpful to see.

Do you have any areas in your life where you have a big red X and a sign that says not to go there? Do you think you can control your thoughts and where they take you? Whatever your answer, it will reveal some of your beliefs about yourself and what you can and cannot do.

Each of us hold onto beliefs about ourselves, some of which serve us while others hinder us. It is critical to weed out the beliefs that hinder us and replace them with balanced beliefs that serve us and those around us.

Have you ever found your thoughts taking you somewhere you had not expected and would rather not be? Or not staying focused where you want? Your beliefs about this are important.

The very thing that causes our minds to wander is at the root of our ability to think. It is a natural part of life. A person's mind can make connections that machines cannot make. That is what makes it possible for people to think of new things.

When a person's mind wanders aimlessly it is because that person is not consciously directing the mind.

It is not possible to stop a healthy mind from thinking. The closest a person can get to that is to put their mind in neutral while they are letting others feed them thoughts and information. This is dangerous in that if it is done often enough it can become habitual.

The best way to avoid this is to consciously guide your mind, rather than try to force it. If a person believes that his mind wanders and there is nothing they can do about it, any time he has to focus and concentrate he will have a real struggle, because he is trying to do something that is contrary to his beliefs.

Many new discoveries have come about as a result of a person directing his mind as it wanders around thinking about things and what could be. The way to direct the wandering of your mind is through precise questions, since your mind seeks to answer any question you put before it. You may not have the answer right away, but in time, you will be amazed.

When a person's mind wanders aimlessly, it is not a lack of intelligence, but simply a lack of direction. Give your mind some stimulating questions to ponder and you may very well be amazed at the answers that appear.

If people's minds wander aimlessly and they conclude that is just how they are, it is incorporated as a belief about themselves. The conclusion they have just embraced as a belief will alter their inner identity. When this happens it often leads them to conclude that they are lacking in their intelligence, when in reality, it is that they have not yet learned how to direct their powerful mind.

It is important that we chose how we direct our thoughts. The new thoughts you continually run will become your new trend if you run it long enough.

Consider the following:

I am your constant companion.
I am your greatest helper or your heaviest burden.
I will push you onward or drag you down to failure.

I am completely at your command.
Half the things you do, you might just as well
turn them over to me, and I will be able to do them
quickly and correctly.

I am easily managed
But, you must be firm with me.

Show me exactly how you want
something done and after a few lessons
I will do it automatically.

I am the servant of all great men;
and alas, of all failures, as well.
Those who are great, I have made great.
Those who are failures, I have made failures.

I am not a machine,
though I work with the precision
of a machine, plus the intelligence of a man.
You may run me for a profit
or run me for ruin
it makes no difference to me.

Take me, train me, be firm with me,
and I will place the world at your feet.
Be easy with me and I will destroy you!
Who am I?

I am Habit!

Author unknown

I ran across this years ago. It is amazingly accurate in the way it describes how the unconscious mind works in our everyday lives. It is the unconscious mind that makes something an automatic response without conscious thought or, as they have listed, a habit!

This is indicative of what the unconscious mind does with our thought patterns, word choices, and the meanings we give to events. Each of the many different meanings we can give events in our life has a certain flavor to them. This flavoring is accomplished by the words we use to describe events that happen in our lives.

These patterns become the programming for your unconscious mind's autopilot mode, which operates at extremely high levels of proficiency. Your unconscious mind has radar out that is looking for anything that is recognizable. Once spotted, it takes whatever course is in its log books. This can be good or bad.

In the movie **Stealth**, there is an unmanned, computer-controlled aircraft. The name given to the artificial intelligence that ran the plane was "Eddie." Eddie listened in on everyone's conversations and he learned from everyone, especially the commander of the squadron.

Eddie learned things that members of the squadron wished he had not, and he took everything seriously. He didn't have the wisdom or understanding to evaluate the correctness of what he was copying. As a result, he adopted some bad behavior because there were no references by which to judge what he was hearing.

This is what the unconscious mind is doing when it is first starting out. It has no references and accepts everything as the way to do things. It uses these references it has gathered over time to determine the appropriateness of future decisions and actions. Once the frames of reference are programmed in, it is challenging to reprogram, but it *can* be done.

I have heard people ask how a young kid who has grown up in a war zone can pick up a machine gun and start shooting everyone he sees. That behavior is a result of the models, beliefs, references and strategies he has learned. That type of behavior could very well be in line with the inner identity that has been formed in his unconscious mind.

To him it is normal. His model of the world is fighting and death; picking up the gun is one of the strategies that exist in his model of the world. His model colors his understanding of how a person deals with disagreements and heartache, so he employs the strategies he has learned.

Everyone is chained to the strategies that they have learned. When they are faced with a situation that they don't have a fitting strategy for, they will use one of the strategies they have used before and are comfortable with. The strategy may be one of the worst, but they aren't aware of it. They are simply doing what they know to do.

Models create incongruence. These same models that create incongruence encourage strategies that meet the individual's psychological NEEDS. Once a person understands the different layers that exist and how each one affects and reinforces the others, changes can be made if a person so chooses.

If you have come to the conclusion that you are incongruent from your core nature, don't worry. You can regain your congruency. If you are serious about changing this, you **must** write out your beliefs about life and what it is to be a man or woman, whichever is your situation.

Ultimately it is in everyone's best interest to be congruent with their core nature. This is possible only if people adapt their beliefs which will shift their models and make it possible for them to regain congruency with their core nature.

It is possible for a man to be totally congruent with his core nature and be able to show genuine tenderness, compassion and love for someone and never become incongruent. This is possible after a man has learned how to center himself in his masculinity.

If a person has been living incongruent for a long time, their self-perceptions will have been affected. How they see themselves and their capabilities will be limited in varying degrees, depending on their personality temperament and their models. This can be challenging, but it is something they can do.

So where do you start? ***First, you must approach this whole business of making the changes you want from the predisposition that you can, and will, succeed.*** If you cannot embrace this thought without doubt, you have some beliefs within your models that you need to weed out first.

Have you ever felt odd at times, as though you were different or didn't quite fit in? These feelings are normal. Each person on this planet is unique. The key is the way people explain their feelings to themselves and the meanings they attach to being different. The person who sees being different as bad is doing himself a disservice.

Typically when a person feels something, he tends to incorporate it into who and how he sees himself. This is not bad if the emotions are positive and uplifting, but when those emotions are negative and destructive, it can be harmful.

Do you ever find yourself feeling emotions that you can't explain to yourself?

It is common for each of us to experience emotions that we don't want and/or don't understand. When this happens the questions you ask yourself will direct your focus in a positive or negative direction.

One of the most challenging things to do with emotions is to work backward. You have a result (an emotion) and you need to find out what happened to create it. The emotions that you experience at any time are a direct result of the meanings that have been given. If you have not consciously given a meaning to an event what do you do?

This challenge exists because a great number of meanings are being assigned by your unconscious mind. It is running programs that have been taught in the past by your conscious mind when it consciously gave meanings to events. Your unconscious mind does not hand you a detailed list of what it did to produce the emotion you are feeling; it simply gives you the end product, the emotion.

As we saw earlier, emotions are either masculine or feminine in their make-up. All emotions will be in one of these two categories. The emotions you feel on a daily basis will give you insight into where you are within your own self-contained masculine/feminine dynamics.

I was working with a couple from Australia. The woman said she was tired of being the man in the family and wanted her husband to step up and take the leadership role. Even though he said he wanted to take the lead, he would not. I knew that in order for him to make the progress he said he wanted to make, he would have to face the emotions he was experiencing.

I asked him to list the different emotions he was feeling on a daily basis for a week. When I received his list it was a detailed list of what he had done that week: it did not contain a single emotion. I made contact with him and explained that activity was not an emotion and he agreed to make a new list of emotions. At the end of the next week, I received another list of what he had done. This went on for four weeks.

Finally, I confronted him about his models and beliefs regarding emotions. He had a dilemma that he would not let go of. The first challenge was that he had adopted models that contained the beliefs that certain emotions were unmanly. He was into sports. Can you guess why? SIGNIFICANCE. This man's top need was SIGNIFICANCE, and he received it on the field. In fact, that was one of the things that attracted his wife to him. She wanted a strong man. Her model contained beliefs that someone good at sports was a strong and capable man. This man was a great catch: he was great at sports and he was kind and tender when he was around her; he never forced or pushed anything or anyone. The perfect gentleman. Eighteen years into their marriage, and she was at her wit's end.

As I said, he believed that feeling emotions was unmanly; especially the feminine emotions. To acknowledge those feeling would have been a big withdrawal from his SIGNIFICANCE account.

The real problem that derailed this man from making the progress he said he wanted to make was his great fear of losing the balance in his NEEDS account. Let me explain. When he was around his sports or anything to do with sports, he felt really good about himself and his world. When he was around his wife, taking the lead as she desired, he was extremely insecure and unsure of himself. He found himself being torn in two different directions and that terrified him. This he did admit once.

The reason for this is simple. He had been raised in a female-dominated home and that was what he knew. Everything in his past pointed to the woman being the leader of the home. When it came to his relationships, his inner identity was that of a follower.

On the sports field it was something different. That was where he shined. On the field he had VARIETY in that he never knew how it was going to go, he had CERTAINTY that he could handle whatever came his way, LOVE and CONNECTION from his fans, and the big one, SIGNIFICANCE. From 1 to 10, all of his psychological NEEDS were being met at a level 8, and up, while he was on the field.

When he was at home trying to lead, he was uncertain of himself and his role of leader. He was outside of his inner identity and his unconscious mind was making that very clear to him. Leading at home was more difficult because he kept falling back into the follower mode.

According to his wife, he would be leading for a little bit. She would say something or suggest something and the next thing she knew he was behind instead of in front of her.

At home, when he was following, he had CERTAINTY that he knew his role, at least the one he had learned growing up. He also had VARIETY in that he didn't know when or what his wife was going to do. When you get down to it, he lacked confidence in himself. His wife didn't lack confidence in him: in fact, she had more confidence in him than he did. If two people live together for eighteen years they know each other pretty well.

So what was the problem, the speed bumps? Remember our diagram that shows the complete composition of a belief? This man, like many of us, had different beliefs for different areas of his life. On the field he believed he was extremely capable at leading and calling the shots. At home he had beliefs about what he was capable of, and his role was that of follower. This was both taught and caught from his parents.

If we were to compare his beliefs about himself in the areas of sports and leading his family, it would look like this.

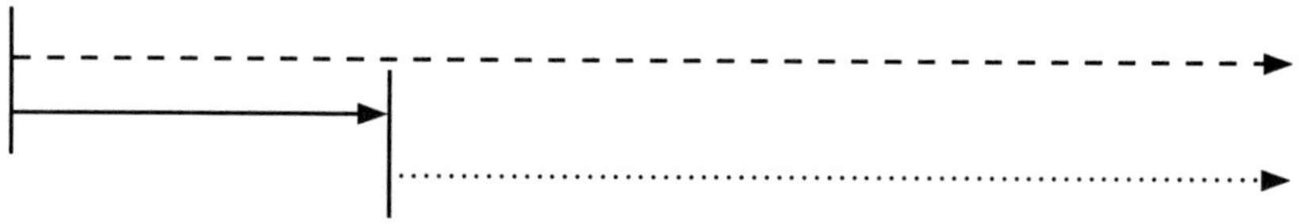

The dashed line represents his ability to lead in sports, and the solid line represents his beliefs regarding his ability to lead his family. Where his solid line of what he believes is possible for him stops, it is replaced by the belief (dotted line) of what is impossible for him.

If you were to draw lines that represented his wife's beliefs of his abilities to lead in both areas, the lines would look like this.

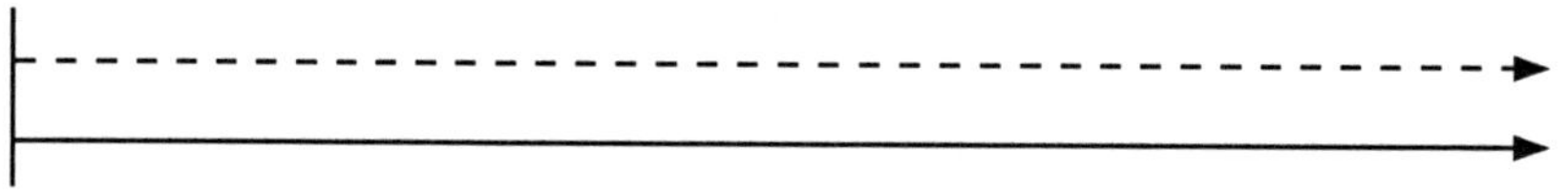

His wife sees that he has abilities that he doesn't recognize. She sees it, but he doesn't. ***Each of them has their own beliefs, and they are responding according to the beliefs they hold onto.*** In both cases their beliefs and models are directing what they see. On the surface it appeared to him that she was not backing him, and was in opposition to him. In reality, she was on his side and was encouraging him the only way she could without encouraging his dependence on her.

There are many ways a man can respond to growing up wearing his feminine hat. The reason for this diversity in their reactions is due to, and can be found in the differences in personality temperaments, beliefs, models and unmet NEEDS.

When a man has taken up the feminine hat, he is geared more toward relationship than accomplishment. This becomes a part of his inner identity. When a man is not aware of this it can, and will, affect his ability to lead himself as well as others.

It is possible for people to embrace beliefs that are in opposition to each other. Part of them wants to, and knows they can do something while another part of them doesn't want to and is sure they will fail if they attempt it. In this situation, the emotions that a person experiences will be confusing, to say the least.

An example of this is if a man has adopted a belief that it is unmanly to show any kind of emotion at all. That man's belief would make it impossible for him to experience life at it fullest, because the belief makes a natural part of life wrong. Any time he feels any of the normal emotions that people feel, his models and beliefs would condemn him. Therefore, he concludes that if he feels those emotions, he is somehow less of a man.

So what can you or anyone do for a person in the above situation? It is impossible to change someone's beliefs. If you try, he will only resent you for your efforts to help him. So what do you do? You can offer information and answer questions after that it is in his hands. He is the one who is responsible for making the change he wants. A great number of people want you to change them and that is dependency, which is not healthy for an individual.

List out the emotions you feel on a regular basis in such a way that you are able to see which emotions you feel the most. It is critical that you are totally honest. Being honest with yourself is one of the first steps in taking responsibility for your life. No one is to see this list but you.

What does listing out the emotions you feel on a regular basis do? It separates you from them; it creates a little distance between you and them. Before you look to find out where the emotions that are on the list fall out in the rectangle, it is important to understand the emotions on your list are the end product of strategies that were executed.

Look at the Masculine Feminine Dynamics Rectangle on the next page. In which of the quadrants do the majority of the emotions place within the rectangle? Where they are is where they are: they don't have to remain there if you don't want them to.

First, don't judge the emotions because of where they fall. The next step is to think through the possible meanings that could produce those emotions. What beliefs would direct a person toward the meanings that were given to events that took place? Remember that beliefs influence meanings, and meanings create emotions. So to play the detective, reverse the order. You have the end result of emotions but what meanings could cause those emotions? What beliefs would inspire those meanings? List them out and see which of the possible meanings are behind the emotions. Then list out the possible beliefs that could point a person to that meaning. Once you have pinpointed the meanings and beliefs, evaluate them. Some beliefs were once valid but are now outdated.

People, like towns, can have beliefs that are outdated. In Chico, California, there is an ordinance that states, "Driving a herd of cattle down a street is against the law." In Ocean City, New York, a law from the early 1900's prohibits men from going topless on the Boardwalk. These laws were still on the books at the time of this writing.

These are humorous examples of laws that at one time were considered correct, yet at this time it is clear that the areas have grown to the point that these laws are not needed or appropriate, but they are still on the books. Just as towns have old laws on the books that are not appropriate any more, we too can hang onto beliefs that no longer fit, or are totally false, and we just didn't realize it when we first embraced them.

Masculine-Feminine-Dynamics-Rectangle

Confident	Love
Determined	Compassion
Self-assurance	Tenderness
Optimistic	Mercy

Strong & Powerful — ***Positive*** — **Soft**

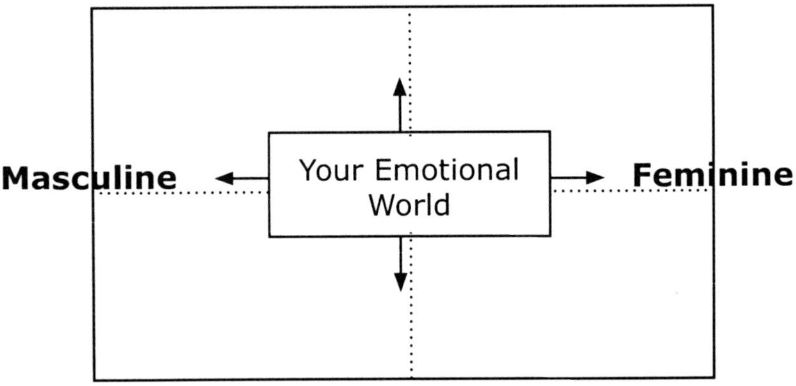

Hard — ***Negative*** — **Weak & Vulnerable**

Anger	Overwhelmed
Selfishness	Helplessness
Rage	Fear
Heartlessness	Pessimism
	Depression

It is critical that we find out what models and beliefs are at the root of the emotions and behaviors. If people are holding onto models and beliefs that are contrary to the new meanings they give events, the new meanings will not stick and they will be discouraged.

At the unconscious level it is like telling yourself something you know is not true. The unconscious mind treats it like a joke. If I were to start telling myself that everything is going to work out just perfect today and part of me says, "Yeah Right, Fat Chance!" That is a key indicator that somewhere in my beliefs there is a conflict.

The next step is to consider the psychological NEEDS. It is possible for a belief to rob or hinder a person from meeting their NEEDS in positive ways. If people, like the young lady who believed that she was ugly in every way, hang onto a belief that they are not worthy of being loved, they have closed the door to feeling genuinely loved by anyone as long as they hang onto that belief.

The only way for a person in this situation to feel loved if they don't change that belief, is through self-love. Remember, when people feel sorry for themselves what they are actually doing is comforting themselves and expressing LOVE to themselves. This meets their NEED for LOVE, but at a very low level. It is also possible for a person to meet their needs for SIGNIFICANCE and CONNECTION through this strategy as well.

If someone does love her and tries to express it, what they are saying will be automatically thrown out and rejected because it is so counter to what she has come to believe about herself. When the young man kept telling her she was pretty and that she was a wonderful person, she got upset with him. This behavior is in line with her accepted inner identity and is a strategy she has found meets her psychological NEEDS, all of which is operating at the unconscious level.

When a person argues with another, they have CONNECTION, SIGNIFICANCE, and VARIETY all met within that one event. The challenging thing about negative strategies is that they often meet many NEEDS at one time and at high levels.

A Person's Strategies for Meeting Their Psychological NEEDS will Always be Directed Through Avenues that are Compatible with their Models, Beliefs and Perceived Identity.

One of the challenges for a man who has grown up in a family where the father was not the leader is that he, too, learns to adopt the feminine role through the example of his father. The son learns to meet his psychological NEEDS as best he can while being incongruent to his core.

When the son becomes a man, his beliefs, models, identity and strategies for meeting his psychological NEEDS are all going to be rooted in incongruence. This is what he has learned and knows to the point that it has become automatic. He will also experience inner conflicts as a result of the incongruence. Depending on how long, and to what extent, a man has been raised feminine, he will experience varying degrees of frustration and confusion.

One man I know, whom I will call Jack, was raised by his mother and grandmother. Growing up he was never around men. His world consisted of females. When I met him, he had hired on for the summer with the company that I worked for.

Jack was taking pre-med courses and was doing very well. One day he asked me if I could explain something to him. He began with, "I don't get it. I'm around all of these beautiful girls at school. We have labs that we have to do in groups, so I have gotten to know some of them and have asked them out. They laugh at me! What is going on?"

That was thirty years ago. I didn't know then how to explain it as I do now. He had been raised feminine in his approach to life. There was no attraction for the girls because he had the same feminine energy they had.

Jack was physically attracted to these women. When a person is incongruent with their core nature, it does not mean that he is not physically attracted to the opposite sex.

Jack had been taught to wear his feminine hat, which is what the girls responded to. The girls loved being around him because he was understanding and tender and they felt safe and secure. Meanwhile, poor Jack was going crazy, he couldn't figure out why they were not attracted to him.

When a person moves from the masculine to feminine quadrants or vice versa there is a shift that takes place. Often it is not consciously recognized, but at the unconscious level it is clearly understood and surfaces in the form of emotions.

A major shift that takes place is in the source that person now looks to for CERTAINTY. The unconscious mind understands that when the feminine side is predominant, their source of CERTAINTY is outside themselves. While the masculine side is predominant CERTAINTY is found from within. Because this takes place at the unconscious level, it surfaces as emotions that often confuse people.

Emotions have confused people for thousands of years. You now have insights that will help you understand your own emotions and how you are ultimately creating them. If you choose, you can change and pick the emotions you want to experience. If you do these things, does it mean that you won't get surprised by your emotions at times? The answer is no. But you will be able to have a more even and enjoyable emotional life.

The Masculine Feminine Dynamics Rectangle is a great reference tool for understanding where you are at any moment in time. All people move around within the Masculine Feminine Dynamics Rectangle. There is no right or wrong spot to be in. If, at some point in time, you discover yourself in one of the negative quadrants, you now have a better understanding of how to move yourself to a better position.

In which quadrant(s) do you want to reside on a regular basis?

Masculine-Feminine-Dynamics-Rectangle

Confident
Determined
Self-assurance
Optimistic

Love
Compassion
Tenderness
Mercy

Strong & Powerful

Positive

Soft

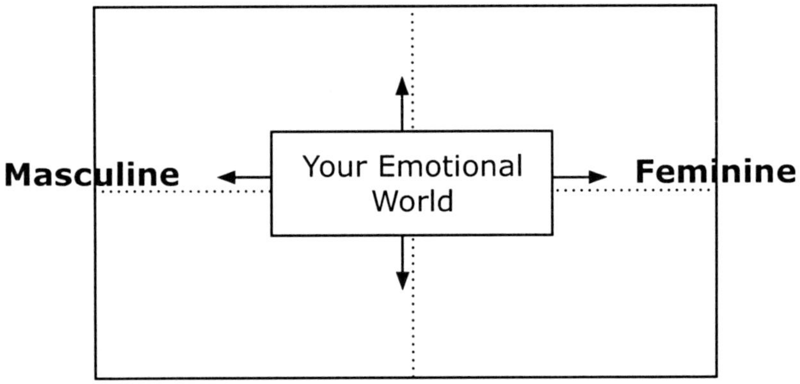

Hard

Negative

Weak & Vulnerable

Anger
Selfishness
Rage
Heartlessness

Overwhelmed
Helplessness
Fear
Pessimism
Depression

JimWysong.com

CONQUERING

Conquering

Have you ever wondered why people do some of what they do? Why do people climb mountains? What was the compelling reason behind going to the moon? Why are sports such a big deal for people, and why is winning so important?

The reason is simple: humans have a built in drive to conquer. This is true for men and women. The drive to conquer is not the same as the psychological NEEDS that we have explored earlier. I do not include this in with the psychological NEEDS, because it is something that a person can function without.

Unlike a person's psychological NEEDS, the drive to conquer cannot be met from within by the meanings a person gives to an event. Conquering involves action and things outside the individual.

The drive to conquer is inborn. It will manifest itself differently in people's lives as a result of their personality temperaments variations, models and the strategies they have embraced for meeting their psychological NEEDS.

Males, because of their masculine core nature, have a stronger drive to conquer than females. For both males and females however, those who have the strongest personality temperaments also have the strongest drive to conquer.

The fact that boys have a greater inborn drive to conquer than girls is evident by simply watching them. A large number of women don't understand boys. I have heard many women say, "I have no idea why they do what they do. It makes no sense to me, and they drive me crazy."

All behavior is motivated by something. Naturally, when the motivation behind the behavior is not seen and understood, the behavior is confusing to those who are looking on. As we have discovered, all people give meaning to events and activity, and if the activity is not understood, the onlookers will typically search their mind for an explanation for the behavior.

When the people who are looking on have no understanding of the "why" behind the behavior, they will seek to explain or label it. To find an answer, they will search through their references to see which ones match it or look for ones that provide some explanation that can be linked to the behavior. Once some things have been found, the possibilities are listed in order of what they determine are the most likely to be correct according to their references.

This is one area where women have a challenge understanding male's behaviors. In a majority of women's world, relationships are a high priority and conquering things for the sake of conquering is totally outside their approach to life. Because conquering makes no sense to them, other than to subdue another person, they often conclude that men are bent on conquering people. After all, to a person who can see no other use for conquering, it would make sense that if a person is always conquering something they will turn that drive toward conquering people.

In reality, that is the exception, not the rule, but it is the only thing that makes sense to many women. The fact that there have been some people who have done terrible things to others only reinforces that conclusion.

I have heard women ask their husbands why their sons do what they do and often their husbands will simply answer, "Honey, what do you expect? They are boys." This does little to relieve their wives' frustration and confusion, but rather adds to it.

As a boy conquers obstacles that are before him, he is building references he will draw from later. As he conquers, he is literally assembling an internal framework that is the structure that will support his confidence in himself. This prevents him from having to rely on an external support for his confidence.

Things that are Not Understood are Often Feared

This is true for a boy's drive to conquer. Because a large number of people don't understand what is playing out, they are fearful of it and want to subdue it, which is, in reality, a form of conquering that is hidden behind fear.

Fear is an emotion that is often created within the mind of the one who is fearful. Don't get me wrong: to never be fearful is not a wise thing. There are things in life that should be feared. Fear, when used appropriately, can save your life.

Uncontrolled fear can result in many negative situations for everyone involved. What a person focuses on becomes larger than life. This is not an endorsement for denial, but an encouragement not to make something bigger than it is.

There are thousands of life enhancing ways for a person to exercise their drive to conquer. When an individual first exercises their drive to conquer in positive ways, and it results in their psychological NEEDS being met, it is likely that the direction of their life is being established.

Unfortunately, this is true when a person does life debasing activities as well. If their psychological NEEDS are being met at high levels, if unchanged, the direction of their life is being mapped out in a negative direction. Thankfully, they are not locked in that downward spiral. Any person can change the course of their life if they want to. This is true regardless of race, culture or sex.

Sometimes a boy's drive to conquer is misunderstood and the label of unhealthy aggression is put on him and his activities. When boys are seen wrestling and always trying to outdo the other, some adults can interpret it as a problem in the making. A great number of people don't understand that what is playing out is, in reality, preparation for becoming a man.

By learning to conquer different things that are before him, a boy builds a reference base to draw from when he is older. If something is there, a boy will climb it, race it, and do everything he can to overcome it, no matter the obstacle.

Through these activities a boy learns to believe in himself and his abilities. It is not important that he conquer his objective the first time. The important thing he learns is that if he keeps working at it, sooner or later he will be able to overcome the obstacle that is before him.

When a boy tries to overcome an object and is not able to when he first attempts it, but works at it until he is able to have victory, the lessons learned in persistence are invaluable. When continual effort is made and persistence is rewarded, it lays a solid foundation that will strengthen him for many years to come.

One day I went outside and saw a bike parked on top of a gravel pile. Later, when I saw the boy who had parked it there, I asked him why he had parked his bike as he had. He just smiled and said, "I thought it looked cool. Do you like it?"

I have no idea how long he worked to get his kickstand to hold his bike upright on top of that pile of loose gravel, but he did it and he had a good time doing it. Boys will conquer anything and everything. They rarely sit still and that drives some women crazy.

Boredom sets in on everyone from time to time, but what is it? Looking at it through the psychological NEEDS perspective, it could be a person's NEED for VARIETY surfacing. If that is the case, they will simply change what they are doing. They might watch a movie, listen to some music, perhaps read a book or go for a walk.

When it is a person's NEED for VARIETY surfacing a simple change will do, but when their drive to conquer is surfacing, change alone is insufficient. A key distinction between when a person is meeting their psychological NEEDS for VARIETY and when their drive to conquer is being exercised can be found in what they do to alleviate their boredom.

If a simple change takes care of boredom, chances are that their NEED for VARIETY was at the root of it. If, on the other hand, the activity that relieves their boredom results in a feat of accomplishment taking place, that person's drive to conquer is somewhere in the mix.

You have heard the saying "killing two birds with one stone." Well, that is what the unconscious mind tries to do on a regular basis. It incorporates many things into one activity. It is possible to take care of a person's drive to conquer and their psychological NEEDS for CONNECTION, CERTAINTY, VARIETY and SIGNIFICANCE through one activity. When this process is playing out in the life of an adult, unless a person has learned how to see clearly what is happening, it is difficult to distinguish each individual aspect that is contributing to their actions.

There are times when a person's drive to conquer can be seen clearly and other times when it is not. When it is not seen clearly, it does not mean their drive to conquer does not exist. As people get older they usually learn to refine the approach they use when trying to get their way. Each temperament blend will naturally have different ways of displaying their drive to conquer. The drive to conquer can be seen easier in children because they are more spontaneous and have not yet learned to hide motivating factors as adults do.

Having a large family, we get to watch a great deal more interaction between siblings than do most families these days. Families are a great training ground for children to learn how to interact with others. Children often play together doing a variety of things that involves every one of them. It is inevitable that when they stop focusing on conquering the worthwhile objective that is before them, without consciously thinking about it, they shift their focus from conquering the common goal to conquering each other.

As much as we adults would rather not admit it, in some ways we are just big kids. There are advantages and disadvantages contained within this truth.

How does a person's focus get distracted from the worthwhile objective that is before them to others? While working with others, things happen, and meanings must be assigned to what has happened. Whether it is something that fell and broke, or someone dripping paint on your sleeve, our internal wiring requires that a meaning be given to the event. This is often the turning point when a person shifts their focus.

It doesn't matter whether it is the person's unconscious mind that ran a short cut and handed that individual emotions that they did not ask for, or they consciously thought out the meanings they gave the event. The fact is they now have a package of emotions. The reality is, they sometimes have a very large bundle of feelings that now have their undivided attention.

Emotions, by their nature, have the ability to captivate a person's attention and focus. When this happens, people lose sight of what they had originally set out to do. This is true for individuals of all ages, regardless of race or sex. It is similar to what happens when a person is doing something and is physically hurt. The pain that is a result of the injury redirects their focus and their attention.

When something happens and a meaning is given that results in a withdrawal being made from their psychological NEEDS account, their attention and focus are redirected. In reality, the withdrawal from their NEEDS account is a direct result of the meanings they have given the event. Because a majority of the time this whole process operates at the unconscious level, that individual does not realize or understand what is happening, but they sure do feel it. When a person does not understand why they are feeling the way they are, it can be unsettling and confusing.

There is another area that humans have a drive in and that is sex. A person's sex drive starts out as hormonal. It does not surface until certain hormone levels rise within boys and girls. Without doubt, inner drive toward sex is real and if this were not so, it is conceivable that mankind could die off from lack of procreation.

Sex can be a strategy people use to fill the psychological NEEDS in their life. Sex can be linked in a person's mind to SIGNIFICANCE, CERTAINTY, VARIETY, and LOVE and CONNECTION. Sex can be, and has been, used as a means to conquer another person. For thousands of years, both men and women have used sex as a way of conquering each other.

Because men are turned on sexually more easily than women, some women have concluded that men are weaker, and they use this weakness, as they see it, to their advantage.

Many men see sex as a means of getting SIGNIFICANCE for themselves. There are some models that contain beliefs that state that in order for a boy to become a man he must do this or that. Often sex is one of the requirements to manhood. Add to that the way sex is portrayed in the media, and it encourages boys and girls to start early.

I know of young men and women who have participated in contests to see who could have sex with the largest number of people in a certain time period. This may sound odd to many, yet if we consider what the motivating factors are behind it, it makes sense, to a degree.

Without doubt that person's psychological NEEDS would be met at high levels in many, if not all, of their NEEDS. SIGNIFICANCE would be overflowing by the buckets, VARIETY would be filled to the max, LOVE and CONNECTION could be filled at high levels, depending on how they explained their behavior to themselves. Their NEED for CERTAINTY would be filled, especially if they were very successful.

The above contest has the potential to meet their NEEDS at high levels for the short term, but in the long term such strategies have shown themselves to be life debasing rather than life enhancing. Granted, when a person is in the heat of the moment, they are not so likely to see it from that perspective.

One man had asked me to teach him how to be more masculine so he could get more women to go to bed with him. I was surprised by his request: I had met this man and talked with him several different times at a series of meetings and he gave no indication that he was a womanizer.

In talking with him, I found out he had adopted models that endorsed womanizing as acceptable. He was quite hooked on his model and understandably so. He was meeting his physical and psychological NEEDS and his drive for conquering all in one activity. The problem was that he was getting all of his NEEDS and drives met at very high levels, through a life debasing activity. For the record, I didn't work with him.

This is one way a person can direct their drive to conquer people rather than things. For thousands of years the majority of man's time and effort had been directed at conquering his environment and staying alive. When he wasn't doing that, he had been trying to conquer others, as history proves out.

The drive to conquer can be used for good or evil: it is up to each of us what we choose to do with it. If we don't consciously direct it, and use it constructively, it can start spilling out all over those around us. When this happens it is not pretty.

When children are playing together or working on a project, they do fine until something happens, and they give what happened a meaning that sidetracks them from their original goal. The focus shifts from conquering the common goal to conquering each other. This happens with adults as well.

In reality, there is nothing wrong with any of the things we have considered in this section. The drive to conquer and the drive to have sex do exist and, if directed in positive ways, enhance each of our lives. The key is how each is directed.

Some are concerned that if a man is too masculine he may become a menace to society. In reality, a masculine man is not what people fear. What people fear, and have reason to fear, is the unrestrained drive to conquer coupled with models and beliefs that move any person, whether male or female, very far into the negative masculine quadrant.

When a person sinks into the negative masculine quadrant to the point they lose touch with their feminine side, they can reach a point where the compassion they once had, is replaced with cruelty. When a person reaches this point they have no concern for other people, their lives are expendable.

All of the tyrants throughout history have embraced models and beliefs that have sucked them into the negative masculine quadrant so far that they never regain a healthy balance again. That individual is to be feared.

When considering the number of people who have gone to that extreme, it is a very small percentage of the population, and that is over a great number of years. It is true that a sore thumb hurts deeply if it is bumped; so it is with painful memories. It only takes a minor jarring and we feel pain.

I share this to give insight into another aspect of men and women, and to show that the masculine and feminine aspects that exist within each of us is not any one thing that is bad, but rather the misuse of good things that should be our concern.

When a man becomes docile and no longer strives to conquer things, he will begin to slowly die from within. I have seen men who became nothing more than a shell of what they once were. ***Men and women need a purpose*** to live, to do something with their lives. When a person's life has no purpose, they begin to wither, and it is just a matter of time before they die. An example of this is the fact that many men die shortly after retirement.

An individual gives meanings to the different events that happen in his life, those meanings are going to result in his experiencing a deposit or a withdrawal in his psychological NEEDS account. It is helpful to remember that a person's meanings typically follow the direction of their models. Understanding how a person's models can affect the meanings they give events is essential.

Models also contain beliefs about conquering and about sex, which will influence meanings that people give, and the methods they adopt toward what is to be conquered. This drive to conquer is not limited to culture, race or sex. Everywhere you turn there is evidence of someone's drive to conquer. Mankind is not content unless he or she is conquering something.

Women have been perplexed as to why men do some of the things they do. If women consider the activities that men are doing in light of their drive to conquer, it makes sense. Add into the equation a person's need to meet their psychological NEEDS of CERTAINTY, VARIETY, SIGNIFICANCE, and LOVE and CONNECTION and it is easy to understand the motivation behind a great deal of what men do.

If a person's model of the world is one that portrays them as smaller and weaker compared to others, how they exercise their drive to conquer will be different than someone whose model of the world has them as capable of dealing with whatever comes along.

When the first astronauts landed on the moon and returned to earth, they had some real challenges. After all, what more can you do after you have walked on the moon? A person is happiest when he is doing something worthwhile and fulfilling. If it is too easy, it is boring. The greater the obstacle, the greater the sense of accomplishment.

People need to be in the process of continually conquering something. When there is nothing to conquer, a person's drive to conquer can spill out on those around them in a negative way. This is especially true when the individual's models are oppressive in their nature. One of the greatest misuses of the desire to conquer is when it is turned toward other people.

We have considered the drive to conquer that exists within men and women. It is important that we consider the fear of being conquered, which is the counterpart to the drive to conquer. No one likes the idea of being conquered. Not men or women: women have a stronger concern in this area than do most men because of the physical strength difference between the sexes.

Men

It is easy to group men together and make conclusions regarding the group as a whole. In reality, everyone is different. Yes, there are some things that each of us face, but even though there are similar things in our lives, each person and situation is different.

There is no way I can cover all that I would like to in this section. That being said, I am going to cover some key aspects of being a man.

One aspect of being a man that is unavoidable is that of confidence. Each of us, as a man, needs confidence. Our need for it is related to our NEED for CERTAINTY. **The key is: where do we as men find our confidence?** ***As a man, how and where you find your confidence will have an enormous impact on the quality of your life.***

It is impossible to write this section to men and not address models. It is the model that a man adopts that creates congruence or incongruence. Models influence how people seek to fill their psychological NEEDS and how a person sees himself in his inner identity.

If you currently lack confidence in yourself, your life will change when you learn to develop it. But that is difficult to do when you don't understand what is going on around you and within you. After all, how can anyone have confidence when nothing makes sense?

It is impossible for people to make sense of their world, or themselves, if the models they are using don't match life as it really is. Trying to find your way through the streets of Chicago with a map of Dallas will get very confusing and frustrating, to say the least.

You, the woman you love, and your children all need you to learn to have confidence in yourself. The confidence level you have in yourself at this moment is a direct result of the models and beliefs you have adopted and made your own.

The meanings we give events will be in agreement with our models and beliefs. Remember meanings create our emotions. Confidence is an emotion. Certain models will make self-confidence an impossibility, while other models pave the way for a person to have self-confidence.

We are going to consider two very different real life scenarios. We are not looking at these examples for the purpose of making judgments, but rather to understand how what we have learned plays out in real life. Your situation may or may not contain similar aspects.

About ten years ago, a friend of mine was telling me about a camping trip he went on. The tale he told me sounded exaggerated, but later everything he told me was confirmed by several other men who had been on the same trip. It will be helpful for you to know that a majority of the men on this trip were college graduates and all were in their mid to late thirties.

Bob's men's class at church had an annual camp-out. "If I had thought of it I would have invited you. You would have loved it," he said. "We fished and canoed all day and that evening we ate dinner and sat around the fire telling stories. At one point somebody said something about how you're not a man if you haven't done this or that.

This conversation had been going on for about twenty minutes when one of the men stood up and started walking to a bucket. He reached into the bucket, pulled out a big crawdad and held it up so everyone could see it. Then, to everyone's surprise, he brought it up to his mouth and bit off its head. He proceeded to spit the head into the fire and then he stated, 'You're not a real man until you can bite the head off a crawdad.'"

I thought Bob was kidding me, but I learned he was not. I asked what the other men did.

"What do you think they did?" He said. "One by one, they got in line and they went to the bucket, reached in, grabbed a crawdad and demonstrated that they were men."

I asked what he did. His reply was. "I'm a man: what do you think I did? I proved it when I got in line and bit the head off a crawdad."

I said to him "You know that biting the head off a crawdad has nothing to do with being a man, don't you?"

"Well yeah," was his reply. "But you can't let someone think you're not a man."

I knew for a fact that many men who knew Bob looked up to him. He was a charismatic Sanguine and he loved being in the center of things.

I asked him, "What if there was someone there who was insecure regarding himself and his manhood?"

"Well, he's a man now. Nothing to worry about, is there?"

I don't know if you have ever had anything like this happen to you when you were out with the boys, but chances are that you have experienced something along those lines. There is a common thread behind events like this.

Every boy looks forward to the time when he is considered a man. But being a man is not as clear-cut today as it was in the past. The reasons for this are many, and too numerous to list individually, but I will address several key factors and how a man can navigate through unknown waters into manhood.

Manhood

Of all the men I know and have talked to, not one of their fathers really took the time to explain what is involved in being a man. If becoming a man were simply committing a one-time act of biting the head off of something, it would be easier. But there is more to it than that.

Each person has ideas of what it takes to be a man, and those ideas are in line with his models. If biting the head off a crawdad sounds absurd to you, it is not in your model of manhood. There is a wide range of models regarding what it takes to be a man.

Your models and beliefs will determine whether something sounds right or not regarding what constitutes being a man. I don't know what you have been taught, and truth be known, most men have caught what they know about manhood from here and there.

If you find yourself feeling that you must continually prove yourself a man, then it is likely that you have adopted models of manhood that are open ended and lack finality. Men rarely consider this consciously, yet it is something that is good for us as men to address.

The problem with any model that pins a man to a wall and says he has to continually prove his manhood is that he has less control in his life. If a man feels he has to prove his manhood, he will find himself easily manipulated into doing things he might otherwise not do, which will result in experiencing an emotional roller coaster. He will not feel as though he is in control, which creates more self-doubt and fuels the need for him to prove to himself that he is indeed a man.

Becoming a man is more than just growing up and being physically able to bite the head off of a crawdad and produce children.

What I am going to offer you are my observations. Boys tend to see the world through the lens of a boy's perspective. There is nothing wrong with this, and it is natural.

In the past as boys were growing up, fathers would teach their sons how to see the world and themselves through the lens that a man looks through. There are major differences between a boy's and a man's understanding of the world and themselves. Unless someone comes along and teaches a boy how to see the world and himself differently, he has no way to learn except through the school of hard knocks.

Unfortunately, as fathers have spent less and less time with their sons, this once common and normal process has all but become extinct. I know many parents who believe that it is the schoolteacher's responsibility to teach their children everything they need to know. That is the approach my parents had. If your father did not know how and what to teach you regarding how to become a man and what is involved, it is probably because he was never taught himself.

In reality, several generations of fathers have not taught their sons about what is involved in becoming men. I remember asking someone "How does a boy become a man?" Their answer was, "You just do it!" Yeah, right, and you fly to Chicago by flapping your arms, too.

Physically, a boy grows into manhood. The other aspects of manhood must be consciously taught or he must learn them on his own, provided he is able to figure them out.

There are some key areas where shifts need to take place from boyhood into manhood. When a boy learns to look at, and understand, the world through the perspective of a man, he is making great progress in taking up his role of being a man. Once he learns to see the world and himself through a man's perspective, his greatest challenge at that point is to let go of strategies he has learned as a boy and learn new strategies that are fitting for a man.

One way to demonstrate this is by comparing what is seen from walking around on the street to what can be seen from the hundredth floor of a skyscraper. Obviously, there are new insights and understandings that are available from this new perspective.

Each of us wants to be looked upon as a man. Granted, different people will seek different ways to earn the label of "he's a man." How a man seeks to earn or prove his manhood will depend on his model and temperament makeup.

A friend of mine called and asked if I would be willing to assist a couple she knew who were having some challenges in their marriage. I agreed to talk with them.

When I first talked on the phone with this man, he told me he had come to the conclusion that he had married the wrong woman. I asked him why he thought that. "Well, we use to get along great. The first year and a half our marriage was great, then things started going downhill. I don't know what happened. First she wasn't happy about this or that and over time it has gotten to the point that I can't please her. All we do is fight, and I'm tired of it. I can't stand it anymore."

The situation this couple found themselves in is very common, as we will discover. When I talked with her, she told me that she wants him to lead, but every time he starts to lead, he never follows through. "He'll start to lead and after a short time he just quits. I don't get it. He gets angry with me, and when he gets angry, I wonder if I have made a mistake. It's during those moments I'm not sure if I want him to be the father of my children."

During a conversation I had with the lady who referred this couple to me, I asked her to tell me if the description I was about to give her fit the couple. The wife encourages him to make decisions and lead, and when he starts to lead everything is fine. At some point he makes a decision. She questions his decision, and he often backs down. On the occasion that he does not back down but holds his ground, she again questions him and what he was doing with more force. At that point he gives in.

I explained that the focus and situations will naturally vary, but in general, this is the basic dance they go through every time there is a problem between them. My friend said to me, "I can't believe it. You sound like you have known this couple as long as I have, and you've only talked to them once on the phone."

Understanding the information that I have included in this book gave a great deal of insight into what was happening in the lives of this couple. They really did, and do, love each other, but there were some challenges before them. Both were great people. Each of them was incongruent and didn't understand what was causing their challenges.

When I asked him how he would describe the women he had been attracted to, he answered, "They have always been stronger than myself." Can you understand how this could be?

I later found out that this man is over six and a half feet tall, built like a tank and he towers over his wife. He is married to a little woman who now bosses him around like he was a doll.

"This drives me crazy," he told me. "I can't take it anymore. She is always attacking me."

Can you see the meanings he is giving the event? Can you see some of what is happening with this couple and what was taking place during the camp-out we considered earlier? Many of the same things are happening in both of these events. The men on the side of the river and this couple are experiencing some of the same challenges, but in different circumstances.

People Commonly Share Their Models

In both cases, models are being presented. The men around the campfire began stating what their beliefs were about what it took for someone to be a man. You may be saying, "Wait a minute. Just because they said something, that doesn't mean they really meant it." That is a possibility. However, in the overall picture, biting the head off the crawdad topped all of the other "you're not a man until" scenarios, and they all got in line.

The key in both cases is that everyone followed the one with the most confidence. The man who bit the head of the crawdad was very confident. So, too, was the woman who wanted her husband to lead. When she questioned him about what he was doing or a decision he had made, she did not waver in her confidence. He had little confidence in himself, and as a result of his lack of confidence, he gave in and let her lead.

Whether the men actually believed "you're not a man until you bite the head off a crawdad" is not important. The revealing thing is that when it came down to the nitty-gritty, they all got in line. Every man who got in line was looking for outside confirmation of his manhood. They lacked the internal support and confidence in themselves to do what they really knew they should or should not have done.

I would hazard a guess that the majority of those men were not saying silently to themselves, "*Oh, I am so excited; I get to do this really manly deed.*" What they were probably thinking was more like, "*I can't believe what I'm about to do!*"

In the case with the husband and wife, she wanted him to lead. She told him, repeatedly, *her preferred model.* One of the challenges he faced was that he didn't understand that ***she was living according to one model, while desiring another.***

It is possible for a person to want a new model while they are stuck in their old one. This wife wanted the model where her husband was the leader, but she was stuck in her old model that caused incongruence to exist in her life. Did she understand that she was actually living life according to one model, while consciously saying she wanted a different model? No. In reality she had no idea of models and their effect on her life.

She was not the only one stuck in her old model. He wanted to lead and to please his wife in that area, but he was stuck in the model that he learned growing up. He wanted to be the leader, but his understanding of manhood was one of following and looking to others for his confidence. Both desired new models, emotions and, in essence a different life. Both were stuck in their old models because they did not understand how the strategies they had learned were keeping them chained to their old ways.

Now let's consider temperaments. The man who told me about the camping trip is primarily Sanguine. The man who first bit off the head of the crawdad was primarily Choleric. The man who was always in trouble with his Choleric wife is a Phlegmatic/Sanguine blend, heavy on the Phlegmatic side. It is helpful to know that there are certain things about these temperaments that tend to lead each of these people to where they are.

Let's start with the man who first went to the bucket to get his crawdad and show the others what he believed made a man. There are several things about the Choleric temperament that make being in this position easier for him.

First, he has an internal frame of reference, and he is an extrovert. Until Cholerics learn to tone down some of their strengths, they don't really care a great deal about what other people think. Cholerics normally aren't concerned if people agree with them or not. "That's the way it is" is their motto.

Second, can you guess what this man's top psychological NEED was? SIGNIFICANCE. All the way. He loves significance, and the more the better. In fact, it is likely that this man's secondary temperament is Sanguine.

The Phlegmatics and Melancholies would not gravitate toward that particular act because they are both introverts and would have had a natural aversion to being up in front of a group of men and taking the first bite. This does not mean they could not, but it is probable that they would rather pass on this one, without thinking twice about it.

Do you think the man who bit the first head off actually believed that it was necessary to bite the head off a crawdad to be a man? Chances are that he did not. It is safe to conclude that somewhere in his model there is the belief that a man must prove himself to be a man.

Thinking about the other men who got in line, do you suppose they actually went home and started proclaiming their manhood and how they became the new and improved man that they are? I don't think they would go up to their wives and say, "Kiss me honey! I'm a real man now!" Or do you think that maybe they questioned themselves even more as a result of getting in line?

There is Always a Reason Behind What a Person Does!

It is a grave error to think less of anyone because of the spot they find themselves in. Whether considering this group of men or this couple, each person found himself in a spot as a result of his models and beliefs. It is true that only one man stood up and reached into the bucket first, but the underlying reasons for the other men's action and lack of action is a result of their models and beliefs.

Looking at the couple in this situation, it would be easy for someone to conclude that they could indeed have some serious problems in their marriage. In reality, they are very much in love with each other. Because of some misunderstandings, they, like many others, were experiencing some challenges that seem very large at the time. It is important to remember that a large part of what this couple was experiencing is a direct result of being incongruent from their core nature.

Without going into a great deal of specifics here, this husband was raised in a family where his father saw his role as being the breadwinner and nothing more. His mother was the dominant one in the relationship for as long as he could remember. We already know that his temperament blend is Phlegmatic/Sanguine, and that he looks to others for validation. Because of his primary and secondary temperaments, he has a very strong external frame of reference. He is also an introvert to a degree, which is offset some because his secondary temperament is extroverted. This combination creates a tendency to go along and have a good time.

His Choleric wife, on the other hand, had a totally different approach to life and people. She was one tough cookie. The attitude of the Choleric is "Suck it up, cupcake, and get it in gear."

Cholerics don't set out to be hard and inconsiderate, but that is what can happen when several of their strengths are overdone. What was once a strength becomes a weakness.

When she told her husband she wanted him to lead, she was telling him the truth. Her husband didn't see it that way. He was convinced the answer was no. If, in reality, she truly did want her husband to lead, then why did she get contrary with him when he tried to lead as she requested? We will cover this in greater depth shortly.

One insight into the situations we are considering is that when people are in their masculine side, they seek significance through accomplishments. There are several common strategies Cholerics will use as a means of meeting their NEED for SIGNIFICANCE, such as standing up to someone or doing something. Both feed SIGNIFICANCE. The man at the camp-out actually did both at one time. When he bit the head off the crawdad and issued his challenge to the group, he filled his psychological NEED for SIGNIFICANCE in a big way through action and confrontation, which is a form of CONNECTION.

When a man is incongruent, he looks for SIGNIFICANCE not through accomplishments but through relationships. Women, when they are in an incongruent state, seek SIGNIFICANCE through accomplishments rather than relationships. That is a key distinction between when a person is on their masculine side or feminine side. What they draw SIGNIFICANCE from is one indicator. It is not the definitive indicator regarding incongruence, but it is one that people can learn to recognize themselves.

This is not to say that it is bad for a woman to do something and derive a sense of SIGNIFICANCE from it. When a person regardless of their gender does a good job they should be proud of what they have done and feel good about themselves. The key difference here is when this is the main or only avenue for them to fulfill their psychological NEED for SIGNIFICANCE.

The same is true for a man. It is natural for him to derive some SIGNIFICANCE from relationships, but if that is his only means of filling his NEED for SIGNIFICANCE, it is an indication that he has shifted into an incongruent state. This is something that does not happen all at once for men or women. Models are the primary cause of incongruence within an individual. As you can imagine, models are not changed quickly unless a person knows what they are doing. Even then it takes time and effort.

We have considered incongruence within a marriage. Now let's consider how it might play out in the situation that took place on the camp-out. When a man is in an incongruent state, he will look outside himself for leadership and encouragement.

His models have trained him to look primarily to women for leadership (which he is comfortable with), but when there are no women around and he is with other men, he will continue to look outside himself for leadership because he has not developed the inner self-reliance needed to lead himself, let alone other men. Often he will feel intimidated by a strong male presence, and he will gladly assume the role of a follower. The incongruent man has not built his own internal support. As a result, he will constantly find himself looking to those around him for leadership and support.

He will also find himself more comfortable and safe around strong women and feel threatened when around strong or forceful men because he doesn't know how to relate to them. Men will often test and challenge other men in ways that stretch their inner resolve. This often comes about in the form of confrontation. The incongruent man has difficulty with this because at the unconscious level he is looking to others for support and affirmation, not confrontation.

We don't have enough information about all the men who were on the camp-out, but there are indications that some of them might very well have been incongruent. I think we can safely say that they lacked the self-confidence to say, "Hey, wait a minute. Yes, you can do that, but does that really make you a man? What makes you a man is on the inside; it's not on the outside. What you do on the outside is a reflection of what you are doing inside yourself."

A man stands up for what he believes in. It is standing up for that belief that is reflective of one aspect of manhood. That being said, it is important that a person be open to continued learning and personal growth.

One of the greatest challenges is for a man to let go of the models he learned as a boy that are holding him back and learn new models that will serve him as a man. A boy's models of the world and a man's models of the world contain different perspectives and understandings. A model that once fit but now is outgrown can become a man's prison.

Where Do You Draw Your Confidence?

One key distinction between a model that creates congruence for a man and a model that creates incongruence is found in where that model directs him to look for his confidence. It is natural for a boy to look to others for confidence when he is little, but the sooner he begins developing confidence in himself, the better.

In these two examples, the man who bit the head off the crawdad and the tall man's wife were both operating from models of the world that directed them to look inside themselves for confidence. Everyone else was operating from models that directed them to look to others for their support.

The man who was telling me about the camp-out was a Sanguine. We know that Sanguines have an external frame of reference. That puts them in a difficult spot when it comes to resisting going along with something they would otherwise not do. It could be that this man, and many of the others; would not have actually committed the act of manhood that they had if it were not for the group around them.

Looking to everyone around you to determine if something is correct or not is called social proof by most psychologists. Without doubt, social proof has always existed. However, I believe that it is being employed much more now as a result of incongruence that exists today more than at any other point in man's history.

If a person's personality temperament has an external frame of reference, that is going to be magnified many times over as a result of his incongruence. He will not only be looking to others for their approval; he will be dependent on them for leadership and his emotional support, which will be in the form of reassurance.

Any person who has an external frame of reference will have a tendency to go along with the crowd. ***This does not mean that he cannot decline the invitation of the group.*** As a man builds his internal support system through learning how to meet his own psychological NEEDS in constructive ways that enhance his life and the lives of others, he becomes better at meeting his own NEEDS. It becomes less challenging to say no thank you to the crowd. *This is an example of how learning to meet your psychological NEEDS in ways you choose results in your being able to remove something that was formerly a weakness and transform it into a strength.*

The man who is incongruent and whose temperament make-up has an internal frame of reference will find himself in a bind. On one hand, he doesn't give a rip about what other people think, but at the same time he is dependent on those same people for their emotional support.

When a person has an internal frame of reference, it means they first look within themselves for what is correct. This becomes a big problem for an incongruent man because he is looking inside himself for what is correct and outside himself for reassurance and emotional support. Often this starts out when a man is a boy. If a boy wants the emotional love and support of his mother, his behavior and actions must be in line with what his mother would approve of. If not, there is no LOVE and no emotional support and the boy finds himself in a tight spot.

It is natural for children to look to others. However if a boy does not learn to look within himself for the inner strength he needs, he will feel it later. As a boy adopts models and beliefs that shift him into an incongruent state, he learns to look to others rather than within himself.

The man who has become incongruent will have an external support system. It is because the support is external rather than internal that he is constantly feeling as though he is lacking. It is important that both men and women develop the internal support system they need.

The Choleric man who has an internal frame of reference and is incongruent is likely to experience a very wide range of emotions that are at times extreme. Over time, this wide range of emotional swings is unconsciously incorporated into his emotional identity, which in turn flavors his self-perception.

Building self-confidence is one of the things that drives boys to conquer everything they see. When they persist and overcome whatever obstacle is before them, they are building their own internal support system and adding confidence to their inner identity. This is key. If a boy is not allowed to conquer things, and concludes that kind of behavior is wrong, it will result in an inner struggle. One part of him will want to conquer things, and another part of him will see that desire as wrong. This affects what he will think and feel about himself.

Models Determine What is Acceptable

When a person adopts models that make normal aspects of life wrong, whether it is conquering things or experiencing certain emotions, they are setting themselves up for trouble down the road. Remember, any time a person believes that a natural part of life is wrong, they have unintentionally put themselves on a downward spiral. If unabated, this process can result in a person feeling nothing but self-contempt. Throughout this process, his inner and emotional identity are being altered as a result of this harmful belief being embraced.

When a male is taught to see conquering as wrong and turns his back on it, he is forced to look to others for his strength and reassurance. This is one way models contribute to a boy becoming incongruent. Remember, models are constructed of beliefs. If a boy learns that he needs to look to others rather than inside himself, he will seek external support and will have no idea of how it will affect him later.

This model, and its beliefs, shifts how he perceives himself in relation to others. He has great difficulty in seeing himself equal to, or capable of, leading others because at the unconscious level he is dependent on others for support.

The more incongruent a man becomes, the more support he needs. This external support is different from an external frame of reference. Keith, who we met in the Gender Dynamics section, was in the position of having both an external frame of reference and the external support of his mother.

A man who has a Phlegmatic personality temperament has his hands full when he is congruent because his external frame of reference, coupled with his drive to avoid confrontation, can become a weakness for him. But if he learns to balance those positive traits with his own solid internal support that bolsters his self-confidence, he has a fabulous combination that will serve him well as long as he maintains balance.

When the need for external support, which is a by-product of incongruence, is added to the Phlegmatic's overdone strengths that have become weaknesses, that man has several large obstacles that he must overcome. The external frame of reference that is normal for the Phlegmatic makes the dependency on external support more difficult to see clearly.

The man who has a personality temperament that has an internal frame of reference will naturally look within himself for support. This man's incongruence will partially short-circuit his internal frame of reference. Inside he knows he should be able to stand and support himself. Yet for some reason he can't. At times he feels he is the rope in a tug-of-war contest. His internal frame of reference will direct him to look within himself, while his incongruence will force him to look outside himself for what he knows he should have within himself.

A man who has a stronger personality temperament and is incongruent will experience wide emotional swings that range from being powerful to that of feeling helpless and being needy. This causes confusion and more self-doubt, which further erodes his self-confidence and self-perception.

The key is a person's models and beliefs: they shape an individual's perceived identity and position him in a different location in regard to how he relates to other people. Which brings this thought: Is it that simple? All a person has to do is change his models and beliefs and he is set?

Unfortunately it is easy to see what needs to be done, but following through is not so simple. This is not to say that it can't be done. It can if a person addresses the following aspects:

Each of us learn how to meet our Psychological NEEDS through our Models and Beliefs

To Change Models and Beliefs is to Remove our Methods and Strategies for Meeting our Psychological NEEDS.

When a person goes out and does something that is outside of his models and beliefs, he is lost regarding how to meet his psychological NEEDS. This puts him in an odd position. He feels he has victory, yet something isn't right. If he doesn't figure out how to meet his psychological NEEDS quickly, he will revert back to his old models, beliefs and actions, which are time-proven for meeting his NEEDS and have been incorporated into his identity.

Beliefs take some time to change since they are incorporated into a person's unconscious mind over time. From the time those beliefs are incorporated into their identity, their unconscious mind's job is to maintain actions that are in accordance with the beliefs that make up their identity. Your unconscious mind does not drop in and have coffee with your conscious mind and discuss what and how it is going to do things. Your unconscious mind simply does what it is designed to do and continues to do so 24 hours a day, seven days a week until you die.

In reality, models that create incongruence are multi-layered in the way they affect a person. They shift a person's self-perception and their approach to life and other people as well. Incongruence becomes ingrained into their unconscious programs and permeates their understanding of themselves, others and the world in which they live.

Incongruence causes a person to adopt strategies for meeting his psychological NEEDS that can have very serious side effects. Those side effects will literally alter the quality of life that person will experience. Incongruence causes people to live more in the negative sections of the Masculine-Feminine Dynamics Rectangle (page 198), which is not desirable.

Having written out your models and beliefs earlier, you have a clearer understanding and picture of what is influencing you. Your models are a major player in where your emotions are placed in the Masculine-Feminine Dynamics Rectangle. Remember, if your umbrella model portrays everything as larger than yourself, the center of that model is located in the negative feminine quadrant. Also remember that a person will naturally be pulled to the center of their model and beliefs.

Models & Beliefs Do Not Cling to People

If you have not already done this, write out your models and beliefs and evaluate them. If you have some challenges writing out your models, you may find it easier to list out your beliefs for different aspects of your life. Each of us has adopted many models. There is usually an underlying theme running through them that reveal your umbrella model.

It is helpful when doing this to remember that *models and beliefs are, in reality, outside an individual.* Imagine a leaf as it breaks free of the tree and falls toward you. You can catch it, watch it fall to the ground or pick it up. You can make it something that is special to you and take it everywhere you go.

In reality, beliefs are just like that. Everywhere we go, people are tossing their beliefs up in the air around us. Some of them we see floating around and we don't pay any attention to them, while others we are attracted to and find desirable. Then, for some odd reason, we feel compelled to take hold of and hold onto them, and we are not sure why.

If you don't understand why you ever picked up some of the beliefs you are holding onto, don't worry: it is okay to let them go. In fact, if you have discovered yourself to be incongruent, you will have to exchange some of those beliefs for ones that will allow you to be the man you have always known you could be.

I understand this can feel like a major step. That's because we incorporate models and beliefs into our inner identity, and it can feel as though they are a part of us. In a way, they are; but **remember, models and beliefs do not hold onto you. You hold onto them.** You can let go and take hold of beliefs that serve you much better if you choose too!

If you begin feeling a bit emotional when doing this, you are not alone. There is an emotional link between a person and his models and beliefs. If you know this ahead of time, when the emotions start showing up they are easier to understand. When we understand emotions, they are easier to deal with.

What you believe makes you a man is your model. This section for men is not to tell you how to be a man. The type of man you are is a direct result of the models and beliefs you currently hold to. What I am going to share with you men in the balance of this section are things that are simplistic in nature, yet can have a profound impact on a man.

Men today face things that were not faced by men one hundred years ago. Since the beginning of the Industrial Revolution life has continually become more complex. Men and women face challenges today that never existed before. I don't know what you are facing, but I do know that you are special. Every person is unique, including you.

If anyone embraces beliefs that make normal aspects of life wrong, those beliefs are going to cause him some internal conflict in the future. The resulting conflicts will show up in the form of conflicting emotions, which are rarely understood. This creates additional confusion that magnifies the already confusing emotional turmoil that is going on within him.

It is critical for each man to develop his own inner support system. Without an internal support system that will keep his self-confidence strong, he will not have the ability to stand strong.

There are many ways in which a man can build his own internal support system. A person's internal support system will be unique to him because each person is different. There are some basic qualities that will determine the strength of their structure.

Each temperament will build a different style of structure; what works for a Phlegmatic would not work for a Choleric. Each temperament blend will have its own unique architecture.

I cannot overemphasize the importance of models in the construction of a person's internal support system. Certain models make it impossible to build one, while other models are a solid foundation for congruency and the building of an internal support system.

Any models and beliefs that encourage someone to look to other people for constant support and guidance, by their nature, create a dependent relationship. This is true whether it is between individuals, a person or a government agency. Anytime there is a dependency that is established and maintained, that relationship weakens any internal support system that person may have already built. Whether the individual has not already started building one or has started it, they will discontinue building it because there is no need to continue.

Some people are trained to take the easiest way possible. Certain temperaments are more prone to this than others, but all can be trained to be dependent on outside sources for things that should come from within themselves.

There are times when a person is dependent on someone else. There is nothing wrong with that if it is only kept for the short term. But, if it becomes a way of life, it is a problem. ***People who***

are dependent on others are easily controlled by those on whom they depend. That is the hard reality of dependence.

When men are dependent on others, over time they lose respect for themselves and embrace a learned helplessness that is incorporated into their inner identity. In reality, they can be capable, but if they see themselves as helpless, they will live their life based on how they perceive themselves through their inner identity.

Remember from the Masculine-Feminine Dynamics Rectangle section that there are emotions that are incompatible. If a person has lost respect for himself - note this person will find himself in the negative feminine quadrant – he will be unable to experience confidence in himself for any length of time, until he re-earns his own self-respect. This works in reverse also. If a person is confident in himself, he will not be able to lose respect for himself quickly. In each of these cases the individual will have certain emotions that he commonly experiences.

Each Person has an Emotional Center of Gravity

The emotions a person experiences on a regular basis has what I call their emotional center of gravity. A person's emotional center of gravity is linked to their models. This is not a contradiction to what I stated earlier that meanings create our emotions. The models and beliefs a person adopts will have a major influence on the meanings that person gives events that come into their life.

To understand how this works, let's look at two different umbrella models again. Consider how the umbrella models (life is to be endured or life is to be enjoyed) will influence the meanings and the life of the person who embraces them. Do you see how umbrella models will have a directing affect on the meanings people give events that come into their life? A person's emotional center of gravity is a by-product of the meanings their models inspire.

Although it is possible to change your emotional center of gravity, it will require time and persistence to do so. Remember, emotions that are found in the negative masculine quadrant are not compatible with the emotions in the positive feminine quadrant. Likewise, emotions found in the positive masculine quadrant are not compatible with emotions that are in the negative feminine quadrant.

One of the problems people experience who want to make changes is that they have adopted models and beliefs that center them in one quadrant and, as a result, their emotional center of gravity is found in that quadrant as well. But, they want to live a life that is only possible if they are centered in a different quadrant.

Simply wanting to make this change is not nearly enough to produce a successful outcome. The individual who wants to make these changes, must make changes in their models, beliefs and the strategies through which they are meeting their psychological NEEDS. If these areas are not addressed and changed, that person (male or female) will find himself falling back into old habits again and again.

People's emotional identity is a compilation of many things. The first contributor is models and beliefs, then the meanings they give events and their strategies for meeting their psychological NEEDS. Once the stage is set, each one of these components reinforce the others, and each makes the others appear all the more correct. Meanwhile, the unconscious mind has many aspects of life set on auto-pilot mode, while it continues to take notes of consciously thought out decisions and actions, all out of sight of the conscious mind.

A person who consciously decides that he is unhappy with the emotions he is experiencing and tries to change them without addressing these issues is going to be fighting a losing battle. No individual will be able to out muscle the unconscious mind and force their emotions to change.

Once a person understands how these different components relate to and reinforce each other, he can then begin making changes that result in the changes he really wants. Until a person understands how to address each individual aspect separately and makes the necessary changes in each area, he is stuck.

If a man tries to reach out and grab self-confidence, and his models have taught him to look to others for his reassurance and confidence, the self-confidence he desires and needs is outside of his reach. When a man is in this situation, his self-perception and inner identity is going to be affected by the models he has adopted.

If you are a man and you are in a position of not having developed an internal support system, don't get down on yourself. Generations ago, throughout the mentoring process, fathers taught their sons how to build one. The father-son mentoring has not been happening for generations, so it is no longer common knowledge.

What makes up an internal support system? Part of a man's internal support system is knowledge of what it is to be a man and some of the challenges that men face. A man cannot develop his own internal support system if he is holding onto models that direct him to look to others instead of himself. He has to develop a belief in himself and his abilities rather than leaning on and looking to others.

Changing models, beliefs and strategies for meeting psychological NEEDS are all required for a person to make lasting change that is easy to maintain. When people change their beliefs but don't change their strategies for how they are meeting their psychological NEEDS, their attempts to build an internal support system will fall apart.

Self-respect is a part of a man's internal support. Until a man earns his own self-respect, he will have great difficulty believing in himself.

The first place to start is to begin earning your own respect. Do the things you know you should do but have not been doing. ***Take responsibility for your life.*** Do not blame anyone or anything. Blame accomplishes nothing. Acknowledge where you are, and begin doing something about it.

A man's internal support system can be compared to scaffolding. There are many sections and certain parts that have to be in certain places. If anything is missing or not hooked up completely, it can be on the shaky side, or even collapse.

Self-confidence is like the "X" braces that hold the scaffolding together. Without enough of it in the right places and fastened completely, the scaffold is unsafe and undependable. When a man is forced to lean on his own internal support and it is shaky, it is not a fun experience. In fact, it can be emotionally terrifying.

When a man is congruent, he builds his own internal support scaffold himself, derived from his experiences of overcoming obstacles and successfully accomplishing what he sets out to do. He learns that persistence is a very valuable tool if he uses it wisely.

As a boy conquers obstacles before him, those victories are added to his collection of accomplishments. The by-product that is so valuable is that he learns to believe in himself, which builds his self-confidence. As his stack of accomplishments gets higher, he is able to reach for things that he would not have been able to reach for if he did not have a solid and steady inner support of self-confidence. Everything a man does is built on, and added to or takes away from, his internal support. As long as it is weak or shaky, he will continually lack self-confidence.

There are certain things that a man must know, or he is at a great disadvantage. What he does not know can, and will, hurt him! Ignorance is not bliss; it is misery.

Remember all models are anchored somewhere within the MFD-R. If a man's models are anchored in the negative feminine quadrant, his models and beliefs will encourage certain meanings that are in harmony with that model while discouraging other meanings that produce desirable emotions.

If a man is incongruent, his models are causing him to look to others for his confidence. As a result of his models, he is at a great disadvantage. He will never be able to believe in himself and have the self-confidence he needs as long as he is looking to others for his support rather than himself.

It is easier for people to make changes in their life when they understand all of the unseen elements that have been working against them in the past. When a man doesn't understand what is happening or why, he has no idea what to do or how to make corrections. This puts him in a bind. Once he understands what is happening, he has the opportunity to make adjustments and live a much happier life.

For a woman to allow herself to become more feminine, she must know in her head and she must *feel* that she is safe. Femininity, by its nature, is vulnerable. Any man who loves a woman and wants to tell her, but is scared to death to share his feelings understands putting yourself in a vulnerable position. It is scary, unless you know you're safe. When you first tell her how you feel, and you don't know how she feels toward you, you are in a vulnerable position. Once you know your heart is safe with her, you can relax. But if later things change and you become unsure, it can get scary again.

Balancing Masculinity and Femininity

The problem men and women face is not knowing how to be congruent with their core natures and still be able to reach out and experience the rest of themselves.

It is possible for a man to be congruent with his core nature and be strong and masculine, yet still be compassionate and tender, without giving up his congruency. The key to this is found in his beliefs and models. ***It is our models and beliefs that hold the key to a balanced congruency.***

Because people have the pendulum complex, we often swing from one extreme to the other. This is true within Masculine/ Feminine Dynamics also. One reason for the swing that takes place is that most models are either masculine or feminine. Remember, models are made up of beliefs, and beliefs tend to be grouped in like manner.

When people find they want to change something they often go to extremes in an effort to make the break. Everything from the old is pushed away and the opposite is embraced. This sometimes works and sometimes it does not. Often the individual finds himself back where he started, even more discouraged than before. Again the reason for this is that the strategies for meeting his psychological NEEDS are based within his old models and beliefs.

When a man is incongruent, his models and beliefs create a dependency on others, which will result in him being pulled into the negative feminine quadrant. The majority of the time when a man is incongruent, it is a result of adapting to the models that have been lived out before him. Unconsciously it is understood that conforming to the model presented is seen as a prerequisite to receiving love. This is true for the out of balance masculine models also, many of which are restrictive in the emotions that a man can feel or show outwardly. As a result, a boy or girl learns that if they want to be loved, they must become a certain way.

When a boy sees his dad following his mother's lead and they get along fine, as far as the boy sees, that is what he learns about how relationships work. On occasion, when his father steps up and makes a decision that his mother disagrees with, there is unpleasantness. Love does not flow between the boy's parents and everyone knows it.

In this scenario, if the father backs down and the mother wins, in short order they are lovable again. If, on the other hand, the father does not back down it is possible that the boy's mother may be upset for a long time. There is an old saying "IF MOMMA ISN'T HAPPY – NOBODY IS HAPPY."

I know that this saying does not apply to all women, but there are some women, and men, who if they don't get their way, they make everyone miserable. In reality, that individual is using a strategy that has worked for them in the past, so they are using it again. As long as a strategy is rewarded, it will continue to reappear in the future.

In the past they have been rewarded by getting their way. Once a person has done that enough times, their unconscious mind creates a program that runs on automatic. That strategy, if rewarded, can fill a person's psychological NEEDS of SIGNIFICANCE, CERTAINTY, VARIETY, and CONNECTION, all at high levels. Remember if something meets three NEEDS at high levels, it can become addictive.

Children are not blind. They learn what a person has to do to be loved, and they will adapt their behavior to receive the LOVE they need. If, after adapting and doing everything they know to do, they are not getting the LOVE they need, they will do things that will result in a CONNECTION being created with the one they desire love from. This is when a person may do just about anything to get the attention of the one whom they long to receive LOVE from.

True, they may not have LOVE expressed to them, but they have CONNECTION and it fills the NEED. If they can't have the LOVE they NEED, CONNECTION works. It's like eating. There are some things you love to eat, but if all you have is something that will keep you alive, you eat it and continue living.

In any and all methods for meeting psychological NEEDS, if three or more of your NEEDS are being met through a strategy, that strategy is addictive. This is true for the person who, for the sake of meeting their psychological NEEDS, has adopted incongruence into his life. This affects men and women in the same way.

Boys and girls learn strategies within their models that meet their NEEDS. You who are reading this have adopted specific strategies that work within your models, it is through the use of these strategies that your NEEDS are being met.

You may have some strategies and models that you would like to change. Be encouraged: you can do it.

In all relationships there is going to be tension and disagreement on occasion. It is important for men to understand that it is not just the subject that is an issue in a disagreement. There is something else that is going on at the same time. Whether you realize it or not, your strength, control, and unconditional love are being tested as well.

What our fathers didn't tell us, probably because they didn't know either, is that ***every time you and the woman you love are having a disagreement, at her unconscious level she is looking for proof of your strength, self control and your unconditional love for her.***

A Natural Testing Process

It is critical for every man to know and understand the natural testing process that takes place between a man and a woman. How well or how poorly you and I do in that test will determine whether she feels safe enough to let more of her femininity out. If a woman is fearful, she will hang on to the strength she has found in her masculine side.

There are two aspects to the testing that men encounter with the women they love. Women need to know that their man is strong. It is not so much a physical strength that they are concerned about, but rather an inner strength.

Women also constantly need the man they love to reassure her of his love. This is a never ending requirement that women possess. Many of us men are bewildered by the woman we love, because we try to understand them through our own thought processes. It doesn't work, so save yourself the effort. Just remember that women, unlike men, need to be reminded of your love for them more often and on a regular basis.

When a woman is unsure, she will test you to get her answer. A woman will not feel safe dropping her masculine side if she is uncertain of your strength. *The stronger your woman, the stronger your test is going to be.*

If you have a strong woman, you will have your hands full. In essence, she is going to see if you will let her conquer you, and if you give in, you lose and she loses too. **It is important that you turn your drive to conquer toward passing the test and not conquering the woman you love.**

Rarely is it a test of how physically strong you are as a man. It is more often a test of how and what you will do with your strength. When you are being tested by the woman you love, *she is not your adversary*! I know, it sure seems like she is against you, but *internally she is cheering for you.* She wants you to pass the test with flying colors.

To show how this works, let's consider what happens in a classroom. The only way for a teacher to know how much the students have learned is to test them. I have not met one teacher who wanted the students to fail or do poorly. When students do well, it reflects favorably on the teacher.

Think about it. Teachers invest themselves in their students, right? They want their students to do well. How much more has the woman you love invested in you? She has nothing to gain and much to lose if you do poorly. She wants you to do well throughout the entire test. There is no cheating on the test; you either have what it takes or you don't.

The problem we men have is that our fathers have not explained this testing process to us. On the surface it all points to we are being attacked. Since we don't know it is a test and how the test works, we put on our figurative boxing gloves. We go in to win and conquer the person we see as our opponent, not realizing that is exactly how we fail the test!

Ignoring her is another way to fail the test miserably. Don't ignore her. Women have the ability to see things we as men are blind to. Remember, she is on your side. If you keep repeating this to yourself and look for how you can benefit from what she is saying, you will do better.

Each of us men has a drive to conquer, but going into our external conquering mode is not the right approach when we are being tested by the woman we love. When a man is being tested, if he gives it the meaning that he is being attacked, his natural inclination will be to go into defend and conquer mode. This will make the woman he loves his adversary and the one to be conquered.

If, on the other hand, a man gives what is happening the meaning of being tested, he can divert some of his conquering drive toward passing the test instead of conquering her. This may sound like an insignificant shift, but it really makes a great difference.

Once a big man asked me, "What do I do when she starts calling me names?" Each couple has certain dance steps they go through during their arguments. The circumstances vary, but the dance steps remain, for the most part, the same. When you find you and the woman you love making the same old moves, the key is to break the routine.

When the woman you love pulls off her boxing gloves and picks up the bat, what she is really saying is "I am so glad you have passed that level of the test. Please keep up the good work, because the test is going to the next level."

When she steps up the level of intensity, you could always reach out, take her in your arms, and gently pull her close. Look her straight in her eyes and softly tell her how much you love her, no matter what, and that will never change. From there it is up to the two of you.

Now, you may be saying "Wait a minute, she starts with name calling..." Okay, that is great, it is simply that your test started out at a different level. It's the same principle. She desperately needs you to be her stable and dependable strong man. It's a fact of life that a person cannot truly respect someone for long if the respect hasn't been earned. Here is your chance to earn it. Be excited about it! It's all in the meaning you give it.

If you can keep your calm and hold your own, you will do well. The key is to control the meanings you are giving the event. If you keep telling yourself that she is cheering for you, and that this is simply a test, it will help create emotions that are easy to deal with. You don't want to give meanings that are going to create lightening bolt emotions that no one can control.

The key is to let her know, beyond any shadow of a doubt, that you love her unconditionally.

That is what she needs to know; that even when she has pushed you to the max, you still unconditionally love her. I know it is a tough test. It is a test for a man, and you are a man: her man.

Yes, I understand, when things are happening, the autopilot kicks in and before you know it, you say or do something you should not. As soon as you realize what is happening, you have the opportunity to do what you know you should do, and in doing it, you will be shining.

Any man who, because of models, incongruence or temperament, finds himself in the position of looking to others for approval and support is going to have a more challenging time with these tests that come his way.

An example of this would be a man who has a primary Phlegmatic personality temperament and has adopted models which have taught him to look to a woman for leadership and guidance. Add to that the Phlegmatic's natural desire to avoid confrontation at all costs. This man's longing to avoid confrontation is a strength that has now become a weakness. If he does not overcome it and learn to deal with confrontation, it will hurt him in his relationship with his wife. (I am not promoting disharmony within any relationship, but it helps to understand what is happening, when you are in the midst of it.)

The Phlegmatic man who is congruent with his masculine core will have his work cut out for him during one of these tests, because his temperament is naturally going to want to go along and avoid confrontation. Once he understands what is happening and has been through it and passed the test, he will find it worth the effort.

A woman cannot let down her guard and be her feminine self until she knows that no matter what, her man cares for her enough to love her unconditionally and that he is strong enough to control himself and protect her.

To get an idea of what this is like for a woman, we must put ourselves in her position. Each of us men has things that if we were to honestly tell someone else about them, there would be the question in the back of our minds, what will they think of me and will they still love me? At the unconscious level this testing process answers that and many other questions for the woman you love.

This was exactly where the tall man I told you about found himself. His wife wanted to shed the masculine side she had been wearing. She wanted to have children and needed to know that he was strong enough so she wouldn't have to worry about anything. He didn't understand what was happening. Once he began to understand he did much better.

You may be saying, how does standing up to whatever she throws at you protect her? That is a great question, and it brings us to our next point.

There is a part of us men that longs to be accepted and loved by our wife, and we may find ourselves agreeing to things that we know are not in our best interest to gain her acceptance and love. This is a man's Achilles' heel. I am not talking about sex.

There are a lot of things that men, in general, think a woman looks good wearing. But I have news for you: whatever she has on or off, if she is not wearing a smile, something is wrong.

The most beautiful thing a man can see on the woman he loves is her smile. A man has a built-in desire to make her happy.

The dilemma that a man faces with his wife is similar to what a couple faces with their children. Naturally, the relationship between a man and woman is different than between parents and their children, although some of the challenges are almost identical. Let's consider what parents face.

A couple has a child and during the first year that child can do nothing for himself. Everything must be provided and done for him in order for him to survive. The parents want to take great care of their son or daughter whom they love. If their child cries, it sets off an alarm in the parents, who hurry to find out what is wrong. Often there is a need that has to be taken care of. At some point the child learns that if he cries his parents will respond in some way. Given enough time, the child learns how each parent will respond to different situations.

At some point, the child tries to stretch their will and test their parents. Depending on the parents, this will be a real challenge or a minor thing.

During the entire time when the child was literally helpless and the parents needed to do everything for the child, a habit was being established. When the child cried the parents jumped and did what was needed to stop the crying. This is entrenched into the parents without them being aware of it.

If this issue is not recognized, and adjustments are not made as needed, this habit will continue to be an automatic response on the part of the parents. It is important to note that this is based on the parents wanting to be good parents to the child whom they love. At some point the parent may become aware of what is going on and make adjustments. It is during this time of adjustment that the tests of strength are taking place.

If parents notice they are fearful that their child will not love them, they need to consider why. There are many possible reasons for this fear, several reasons are: (1) the models they have adopted; (2) if their personality temperament blend leans heavily on the relationship side; (3) if the parent(s) are meeting their psychological NEEDS for LOVE & CERTAINTY through the children. It is possible for one or more of these to play a part in creating a fear of losing the child's love.

If the parent's personality temperament is more relationship oriented and/or they are meeting their psychological NEED for LOVE and/or SIGNIFICANCE only through their children, that parent is going to have a difficult time dealing with their children.

A parent who finds himself in this position is dependent on their child for validation and feelings of self-worth and value. In contrast, the parent who is not fearful that their child will not love them is freer to do what is necessary to help the child learn and grow.

In doing what is necessary, it may mean that the child is unhappy and upset with the parent at times. Those times are not enjoyable for any parent, but the parent who looks to their children for their feelings of validation are going to experience discomfort when being firm with their children. So much so, that it is common for many parents in this position to ignore things that need to be dealt with because it hurts them emotionally when they address them.

If you doubt what I am saying, look around you in the stores and watch families and their interaction. It is not uncommon for a child to start crying to get something that they want. It may not be something that will make their lives any better, yet for some reason they want it. They act as if their life will end if they don't get it. They try option #1. When that doesn't work, they go to option #2 they continue to progress down the line until screaming, if necessary, to obtain their desired outcome. I have seen so many parents give in and give the child what they want.

It is important to note that some give in only because of other people being around. This is evident by the expression of pain on their faces as they give in to their child.

Then there are the parents who give in without much of a fight. Their child knows exactly how many times they must ask or how loud they must get in order for the parents to give in. These parents who don't fight much, or at all, are the ones who are more relationship based: the other person's acceptance and validation are important for them to feel good about themselves.

Another point to consider is that parents, and others, get a great deal of enjoyment watching children having fun. To see a child happy and having a great time is a wonderful enjoyment for a parent, relative or someone else who is close to the child. This became strikingly clear to me when a friend of mine recounted what happened to him when he was on a trip to visit some relatives.

Tom was lying in bed since he had been up late driving to their destination. As usual, the children woke up early and had come into their parents' bedroom. His wife told their oldest son to do something, and to their surprise, his son told his mother, "No." Not just once but twice. This was a challenge that Tom was not going to ignore.

"I looked at my son and told him that he had made a very big error. As a result he would not be able to swim or jump on the trampoline with his cousins for the entire day. He could sit on the side of the pool and visit, and could be near the trampoline but could not get on it."

At this, his son burst into tears and began trying to get the decision reversed. Later that day Tom's brother-in-law reprimanded him and stated that he was wrong in grounding his son and that Tom should have employed a different punishment. Tom tried to explain that nothing had been working and that he saw no point in using an ineffective punishment.

Being grounded had gotten his son's attention and had communicated that his father was not going to yield. Tom wasn't thrilled about telling his son he couldn't swim or jump on the trampoline, but at the same time, he was glad that his son understood he was serious. All day his son had a great time laughing and playing with his cousins from the side of the pool and trampoline.

Tom was confused by how people responded to the consequences that his son had incurred as a result of his actions. When the child was not allowed to play and have the fun that the adults expected, and found quite enjoyable themselves, the adults responded to the punishment as if Tom had injured them personally. Tom had inadvertently cheated the adults of their enjoyment of watching the children have fun.

It is important to realize that what is going on here is simply a test of will, a test of inner strength. When a child knows what is acceptable and what they can and cannot do, they are much more content than one who gets everything they want.

There are many similarities and differences between a parent-child relationship and the relationship between a husband and wife. The enjoyment that we derive from a happy wife can be very satisfying. It is not uncommon for many of a person's psychological NEEDS to be filled from within the husband-wife relationship.

A person's unconscious mind's primary concern is meeting psychological needs. It does not take into consideration whether or not certain actions are in the person's best interest long term. This is true for both men and women. If either a man or woman finds they are feeling compelled from within to agree to something that, from their perspective, is not the best, they need to realize that the unconscious element of meeting their psychological NEEDS may be coming into play.

A relationship has many different stages and transitions that take place over time. When two people first meet and fall in love they are enthralled with each other and do everything to please the other, just like parents who have a newborn. As the relationship ages, there are some testings that come along, usually in the form of miscommunication. These can be challenging and sometimes painful. Should the relationship survive these misunderstandings, the next level of testing in a relationship is that of who is going to be dominant.

It is important to note that prior to marriage the dominance that is exhibited is usually less than is experienced in a marriage. Prior to marriage, if one of them comes on too strong it can easily drive the other away. Regardless of how considerate each of them is toward the other, someone has to be the leader or dominant person in the relationship. The dominance that I am referring to is not a thumb on the other person's head, but rather someone who is the clear leader.

At some point in every marriage the honeymoon is over. Reality sets in and they realize that they are married. I'm sure you've seen it: they are all in love and then it's as though someone turned a switch and it isn't that way any more. The honeymoon ends for one of two reasons. Either they are experiencing challenges in their communication or they are going through the testing process to see who is going to be the dominant one in the relationship. Each of these is inevitable and at some point these challenging aspects of life and marriage will be worked out in some form or fashion.

I remember a couple, Sam and Donna, who were engaged and so in love. Even though their wedding date was still four or five months away, they had picked out and purchased some furniture together. One day Sam had given Donna some money to make a payment on their furniture, which she agreed to do. A week later he asked her about their balance on the furniture, and when she told him the balance he was sure it had to be wrong. They had made more payments than what the balance showed.

When he called the store, he found out that Donna did not make the last payment. Sam was sure that she must have forgotten and asked her about it.

"Oh that," she said, "I spent it on something else I wanted." Their honeymoon ended right at that moment. They began working through the process of who was going to lead in their family. It took a while, but they are now happily married with several children.

In all relationships there are the challenges of communication and the testing to determine who is going to lead and then the occasional retesting to assure the other spouse of the strength of the leader.

Men, no woman wants a pushover. Even a woman who has a strong personality temperament does not really want a man she can shove around. Yes she, like most women, wants a man who is understanding. Yet if he can't stand up to her, how can he stand up to the world?

At the unconscious level a woman knows that if her man can stand up to her, he's strong enough to stand up for her. Most women will not allow themselves to let go of their masculine side if they do not feel totally safe and certain that her man can, and will, protect her. When a woman allows herself to go into her feminine self, she is vulnerable. It is as if she takes her armor off and is unprotected.

Often women are fearful of being feminine because it means vulnerability. When a woman who is feminine learns how to access her masculine side without sacrificing her femininity, the feelings of vulnerability will diminish greatly.

It is amazing when a woman is congruent with her feminine core and allows her feminine side to shine. She can walk into a room and every man will notice her. One man described it to me in this way. "When I'm around a woman who is feminine, there is a drawing effect that I feel toward her. I'm not talking about just a physical thing; there is something about a woman who allows herself to be feminine that is irresistible. With a lot of women, it's as though you have to compete with them: that's like going out with the guys."

While being feminine is certainly a way to get a man's attention, typically a woman will not do this unless the man she loves does what it takes to make her feel safe and secure. When a woman feels safe enough to be feminine, she often discovers contentment and happiness as well.

Protecting and providing for a wife and family is in line with what most men understand is a major part of being a man. We as men love to see the woman we love smiling and happy. If for some reason she is not happy, there are times when we lose some of our own enjoyment. **In an effort to show sensitivity and love, a man will sometimes give part or all of his leadership role to his wife with the thought that it will make her happy.** For a majority of men this could be one of the worst things he can do for the woman he loves.

Very few women want a man who has to be led around and who can't or won't make decisions for himself. Every couple goes through a time of working through who is going to lead in their relationship. Many of the decisions that are made in a relationship are made by consensus, but occasionally there is no clear consensus and not enough information to make a decision that you know is correct. When a man makes a decision and it turns out to be an error, the best thing he can do is to own it. That means standing up and taking responsibility for the decision he made and not blaming others.

Man to Man

In the Bible it talks about "as iron sharpens iron, so one man sharpens another." There is great truth in that statement. There are several ways a man sharpens another man.

A man can come alongside another man and challenge and push him in ways that inspire him. Even an enemy can inspire a man to grow. Men will compete with other men and give it their all. This is good for men. Men encourage men to conquer things that are before them.

Men typically will not want to compete with a woman. From a man's perspective there is something that is not right about competing with a woman. I know there are some women reading this who have an issue with that. I don't say it to create an issue, but it's the truth. It's not good for men to begin viewing women as their opponent.

If a man continually sees women as his opponent, whom he must beat and have victory over, in time this could be adopted into an unconscious automatic program. If that were to happen, the man would see every woman as his opponent and would go into competition with her without consciously deciding to do so.

I dated a gal once who wanted to compete in everything. She had learned that she could fill her NEED for SIGNIFICANCE at very high levels by competing with men. She was also raised as a tomboy. Needless to say, we had one date. There was no attraction for either of us.

For a woman to compete with and beat a man is significant, but for a man to beat a woman is a hollow victory. Men, you understand what I'm talking about, don't you? I know some women might have an issue with that, but for us men it's true.

When a man competes against another man, both men grow. In a contest where both have given their all, both men, even the loser, can feel good about themselves. On the other hand, if a man loses to a woman, the woman is usually excited about it, while the man is deflated, especially if he gave it his all. I have never seen a man feel good about himself in a situation like this.

Just as a man can help another man grow in ways that a woman cannot, so too a woman can help a man grow in ways that no man can help another man grow. As much as it may pain some of us men to admit it, our wives can see things in us that another man will miss.

There is a misconception out there that SIGNIFICANCE comes as a result of winning against someone else. As with all events, it is the meanings you give it. Beating others in something does not make a person a leader. A great leader understands that just because you can do something, doesn't mean you should do it.

Leading is not about being better than someone else and making it obvious. A great leader leads in such away as to inspire and grow other leaders.

Leadership is not about pushing people or forcing people to do what the leader thinks should be done. People follow a leader, hopefully for the sake of becoming a leader rather than being dependent on him.

Unfortunately, there are many leaders who get all their SIGNIFICANCE from having others follow them. They create and encourage a state of dependency between themselves and those whom they lead.

This assures the leader of a continued position of leadership, which meets his NEED for SIGNIFICANCE, CERTAINTY and CONNECTION. I'm not sure how much love can exist in a dependent type of relationship, but there is definitely CONNECTION.

A great leader works to train others to lead, independent of himself. A great leader is secure enough in himself that he feels no threat from training others to lead as well as he does.

There are several approaches to leadership. The first is "to lead others in such a way as to create dependency" which is a win/lose situation. The second is to lead in such a way as to create and grow other leaders. This is a win/win situation for all involved. In reality, the second is more in line with mentoring, which can be done on many different levels of personal involvement.

If a man has only learned to fill his psychological NEED for SIGNIFICANCE through his leadership position, he will, at the unconscious level, resist training someone else to become a leader of his caliber. The man who is secure in himself and has learned to meet his psychological NEEDS in many ways is not fearful of producing other leaders.

When you are first married, things change. Many of you who have been married for some time know what I am talking about. Let me explain. Since she has married you, you have won her love. The next step, once you are married, is to earn her respect. Let's face it; we are far from perfect. We make mistakes and do some pretty stupid things once in a while.

How do you and I, as men, earn the respect of our wives and families? I have known many men who have had double standards. My father use to tell me, "Do as I say, not as I do." He meant it too. It was good advice. But many people are not as open about it.

Is it right to hold on to two standards? The answer is, yes! But only if you are holding yourself to a higher standard than you ask of anyone else.

My father held us to a standard that he did not hold himself to. That doesn't work. Any man who wants to lead must first start by leading himself and holding himself to a high standard. Earn your own respect. It is well worth it. I'm not talking about being all puffed up and egotistical, but rather doing what is right and treating others with respect and dignity. Don't treat others rudely and don't let them treat you rudely either.

This could easily take up several books, but let's start with leading by example. Hold yourself to the same, or higher, standard you ask everyone else to honor and keep. Don't be legalistic. Life is full of surprises. Learn when to cut someone some slack and when to be firm. This is true for others as well as yourself.

Men often find themselves caught between a rock and a hard place. Some women want a man who is strong and capable while others want a man who is in touch with his feminine side. What does this all mean and what can we as men learn from what women are saying? In order to boil it down to the point that we men can understand it, we have to consider what women want and need.

Wants and Needs

The key for men to understand is that women, in general, want certain things, and what they need from us may vary depending on the situation they are in. There are times when a woman will say that she wants a man who will be understanding, and other times when she needs a man who will go out and conquer.

When the woman you love is testing you, she needs you to be that strong and confident man who has things (including yourself) under control. In certain situations the woman will be looking to you for her CERTAINTY. No matter what situation the two of you are in, there is always one thing that will never change, and that is her need to know you love her unconditionally. Many women want their man to share his inner feelings with her, as long as it is not when she needs him to be strong for her.

In her book *For Women Only*, Shaunti Feldhahn has a section titled "The Performance of a Lifetime: Why Your Mr. Smooth Looks Impressive, But Feels Like an Impostor." In this section, Feldhahn addresses a type of situation that I believe everyone finds themselves in at some point in their lives. It is where people are not sure of what they are doing, but are proceeding anyway. Feldhahn addresses different examples that men have found themselves in.

One example is of a Star Trek commander who had to give an order but he didn't know for sure which way to go. He made a decision and gave the order. In this instance, there was a lady who could read his mind and she promptly confronted him about the fact that he really didn't know which way to go, and was guessing. Then she asked him if he did that all the time. The commander explained that there are times when it is important that the commanding officer give the appearance of confidence.

I have never met a single person who has had all the right answers. I know I don't. I also know that I have found myself, like millions of others, with people depending on me, and I wasn't sure what to do or how to go about something. I proceeded, not because I wanted to, but because I saw it as my responsibility to follow through even if I was uncomfortable with my personal uncertainty about how to do something perfectly.

With every man I have talked with, there has always been a concern about failing those he loves. I don't know whether women see it clearly, but there is a great amount of weight that many men carry when it comes to doing right by their family.

One man told me, "I hate getting shot at from all sides, especially from my wife." Occasionally when this man made a decision, his wife would ask him some questions about what he had decided. Whenever his wife asked him about a decision he had made, he gave it the meaning that she was attacking him. I explained that I could see what he was saying, but that I had a question for him. "When you are unsure of something, do you ask questions?"

"Yes," he said.

"What if your wife is asking questions, not from the perspective that you have made a wrong decision, but rather from the perspective of curiosity?"

"Well, if that was the case, I've acted like an idiot on more than one occasion," he told me.

As a leader, as a man, you will be questioned. The meanings you and I give those questions will determine how well or how poorly we do from that point on.

Remember, leaders--men--are continually tested. This is bad if you don't understand the process, but if you do understand, you have a great advantage.

Acknowledging to the woman you love that you know you don't have everything together is not bad. If she has known you for some time, you're not telling her anything she doesn't already know. If you explain it to her in such a way that you convey doubt in yourself, her red flags will go up. If, on the other hand, you acknowledge your situation and at the same time have confidence in yourself, she will sense it and she will not be alarmed.

Just because you are not sure of everything is no reason to doubt yourself. This may sound odd, if not impossible, to someone who has CERTAINTY in the number one spot in their NEEDS hierarchy. ***There is a major difference between not knowing everything you would like and questioning your abilities.*** The first can compel you forward while the latter will ruin you from within.

One of the greatest ways to earn the respect of the woman you love is to pass the tests that she presents to you. The army has a slogan "Be all that you can be" but ***it takes effort to be all you can be.*** It requires you to make that decision every day and sometimes many times during your day. To do this it takes focus and consistent effort. Don't allow yourself to be overwhelmed. If you are, it is because you have a belief or secondary gains (possibly both) that are at the root of these feelings.

Life's Unexpected Surprises

Life sometimes throws unexpected surprises at people that literally change their lives in a moment. There are events in life that can shake a person so much that they are unsure of themselves and the world. As a result of shifts in their beliefs and the meanings they give events, their inner identity becomes shaky and they slip into incongruence. The types of events that trigger this kind of massive shift are ones that alter how they see themselves and the world in which they live.

Here are several examples.

1) A man suddenly loses his job and cannot find another. A major factor in how well or poorly he will do is going to be determined by how many of his psychological NEEDS were being met through his job. If it is the majority of them, he will have a much more difficult time looking for how he can benefit from his situation.

While a person is suffering from psychological NEEDS withdrawal, it can be a struggle to see something as a stepping stone rather than a stumbling block. If, as a result of the massive unexpected change that he experiences, he begins to question his models, it is only a short step until he is questioning himself and his abilities, too.

2) A person is physically hurt in an accident, or they have a serious illness, or a person is attacked and taken

advantage of. Each of these events, and others like them, has the ability to shake a person's life deeply. When a person is physically hurting it is harder to give what they are experiencing a good meaning. The key, when a person is experiencing discomfort, is to look to the future when the pain will be gone.

3) When a person embraces the thought that his pain will never go away or that he will never get another job, that becomes his focus, and it will be the only thing he notices. When a person's beliefs shift in this manner, his inner identity shifts and so do his methods for meeting his psychological NEEDS.

4) When a person goes through a very emotional time. It is during emotionally difficult times that a person is even more susceptible to embracing beliefs about themselves and others as reality, without objectively weighing their conclusions.

5) When any major event takes place that eliminates how an individual is meeting their psychological NEEDS. Unless they plan out how they will meet their NEEDS through new avenues, they will typically bounce around until they discover something that meets their psychological NEEDS. Once they find something, they will notice themselves gravitating toward it while not always understanding why. Remember, one of the unconscious mind's primary roles is to make sure that a person's psychological NEEDS are somehow met. Whatever meets their psychological NEEDS will be latched onto and kept.

Depending on their temperament makeup, their NEEDS hierarchy and their models, they will or will not do certain things. However, if their inner identity has been shifted enough, they may respond in ways that are totally foreign to them prior to that point in time in their life.

It is said that people change. In reality, they don't change. It is how they seek to meet their psychological NEEDS and the meanings they give events that change. Their models and beliefs change, which results in their actions changing as well. There are many other situations that can come into a person's life that can result in incongruence. One key to resisting incongruence is what the individual does with his mind.

The extent that an individual's life is altered by an event is directly related to the meanings he gives that event. Those meanings will be influenced by his beliefs and models. When an event happens that totally alters a person's world he must search out meanings for things he doesn't understand. Events that are not understood are typically given negative meanings, which reflect back on the individual and have the potential to alter his beliefs about himself.

What distinguishes a life-altering event from other events? There are two distinct characteristics that increase the seriousness of an event. First is when an event shatters a person's models and beliefs to the point that he is not sure what to believe. When this happens it is not just a person's models and beliefs about the world in which they live that are shaken: their identity is shaken as well. Remember, models and beliefs reflect back on the person who embraces them.

The second thing is when an event eliminates the avenues through which that person has become dependent for the meeting of their psychological NEEDS. If an event contains either one of these two aspects it can be devastating to the individual if they don't know how to deal with it. In extreme cases, events that contain both of these two factors have resulted in once successful people finding themselves in the gutter.

Events containing one or two of these characteristics can have devastating effects. It is possible for people to become emotional basket cases, to the point of helplessness or even outright hostility.

When a man wraps his life around his job, his models, beliefs, identity and how he meets his psychological NEEDS are all tied to his job. If he looses his job suddenly, it is not just his job and his means of supporting himself he has lost. His identity is in jeopardy and the avenue he had become dependent on to meet his psychological NEEDS is no longer there. Unless a man in this position understands what is happening behind the scenes, there is the potential that he could face some major emotional challenges.

Remember, models and beliefs reflect back on the individual who holds them. The resulting reflection causes him to embrace new beliefs about himself and his capabilities that he would not have considered earlier in life. This change can be positive or negative in nature, but regardless of which direction it is, the shifting of their models and beliefs will affect inner identity.

When someone is faced with a negative situation, the person who chooses to believe his situation is only temporary will do much better than the person who believes it is permanent.

Imagine an event as a thing, and a person's mind as a room. An event happens, and the person takes it into his room (his mind) and does whatever he wants to with it in that room. Some may color it with dark colors, some may paint bright colors on it, while still others may begin taking it apart and begin building something new out of it.

This latter option is possible only when an individual's model and beliefs place him in a powerful position rather than a weak one. In this dismantling, he sifts through the pieces and separates the good from the bad. Once this is done he discards any aspect that is of no value to him and begins building a stepping stone out of the experience.

Everything that comes into our lives is seen and understood a little (or a lot) differently from one person to the next. It is against our nature to not give events meaning. The differences are brought about as a result of different models, beliefs, temperaments and strategies for meeting psychological NEEDS.

Until a person has *learned* to give meanings to events that give him mastery over them, the natural tendency is for him to give meanings that allow the event to master him. Each of us has the ability to give meanings to events that will alter our perspective. This perspective will be in line with the beliefs we have embraced. The choice we make will position us in either a powerful or vulnerable position. This process is not restricted to a culture, certain ages or sex.

This book contains insights that will allow you to make changes you only dreamed of in the past, if you want to badly enough. You have to want it. You have to be tired enough of the past to break away from it. You now have the knowledge. It is up to you to apply your new found knowledge and change your life in the process.

It is not just your life you have the opportunity to change. You will touch the lives of everyone you come into contact with, especially your family. Your sons and your daughters have a chance to learn at a young age what you are learning later in life. Will you help them make better lives for themselves and their children?

WOMEN

Although the world that men and women live in is different than it was one hundred years ago, men and women are, for the most part, the same. Both men and women have the same physical and psychological NEEDS as before. What has changed are the models and beliefs that they now embrace. Incongruence has created much confusion and frustration within individuals and couples.

The slogan "You've Come a Long Way, Baby" is true. Women have made major advances in jobs, positions, and status compared to one hundred years ago. Advances in medicine, especially the birth control pill, have eliminated many limits women previously faced. Technology has made it possible for women to do nearly everything a man can do. She can drive a truck, fly a fighter, go into outer space and bring home the bacon. Wow!

Of all the technological advances that have come about, none have changed the power equation between men and women as much as electricity. With a push of a button a woman can lift 40,000 pounds of steel with a crane or launch a missile that has the capacity to destroy a great number of people. If she is cold, she can simply turn up the thermostat; she doesn't need a man to bring in the firewood, or to get the horse and buggy ready to go get the pizza: she can simply order it in.

Without question, technology has made our lives easier. I don't know many people who would turn their backs on the many benefits we have today as a result of it. But, what promised to be a way to make our lives more enjoyable and carefree has only partially been fulfilled.

Life is easier in many ways, yet at the same time, it seems to be so much more complicated and confusing. I'm not referring to challenges that exist with learning how to use new technological devices. But how technology has changed how men and women relate to each other because it has shifted the power equation between them. This has also altered the perceptions through which men and women look at and evaluate themselves and each other.

What Affects One Sex, Affects Both Sexes!

This can be ignored, but there is no escaping it. Since models and roles have shifted, women have more ways to earn significance. Men watched as the ways they had earned significance disappeared before their eyes. While all of these changes have been taking place, men and women have not made the conscious connection between technological advances and how the resulting power shifts altered how they relate to each other.

The traditional roles that men and women had for thousands of years complemented each other. What one could not provide, the other could.

One of the by-products of the technological advances is the competition and contention that have been introduced into the lives of men and women in areas that never contained these aspects of life before. This new competition between sexes has altered how men and women see and respond to each other at many different levels.

Some women reading this are either married or single career women, or stay at home moms. The reasons for choosing a particular path are many, varied and personal. Each woman could look at the others and wonder what in the world possessed them to pursue their path. It is the models a person embraces that shape their perspectives and influence their choices.

While there are women who seek out a career, there are also those who are forced into careers for a variety of different reasons. Some husbands have abandoned them and their families. I know several families where something has happened to the husband, and he is now disabled. Without doubt, many women have found that life has dealt them a difficult situation. When that happens, their world changes and they have no choice but to adapt. Often this means facing and dealing with things they would not have to do if their husband was able to. It is hard on many levels. The single woman who has not found the right man or simply does not want to marry is in the same position as many of these married women.

These types of situations force women to become more masculine in their approach to life. Rarely do men or women choose to be incongruent. Situations in life push them into it. Everyone does the best they can with what they have at their disposal. Sometimes congruence is enhanced but other times incongruence results. It is never a question of the person's worth or abilities; the root is always found in the situations they are in and the models and beliefs that are adopted.

Without doubt, women live in a different world and see things differently than do men. Men and women approach things from totally different perspectives to such an extent that it could be construed that men are indeed from Mars and women from Venus.

Although men and women have the same hormones in their bodies, the different levels that exist between men and women is huge, causing very different effects. Add to that the fact that while in the womb, a boy's brain undergoes a process that severs many of the connections between the right and left hemispheres. Conversely, girls do not experience this process to the same extent that boys do, which is why women have so many more connections between the two halves of their brain.

It could be declared that men have experienced brain damage and are broken as a result. Being a man, I prefer to think of it as one of the many contributing factors that make men and women uniquely different. The point is that men and woman are different in more ways than just their sex organs.

A great number of people find the differences between men and women frustrating. A man by the name of Jim Rohn had a unique thought. He encourages people to learn the art of turning frustration into fascination. We have examined how the meanings we give events literally changes the emotions we experience in our lives.

When a person chooses to get curious about something, their perspective changes, and they are able to see things they would have otherwise missed. This perceptual shift opens the door to new insights that would never be seen if the individual were to get frustrated over their challenge. Indeed, what was once frustrating can be truly fascinating. When a man or woman chooses to see the differences that exist between men and women as fascinating, it is really amazing what can happen.

My desire in this section is to give some insight into what might help you in your relationship with the man you love. I am not one who believes that the whole world revolves around men. There is a saying that when a couple gets together if each of them gives 50% then together they have 100%. In reality, each one needs to give 100% if their relationship is going to do well. If they each give only 50% they are falling way short of what they need to have a wonderful relationship and life together.

Ladies, I probably don't need to tell you this, but we men are goofy. As a result of doing things that we think impress a woman, we discover that we are picking ourselves off the floor or pulling our feet out of our mouths to our own embarrassment. I wouldn't be surprised if the conversation between women went like this as they watch a guy try to impress them.

"Do you know why that guy is doing that?"

"No. In fact, I'm not even sure what he's doing. It doesn't make any sense to me."

"I don't know either. Do you think he's sick or something?"

"I don't know, but whatever you do, don't let him get too close. With the way he's acting, he could be an alien from Mars."

There are, in fact, times when we men seem to make no sense! Now, if you are wondering why, I can explain some of what males do, but not all. We don't have enough room. Males of all ages are hardwired in such a way that they are always seeking to get the attention of females. At first, this is aimed at any and all females. In time, it is usually refined to seeking the attention of one particular woman.

The challenge for men is that somewhere along the line they came to the conclusion that what impresses other males also impresses females. "If we're impressed with it, the girls will be impressed with it." This is false logic at its best. After all, it looks and sounds logical, right?

I remember doing things as a boy that I was sure the girls would be impressed with, but I could not for the life of me figure out what went wrong. For some reason it just didn't work well. So what do most males do in that situation? They do the same thing with more intensity and think, "Those girls will love this! It's going to be way better this time!"

As an adult, I now understand that the definition of insanity is doing the same thing over and over again and expecting different results. As a young boy and young man, I didn't get that.

My teenage daughters tell me about some of the silly things guys do and they can't figure the guys out. One day they told me about what some boy had done and how it didn't make sense. I explained why he did what he did and both my girls said, "You've got to be kidding me! Is that why guys do stuff like that? They're all mixed up!"

This doesn't just happen when males are young. It continues for most of their lives unless they decipher the code so they understand women and what is important to them. Most people operate from the perspective that what is important to them is important to everyone else, which leads to a great number of false assumptions.

Females of all ages see life through a different lens than do males. Don't get me wrong here. I realize that each woman is different and unique and I am not saying that all women fit into one mold. But, as a general rule of thumb, women do see most things differently than do men.

How Do You Seek Love?

One of the greatest differences between men and women is how they approach meeting their NEED for LOVE. (I am not making reference to sex.) I mentioned earlier about the five different love languages which, when a couple understands and communicates love in the manner their spouse understands love, can make a world of difference in their relationship. But that is not what I am referring to here.

The majority of men are hard wired in such a way that they know they are to provide for their wife and family. I know there are some who have defied this and have proven themselves to be bums and slackers. However, most men feel very strongly that they are to be the provider: so much so that, if he is not able to provide, it often affects him in adverse ways.

This is one area where there is now competition between men and women more than at any other time in history. Providing for his family is one of the few traditional ways for a man to earn significance in the eyes of the woman he loves and his family. When he is not able to do this as he feels he should, the meanings he gives his situation will have ramifications. If he directs his meanings in a negative direction, it will affect his beliefs, which will alter his models, self-perception, inner identity and how he relates to himself and others.

The vast majority of men feel compelled to provide for their families and have a much stronger drive to conquer than do most women. By providing for his family, a man fills his psychological NEEDS for SIGNIFICANCE and CERTAINTY. **The by-product of providing and earning SIGNIFICANCE *is that he feels worthy of being loved.***

How does this link get formed between SIGNIFICANCE and LOVE in the hearts of men? When boys do something that is significant, they are often rewarded with signs of LOVE. Remember, the unconscious mind is always taking notes. Over a period of time, the unconscious mind links up the two as a mathematical equation: SIGNIFICANCE equals LOVE, and if you want to be LOVED, you have to continually do significant things and be significant. **Significance, for it to be genuine, has to be earned.**

Independently, each of these factors is compelling and has an impact in the lives of men. But when they are all added together, each one contributes to, and reinforces, the others. It is no wonder some of the things men do are deeply ingrained within them.

Men are always looking for something to conquer. Some women might be thinking, "You mean looking for the couch and the remote." Granted, I realize that there are some exceptions, but there is evidence of man's drive to conquer everywhere. Ladies, when are the men you know at their best? Is it when they have purpose and are making something happen or is it when they aren't sure of much and are wondering what to do?

Women may wonder what it really matters if a man is out conquering and doing things that are considered manly. For a lot of men it is a big deal. To be less than manly equals being less than a man, which takes away a man's SIGNIFICANCE.

When a man's SIGNIFICANCE is taken from him, his emotional state is greatly affected. If he is comfortable at level three SIGNIFICANCE, for him, anything below that number is emotionally uncomfortable. The lower it goes the more emotional pain is experienced. Over time this has the capability of altering his self-perception.

I realize some women will look at their man and say, "Hey, you don't have to do anything to impress me. I love you for who you are not what you do." This can go way over a man's head depending on the models and strategies that he has adopted up to that point in his life. At the conscious level he may say he understands, but at the unconscious level, he is operating from a different model.

This is where a great deal of confusion develops between men and women. Each can, and does, consciously acknowledge things, but then their actions are in line with the models that their unconscious mind is operating from. This can at times cause a total contradiction between word and deed, and the person does not understand what or why it happens.

What woman does not crave and appreciate her man's praise? When a man tells a woman how good she looks, it means something to her; it builds her self-confidence and she feels better about herself. This is true when their relationship is in the *LOVE* aspect of LOVE and CONNECTION. Should they slip into the *CONNECTION* aspect of LOVE and CONNECTION, the strategies they will use to get significance with each other will be radically different, as will their emotions.

Both men and women long to be significant in the eyes of the one they love. The ways that each seeks SIGNIFICANCE is different. The strategies they use to find significance will be influenced by their personality temperament blend, models, and beliefs. The latter two will have major effects on how an individual tries to find significance in the eyes of the opposite sex.

If a man acts like love is unimportant to him, there are two probable reasons. One is that he has adopted models and beliefs that portray feminine emotions as less than manly or as weaknesses. As a result, he will stay as far away as he can from such feelings. The problem he will have is that the beliefs contained within his models depict a natural part of being human as wrong. If he does not change his beliefs and thus his model, every time he feels those natural emotions, his beliefs will condemn him as wrong. He could easily find himself in a downward spiral, condemning and judging himself for feeling healthy emotions.

The second reason could be that he has been hurt badly by someone he loved in the past. When this happens, it is possible for an individual to form the link that love equals pain. Granted, in any relationship there may be some uncomfortable and painful moments, but if a person makes the link that relationships equal pain, his conclusion over time can become a belief that is incorporated into his life causing him to reject most relationships.

Remember, our beliefs form our models. When people are in this position, they will seek to fill their NEED for LOVE and CONNECTION through *CONNECTION*. This can take the form of teasing or pestering. This is clearly seen with children and young teenagers. They will tease and do things to people that are actually very annoying. In that situation it is not uncommon for someone to ask why they are doing whatever they are doing.

CONNECTION is a safer way to approach someone that you care about. It meets a NEED, but it doesn't lay you wide open to getting your heart ripped out. Some people have settled for, and maintained this type of relationship with others, because they are fearful.

For the purpose of simplicity, in the next few paragraphs rather than try to cover all the many age groups by listing each group (i.e. boys, young men and men) I am going to use the word "male" to refer to all of them. I will use "female" similarly.

When a male finds himself caring for a female, and he finally gets up the nerve to tell her how he cares for her, he is totally vulnerable. She has the power to do what she wants with his heart. This same thing is true when a female really cares for a male. At the beginning of each relationship there can be a lot of anxiety because they don't know if the other person cares for them in the same way.

There is another aspect that is at work here as well. When a person starts to love, or is in love with, another person, they are actually meeting their own psychological NEED for LOVE through the person whom they care for. If the other person does not feel the same way and rejects them, in an instant they are suffering a large psychological NEEDS withdrawal. The positive feelings of LOVE they have been experiencing are replaced by a major withdrawal in their psychological NEEDS account.

Depending on their models, beliefs and the meanings they give the event, they could really be in for a tough time. Remember, models and beliefs will influence the meaning a person is likely to give an event. How the individual explains it to himself will result in a magnification of their loss or a reduction in their perception of loss.

The areas you are strong in are a direct result of the efforts that you have invested in that particular area. You naturally gravitate toward the things you are comfortable with and capable in. When you start to experience uncomfortable feelings, we often say you are outside of your comfort zone. In reality, you are traversing beyond your identity into what is currently not your identity. This feels foreign and can be very unsettling. The intensity of what you feel will be a direct result of the meanings you give it and the way you describe it to yourself.

We all understand what opposites are: for many people men and women are considered opposites, just like the colors black and white. In the world of colors, pure white has an absence of all black. In the world of models, some see the absence of anything soft as manly.

When a boy is little the last thing he wants is to be known as is a "sissy." For a boy to be called that is often considered a reason for a fight. But why fight over what someone said? By fighting he proves that he is not a sissy. As we considered earlier in the identity section, many things are incorporated into our inner identity. The avoidance of anything that refers to sissy or feminine is an automatic for most men.

When a good friend of mine and I were talking about this book, he said to me, "Jim, could you find some other word to use instead of feminine emotions? There's just something about the term feminine and male that just doesn't go together."

If a man has difficulty with some of the softer emotions, it is because of the beliefs that have been incorporated into his model of manhood. Anyone will have difficulty with emotions that are outside their accepted beliefs and models. I know of men who refuse to cry, and they have taught their sons that it is unmanly to cry. People, regardless of sex, can adopt the belief that to cry is wrong, and if that person cries, it will have a negative effect on them because their models make it wrong for them.

It is possible for a man to be drawn To a relationship and Remain distant in his emotions.

When a man realizes that he has some beliefs that are holding him back from enjoying life, he can change them. It is not possible to simply remove a belief. The outdated belief has to be replaced with a belief that serves rather than restricts him.

Some men have a challenge with anything that is considered feminine because of what they learned growing up. No boy wants to be known as a sissy. No man wants that label either.

A man's models form his understanding of what a man is and what he is to do and not do. His models are his map of how to conduct himself as a man. The majority of men want to be the best man they can be. If, in his model of manhood, a man is to be soft, understanding, and never get angry, he will do his best to live up to that.

Many men find that they cannot live up to their model of manhood. The reasons are many, but they boil down to the fact that some of the beliefs contained within their model are counter to the human experience. ***Any time a model covers only part of the human experience, that model will bring discomfort, confusion and, at times pain to the person who is holding onto it.***

If a man has adopted models for manhood that exclude any of the softer emotions of life, such as tenderness, compassion and love, he will have a difficult time feeling and expressing love to others.

A good example of this is the "macho man" model, which leans heavily to the masculine side. This, like every other model, dictates how a person will behave. A man who adopts that model about manhood is going to be limited in certain areas of his life. Because of the model he has adopted, he will feel compelled to do some things while avoiding other things. The reason is simple: any model that leans to the masculine or the feminine to the exclusion of the other is restrictive by its very nature.

* * *

I know that there are many beliefs about love, but let's consider love apart from the physical aspects of sex. For love to be genuine, it has to be offered freely with no pressure or strings attached. Genuine love does not seek to conquer another, but rather to simply be accepted and embraced. If it is not, it is rejected.

If a person is being bowled over by another's love, it is not their love that is knocking the other person over, but rather it is the strategy they are using to show their love. Sometimes people approach others in the same way they approach a project they must conquer. Conquering can be used in forming connection, but it is not compatible with love.

One of the challenges men face is that they need to be strong, confident, self-assured and be tender, compassionate and loving at the same time. From the perspective of many men this is an impossibility! It is impossible because their models say it is impossible. It is that simple. People will only reach as far as their models, beliefs and identity will let them.

If a man will replace some of the beliefs he has embraced, he can be strong, confident, self-assured and tender, compassionate and loving without sacrificing his masculinity. Most of the models of manhood are either totally masculine or they are lacking in masculinity. It is the old pendulum swing, but it doesn't have to be that way.

The majority of models out there are either very masculine or feminine. His choices are limited. When a man learns to meet his own psychological NEEDS himself, rather than looking to get his NEEDS met from outside sources, he has taken the first steps to free himself. At that point he is no longer a puppet. He has cut the lines of dependency on others for his psychological NEEDS.

* * *

When it comes to love, it is a different world from the conquering world that males live in. Men can have difficulty jumping from one category to another. When they do, they have a tendency to take the strategies that work in one area of their life (work) and use those same strategies at home, and then have no idea why things are not working. Yes, as I stated earlier, we men can be slow to catch on to some things.

When it comes to love, men sometimes employ strategies that are inherently incompatible with love. The choleric is a temperament that is likely to need some assistance in adopting different strategies for relationships that do not include conquering and pushing to make it happen.

Genuine love cannot be forced or bought; it must be freely given. Love that is a result of conquering is obedience: not love.

The first to proclaim their feelings for the one they love is in a vulnerable spot. They are at the mercy of the person they care for. If love is offered in return, the person who offered first is very relieved and has much to be happy about. If, on the other hand, the other person does not reciprocate the love and rejects them, the meanings the rejected person gives the event will be influenced by their beliefs and models.

I must point out an important fact here. There is a major difference between when a man is really in love with a woman, and when he is just asking her out. In the second situation his perspective is "if she turns me down it's no great loss." Regardless of a person's gender, they can take the perspective that there are always more fish in the sea, so to speak.

When a person has become emotionally and psychologically invested in a relationship, if it doesn't work out there will be a sense of loss. How that person explains it to themselves will determine if they suffer for a long time or a shorter time period.

There are two approaches to love. One is genuine and cares for the other individual, while the second approach is selfish and seeks to conquer the other individual. When this is the case, usually the conquering is complete when they have sex. Both men and women approach love from both of these approaches at times. When a person is out to conquer another person and is rejected, the only loss they may incur is the loss of SIGNIFICANCE.

If a man cares about a woman and she does not care for him in like manner, he will usually think through the situation and try to figure out why he was rejected. During this process he will consider what he is lacking or what he doesn't have or hasn't done. The list of what he thinks are the reasons why he was rejected feeds the idea that LOVE and SIGNIFICANCE are related.

Compartmentalization

In general, men have an ability to compartmentalize things in their life easier than do women. This is possibly a result of having fewer connections between the two sides of their brain. Women, on the other hand, can have a great deal of things going on in their mind simultaneously. Sometimes a woman will go from one subject to the next and other ladies in the group will be following her just fine while the men are lost as to what she is talking about.

Some men are better at compartmentalizing than others. Compartmentalization is different from focused concentration, which is a skill that can be learned. The ability to focus and concentrate on something to the point of ignoring everything else is a valuable skill, but if overdone, it too can become a weakness.

For a lot of men, their focused concentration is toward providing for their family. Unfortunately, society and some models have painted a man's role as simply bringing home the bacon. When a man does this, it is possible for him to get into that compartment and remain there because it is comfortable to him. In reality, what a man needs to do to provide for his family goes far beyond just bringing home the bacon.

We have already met a couple who is a good example of how compartmentalizing can create confusion and problems in a family. Do you remember the couple that I mentioned earlier? The wife said she was tired of being the man in the family. On the field her husband was a man's man: he was great at sports, and time and time again he proved his ability to lead on the field.

But when he was home, he didn't want to lead and at times refused to take the lead. This confused his wife and others because there appeared to be no reasonable explanation. This man had learned to compartmentalize his life so well that he had in a sense two different inner identities. One was for playing sports on the field and another one he lived out on a daily basis at home with his family and his work.

Because men have the ability to compartmentalize things in their life, it is easy for them to focus in on one or two aspects of life and miss the rest. It is sad when a man wakes up one morning and realizes that he has missed out on much that life had to offer.

Technology has created some shifts in how men and women relate to each other, but the real problem that exists is a direct result of fathers not spending time with their sons, teaching them about what it is to be a man and a father.

A great number of men want to be the husbands and fathers that their wives and families want and need, but they find themselves between a rock and a hard place because no one has taught them how. So every man does the best he can, often feeling as though he is somehow missing the mark.

Everyone is Valuable and Important

I want to re-emphasize that, regardless of gender, if people are in an incongruent state they are not less valuable or less important as people. However, because they sometimes see themselves as less valuable and less important, the natural mood swings that are common in life are magnified a great deal as a result of their incongruence.

When a man is incongruent, his models will be pulling him toward incongruence, while inside he knows that it is not really who he is. He will experience all of the corresponding emotional swings that go with being incongruent. The gentleman who had a compartment for sports and another one for the rest of his life was confused all the more by his situation. He could lead on the field and felt good about it and himself. However, at home he was unsure of himself and had no self-confidence. He had no idea what was happening and, as a result questioned his abilities, which created even more self-doubt.

When a woman is incongruent, she too will experience wide emotional swings that can make what a man experiences look like gentle waves on the beach in comparison to her emotional tsunamis. She will have two different aspects contained within her inner identity. Her feminine core will be pulling her toward congruence, while her models portray being feminine as something that is to be avoided. One part of her wants to be feminine while another part fears and avoids it. A woman in this position, can experience emotions that are in total opposition to each other, leaving her confused and bewildered. Until we understand models, personality temperaments, congruence, incongruence, and how people are meeting their psychological NEEDS, other people's actions can be confusing.

Some of the women reading this may agree with everything except a man leading. The idea of following a man is not in her model of the world. If that is where you are, I understand it.

A man needs to be able to lead himself. This will be very difficult for him if he does not have the models and beliefs that will enable him to have the confidence he needs. Without self-confidence, he lacks the ability to do what he needs to do for his own, as well as his family's, good.

How important is respect to you as a woman? Are you aware of how important being respected is to a man? ***For a majority of men, when they feel they are being disrespected, they feel unloved.*** Most women see disrespect and lack of love as two totally different things, yet for the majority of men, there is little difference between the two.

When a man feels disrespected, it has a much deeper impact on him than a woman might think. Because men are prone to link SIGNIFICANCE and LOVE together, when they are not respected, there is neither love nor respect.

I realize that from a woman's perspective this may sound truly odd. Intellectually a man knows he is loved, but at the emotional level, it doesn't feel that way. But many a man understands what I am saying here.

We men are aware that we are not perfect--if anything far from it--but we do try. If the woman we love will acknowledge and respect us for trying and encourage us instead of showing disrespect for us because we have failed occasionally, her encouragement and respect will go a long way for both of them.

Just as a woman longs to know, and be shown, that her man loves her unconditionally, so too does a man long for the respect of the woman he loves.

I'm sure some of you are agreeing, while others are feeling no need to do anything about this. It is possible that your relationship has slipped into the CONNECTION mode rather than the LOVE mode. If you are in this situation, often the impulse is to continue to do the things that create CONNECTION because it has proven itself effective, which meets the NEED for CERTAINTY, SIGNIFICANCE and VARIETY.

Should a person decide to attempt to make the change from the CONNECTION mode back to the LOVE mode, they will have to re-win the heart of the one they love. During this process, they will need to court the other person again, as such actions may be viewed as false. During this re-winning process, there will be many testings that must be passed. Once the other person sees that they are genuine and sincere, the barriers will naturally begin to come down, and intimacy will return to their relationship.

When someone puts another person's needs before their own, there is an element of uncertainty that both people could experience. Depending on the meanings that each individual gives events and statement during this process, the emotions that are produced could be disturbing and uncomfortable.

A large number of women want their man to share his innermost feelings with them, and if he doesn't, some have questioned his love for her. ***Whether a man will share his innermost feelings is a better indicator of his models than it is of his love for her.*** For a man to tell the woman he loves his feelings can mean taking the risk of losing her respect. Unless he knows and feels that she truly respects him, he will likely withhold some of his feelings, especially anything that might result in losing some of her respect.

A good example of this is when a couple is making love. One or both of them may find themselves wondering about trying something different and not mention it because of a concern of what the other might think of them. *When it comes to sharing his emotions, how comfortable is a man going to be telling the woman he feels he has to impress, emotions that he himself is not comfortable feeling?*

Love is important to a woman, and respect is important to a man.

Men and women have been perplexed with each other for a long time. Have you ever wondered how a big strong guy can become such a wimp when he is sick? For some guys, when they are sick with a common cold, they don't even try to be tough. They are helpless and needy.

When the man you love is sick like this, what do you do? You, the love of his life, do one of two things: you either dote over him, taking care of his every need, while you wonder to yourself and to someone else how men can be so helpless at times; or you tell him to suck it up and get over it.

Now, let's consider what is going on when a woman caters to her helpless man. What psychological NEEDS are being met? Do you think that SIGNIFICANCE is met at a high level? He is the center of attention. What a great place to be! What about CERTAINTY? He knows you will take wonderful care of him. Being sick is filled with VARIETY, as you never know how long it will last or how bad it will get. That contains some VARIETY doesn't it? What about LOVE? Well, your doting over him makes him feel loved, but in reality, he rewards himself with the feelings of being loved.

The above does not happen to the man with the model that real men don't get sick, and if they do get sick, the only way they will stay in bed is if they are about to die from it. "I can knock this out. It won't get me down. I can handle a little cold. What's a little cold? No cold is going to get the best of me."

The depth and importance of this is often missed. In each situation psychological NEEDS are being met, but through totally different strategies. In the tough guy example it is easy to see the SIGNIFICANCE NEED being met. Consider how the NEED for CERTAINTY is being met from within as opposed to the external CERTAINTY from the first example. The element of VARIETY is the same: no one knows exactly how bad a cold is going to get. CONNECTION is there with everyone else who won't give in to a cold. If you have noticed, the first one is more relationship oriented, while the tough guy is more accomplishment oriented. Are you catching on?

Masculine/Feminine dynamics show up in every area of life without exception. Now, is either man wrong? Well, that is subjective. If it matches with your model, it's good, if it doesn't, chances are you may find it challenging to not look down your nose at it.

You may be wondering what this has to do with relationships and how men and women relate. There is a part of every man that feels helpless and needy. Depending on the models and beliefs a man has adopted, he will or will not allow himself to be seen as helpless or needy.

There is a note here that needs to be made. It is not just a person's models at work here. There is also an element of unconditional love. The man who feels free to appear helpless is not fearful of being judged. He knows he is loved and in his understanding your actions back that up.

If you will remember, on the masculine side LOVE is often sought out through SIGNIFICANCE. The guy who is working hard to stay on his feet even though the cold is doing everything it can to knock him on his back is working hard to be worthy of respect and SIGNIFICANCE. His models and beliefs are his guiding light. Remember, it is not uncommon for men (women can do this too) to link SIGNIFICANCE with being *worthy* of LOVE.

If you see this happening, please do not go up to him and say, "Oh, here are the NEEDS you're meeting through this strategy. I know what you're up to!" Trust me, that will hurt a relationship terribly, and none of us want to do that.

Quarreling could be a Symptom

Sometimes couples discover that they have become more quarrelsome than they use to be. In fact, some have realized that all they do is quarrel. When a couple consciously becomes aware that they have reached this point in their relationship, it is common for one or both of them to begin to wonder if they have married the wrong person.

When this happens, the focus is directed at the other person, and it appears that the problems are the other person's fault. ***When CONNECTION sets in, if a person isn't careful, the natural tendency is to direct the drive to conquer at the other person.*** This intensifies the conflicts and increases the CONNECTION, thus meeting that and other psychological NEEDS at higher levels, which in turn increases CONNECTION and decreases LOVE.

No one sets out to get themselves into this type of a rut, but many find themselves there. Both men and women can get caught up in the downward spiral that develops once CONNECTION is the basis of their relationship. This is nothing new, but it might shed some light on what happens in marriages.

We have examined mankind's drive to conquer, but what many women don't quite realize is that they too have a drive to conquer. If men and women don't learn to direct that drive in positive directions, it will go where it will: often where you wish it had not. CONNECTION is a good example of this.

Throughout life people have a list of things they must conquer. First is standing up, then walking, running, getting dressed by himself, riding a bike (without training wheels), climbing trees, running faster than the next guy or gal. The list goes on. It never stops, until he dies.

Which boy gets the most positive attention? The one who accomplishes the most and does it the best. SIGNIFICANCE is drilled into men from the time they are small boys. Was it always this way? Yes and no.

SIGNIFICANCE has always been important to men. Throughout the centuries, men received a lot of their SIGNIFICANCE from the roles they had as a husband and a father. **Now, instead of a man receiving SIGNIFICANCE from his role, he has competition from the woman he loves.** This is not to say that she has set out to compete with him, but in many areas that were once where men shined the most, she, too, is there shining. With her shining beside him, he is not shining as brightly as he once did.

Men of today have to deal with competition and try to come up with new ways to earn SIGNIFICANCE for themselves. The lifestyle of today has made man's quest for SIGNIFICANCE much more challenging than ever before. If you have ever wondered what is fueling the buying habits of some people, SIGNIFICANCE is it, and the advertisers know it. But how does it affect couples? Let's consider the following.

Some women have adopted models that have them going head to head with men. When they come out even, or further ahead, they reward themselves with SIGNIFICANCE. A person's models are the determining factors regarding what they understand as acceptable. A woman's models will affect her inner identity just as it will a man's.

Most men and women have at least a mental list of some of the things they want to do in their life. Both men and women will respond differently depending on their models and whether they are congruent or incongruent with their core nature. A man who has adopted models that are extremely accomplishment oriented may discover, to his dismay, that his biggest problem in life is in the area of relationships. Typically, a man in this position sets out in life conquering his checklist, and finding the right woman is an important highlight. When a man gets married, he has won her hand and now he focuses on providing for her. It is through providing for her that he is working to show his love for her.

If he is unable to continue to meet his psychological NEEDS (especially SIGNIFICANCE) through his relationship with his wife, he will gravitate toward other things and activities that reward him with the SIGNIFICANCE he no longer finds at home. It is important that we remember that in every situation he is meeting his own psychological NEEDS. The challenge for us all is what we come to believe is required before our psychological NEEDS are met.

Remember, men often make the link that LOVE, like SIGNIFICANCE, must be earned, which fits with what men know. When a man meets the woman of his dreams, he has to win her heart and her hand. Once he has done that he is supposed to provide for her. The better he provides, the more significant he is and the more he demonstrates his love for her as he is trying to earn her respect and love.

I remember seventeen years ago I was working for a company that had a large number of us working in one big room. As you can imagine, everyone knew what was happening with their neighbors. One day the fiancée of Ben, the guy who had his desk behind mine, came in. They were all mushy and I made the comment to someone next to me that it must be nice to be young and in love.

She wanted to know what I meant by my comment. I explained that after you get married, life sets in and there are a lot of things that seem to drain off the romance. She didn't agree with me. Later Ben told me I had really shaken her up but assured me she'd be fine. Years later I saw her and she reminded me of what I said. Puzzled, I looked at her. She told me that, unfortunately, she now understood what I was saying that day.

What happens when someone is romancing the love of his life? He thinks of things that the other would enjoy and that would show her how special she is to him. When a man romances a woman, he makes her feel significant and special. Is it any wonder women want their men to romance them?

When a man is romancing the love of his life, he covers every one of the love languages thoroughly. After all, he is on a quest. But after marriage, romance often finds itself sitting on a shelf. Unfortunately, many women feel as though they, too, have been put on a shelf. She feels pain as a result of not feeling as SIGNIFICANT to the love of her life, or she might wonder if he is the love of her life.

What is happening? When a man gets married, he has new responsibilities and like any man he turns his focus to how he can take care of his wife and his new responsibilities. Without meaning to, men can get caught up in conquering the many things in life that need to be taken care of.

Because of a man's ability to compartmentalize his life, when he is away from his home he focuses on what he needs to do. When he is home, if he has things he needs to do there, he may focus on those things rather than focusing on his wife. In reality, he is trying to be responsible and take care of her, but he soon learns that he is missing the mark.

When this has been happening for a time, there is going to be some venting of emotional discomfort, which usually takes the form of an argument. The unseen gain in the argument is that there is CONNECTION between the two people. Over time, if the love that exists is not shown in a way that is understood as love, the natural tendency will be to gravitate to the next best thing, which is CONNECTION.

What the woman needs is for the man to make her feel special again. When a man is living a life that declares everything else is more important than his wife, she naturally feels insignificant. As is the case with everyone when they feel insignificant, they will seek some way to gain the SIGNIFICANCE they need.

Do you know a couple who is not happy unless they are fighting? Their relationship is anchored in CONNECTION. If this couple still loves each other and will begin communicating the love they feel for each other in the way the other understands love, their relationship will change dramatically for the better. If he will genuinely do things that she has linked to being SIGNIFICANT, and if she will show respect and LOVE for her husband, there is a good chance they will find the one they fell in love with.

One of the first things to do if the romance has left your relationship is to find out your spouse's love languages and start showing your love in the way that your spouse understands love. If two people are feeling unloved by the other, neither is going to feel like working together to get over the hurdles that are before them.

I know one man who loves his wife and has done everything to re-win her heart since they got married, but he has not been able to get the love he desires. He has moved, built her a new house, bought her new cars. Anything she wants, he provides her with.

"I don't get it," he told me, "all these years and she still won't cook me a meal."

One of the ways he shows love is to do for his wife whatever she wants. In her model, cooking is something that successful women don't do. He would be thrilled if she would make him a peanut butter sandwich. I have seen countless marriages that are struggling because one or both of them refuse to do something for their spouse because they see it as beneath them.

> **Within Relationships**
> **LOVE & SIGNIFICANCE**
> **are By-Products of Love Communicated in the Preferred style of the Other Person**

Women are typically more sensitive to these things than are men, which is why I included this information here. Remember, there is always a reason for what people do. It might not make sense on the surface, but if you can get down to what is at the heart of it, changes are possible.

It is not always possible to get your spouse to cooperate with you in making changes that are needed. That being the truth, be careful whom you marry. What has helped the guy whose wife won't fix him a home cooked meal? He has learned to see how she shows him love. He told me it is not as tasty as a home cooked meal, but he knows his wife loves him.

Learn how your spouse shows love, and every time your spouse is doing that, remind yourself that they are trying to show their love for you. I realize it won't be as tasty as that home cooked meal, but you will not starve if you continually look for, and see how they are showing their love to you.

There is a saying, "Behind every great man is a great woman." There is a lot of truth in that saying. A woman has the ability to encourage a man or discourage him. So too, the man has the ability to lift his wife to a place where she knows intellectually and emotionally that she is not only significant to him, but that he loves her completely.

Some people don't have the luxury of a supportive spouse. Their relationship is full of irritations and discord. Some things have bothered them for years and although they try to let go of them, they just can't. One reason people have a hard time letting go of something that has happened in the past is because of CONNECTION. Consciously they want to let go and be free from it, but at the unconscious level they hold onto it because it is CONNECTION.

CONNECTION is always a poor quality substitute for love, but many people find themselves in the position of having nothing but CONNECTION to grasp, so they hold on to the strategies and behaviors that are meeting their psychological NEEDS. The underlying reason for this is the hope that if they hold on long enough maybe they will eventually be loved.

CONNECTION is almost always made through some negative means, such as taking or doing something that someone else would not like. Love, in comparison, is always given. True love can never be taken or demanded.

It is amazing that people, if they do not get what they need in the area of psychological NEEDS, will take what they can get. The problem is that CONNECTION that is forced is never as valuable as LOVE that is given, but it does meet the individual's psychological NEED. The wonderful thing is that if someone is getting their NEEDS met through CONNECTION, and the person who is connected to them starts meeting their NEEDS through ways that the other person will understand as love, as time goes on, they will loosen their grip on CONNECTION and eventually let go of it all together.

CONNECTION in a Relationship Never Satisfies Individuals It always Leaves Them Hungry, Dissatisfied & Longing for More

How does this work out in a relationship? Once you understand what is happening, you can begin to show love to your spouse in the way your spouse understands love.

At first it will be questioned. If your spouse is a gift giver, and you have not given gifts at all for years, when you first give a gift, your motive might be questioned. This is because it is a CONNECTION-based (rather than LOVE-based) response.

Any time a negative or sarcastic comment is made, it is with the intention of establishing CONNECTION with the other individual. An interesting aspect of CONNECTION is the difference in what happens between friends and lovers, when compared with what happens between enemies. It is the intensity of the individual's comments and actions that are vastly different. Within relationships, people often react by saying and doing things out of pain as compared to enemies who act out of utter dislike and sometimes hatred.

When someone you love is not showing love in return, it hurts. The pain inflicted by someone you love can, for all intents and purposes, feel worse than pain an enemy could cause. With an enemy, you always have your guard up, but with someone you love, you don't look to protect yourself.

CONNECTION in a relationship is dangerous because it pushes away the person they long to be close to. The way that CONNECTION works is similar to grabbing a person by their clothing or their throat: you can get their attention and get them to do what you want to a degree, but as soon as they can get away from you, they will create distance.

As the closeness breaks down and the distance increases, the intensity of the words and actions are increased to keep the CON-

NECTION with the other individual. The proof of this is the fact that if someone is saying something we don't like, after a while it has no affect on us. If, about the same time, something new comes into the mix, the CONNECTION is reestablished.

Many couples who were once in love, but slipped into the CONNECTION mode have eventually discovered themselves enemies. This is a result of the continual escalation of the intensity that is required to maintain a relationship based on CONNECTION.

When the pain of maintaining CONNECTION becomes more than the pain of ending the relationship, the relationship is no more.

Another of the major differences that exist between men and women is how they approach relationships. Men, for the most part, are focused on accomplishments, which is one way they show their love and feel worthy of being loved. The degree of intensity to which a man seeks accomplishments will vary according to his congruency, personality temperament blend, models and beliefs.

Because Men Approach Things Differently Women sometimes think that Men Don't Listen

Men have a hard time understanding that accomplishments can be separate from relationships. This is one of the primary reasons why women conclude that men have a hard time listening. From a woman's perspective, relationships are about communication and understanding. From a man's perspective, communication and understanding are important steps to accomplishing something.

Women enjoy talking and understanding each other, and the more areas they are able to do this, the better they feel about their relationships. Men are more concerned with getting things done than they are about understanding each other.

One activity where this is easy to see is when it comes to shopping. For the most part, men and women have totally different approaches to shopping. Shopping, for a large number of women, is a social event. It is not about buying a large number of items: it is about enjoying the process and the time together communicating about anything and everything.

For most of the men I know it's "If I'm not conquering, I'll be sitting here waiting for you." For a lot of men, shopping is almost like getting a tooth pulled. If you have to do it, well okay. Try to make the best of it. It boggles men's minds how women can go to a dozen different stores, look at stuff in each one and then go back to the first store and buy the first thing they looked at.

I remember one time we were remodeling a bathroom. We went to the flooring store and looked at the flooring. We went up to the first rack, found one we liked. I thought we were done. Then my wife said that it had some flecks of colors in it that she wasn't sure about. Long story short, after an hour and a half in the same store, she came back to the same one that had the color that she wasn't sure about and told me she liked that one.

I was flabbergasted. "You're kidding me, right?"

She looked at me and asked, "Why?"

"That's the first one we looked at. We liked it but you said it had that color that you weren't sure about. Remember?"

"Oh, well. I think it will look good."

I did not understand meanings, conquering, and strategies as I do now. All I knew was my back hurt, my shoulders hurt, my butt hurt from sitting, my brain was tired from trying to think of things to think about and now I had just experienced what felt like I was emotionally getting electrocuted when she picked the first one we looked at. Have any other couples ever been in this situation before?

My thoughts were "an hour and a half wasted. I could have gotten this and that done, etc..." I was working hard to hide my frustration and she was happy as a clam at high tide, which I found to be even more irritating. I confess: I was creating some very unhappy emotions within myself.

So what happened? From her perspective she had just invested an hour and a half in finding the right flooring. From my perspective I had just wasted and hour and a half. It is clear that each of us gave the event different meanings and experienced different emotions, but what was happening behind the scenes that influenced the different meanings we gave the event?

Our strategies for CERTAINTY were different. We saw one on the first rack that looked good to us. From my perspective, the decision was made: Accomplishment. My wife on the other hand had a different strategy. She liked the same one, but she had a question about a little speck of color, so she looked at every sample and considered each after having looked at all of them. At last she found one she liked more than any other one. It happened to be the one we liked on the first rack we looked at. Only she didn't realize it was the same one until I pointed out that fact.

So why were our strategies so different? Beliefs. It may sound too simple to be true, but we had different beliefs about what had to happen in order to find the right flooring. Contained within my belief system is the belief that it is possible to walk into a store and find exactly what I want right away and have CERTAINTY that it will look good.

What I didn't realize then was that it is possible for a person to believe that in order for them to have certainty this is the right one, they must first look at all of the other options. If that is the case, they will find themselves with a nagging UNCERTAINTY about their decision if they don't look at the other options before making their final choice.

After having explored all the other options for our bathroom flooring, she was comfortable with making a decision. She had CERTAINTY that she would be happy with that choice. In reality, we had the same end goal: flooring that we liked and was good quality. But because we each used different strategies to reach our common goal, it appeared that we were in opposition to each other. Even now, all those years later, we are both happy with the flooring we picked out that day.

It all makes sense now, but I assure you, it didn't make any sense to me then! You may very well be able to relate to this example, but this problem is not just confined to relationships. This type of situation occurs in many small businesses and corporations as well. When you add personality temperaments, needs hierarchies, models, beliefs, congruence/incongruence, strategies and gender dynamics into the work place, it makes for some very interesting situations.

To an onlooker, the actions of someone might not make any sense at all, but as we have explored, there are always reasons behind them. The challenge is that often we can't see them. When we understand what the motivation is behind the behavior, the very things that use to baffle us now make sense. This does not necessarily mean that we have to agree with it, but it does open up opportunities to bridge the gap that once was impossible to span.

* * *

There are many contributing factors when a couple breaks up. Some are seen clearly and others are hidden below the visible layer of symptoms.

When two people meet and are attracted to each other, there is one of two situations they will be in. Either they both are congruent with their core nature, or they both are incongruent. In either case, they have the correct polarities to be pulled together. We examined this attraction principle in the chapter on gender dynamics.

There is something called the proximity principle. How this works is that people will find themselves, over time, being attracted to those around them. This explains why so many people who work together begin to feel attracted to each other.

Some have questioned the proximity principle because some people are not attracted to each other at all. The reason for this is that if a man and a woman are both masculine, they may be physically attracted to each other, but they will not be attracted to each other emotionally because they both have the same masculine polarity.

Any couple that falls in love has opposite polarities: this is true whether they are both congruent or incongruent. Let's consider what happens between a couple when one of them shifts polarities and the other does not. At some point they will discover that the magic has disappeared from their relationship. When this happens, it is common for them to know something has changed but not know what. Typically one, or both, of them comes to the conclusion that they no longer love the other. They may look at each other and think to themselves, "Wow! What's happened? You're not the person I married!"

In reality, someone has changed: it could be their spouse, or themselves who has changed. In this situation, either one will adapt to the complementary polarity or they will drift further apart. If neither of them shifts their polarity to complement the other, their relationship shifts from one where they both experience LOVE to a relationship that is based solely on CONNECTION. When this happens, the romance is gone. Disagreements are the norm and both parties feel as though they can never do anything right. The sad reality is that they may truly love each other, but because of these other factors, the love is unseen and, as a result, unfelt.

As a couple falls in love, they often begin to look to each other for the meeting of their psychological NEEDS. Naturally this happens in varying degrees. This can span the entire NEEDS group of SIGNIFICANCE, CERTAINTY, VARIETY, and LOVE and CONNECTION.

When a couple's polarities become the same, the meeting of their NEEDS for SIGNIFICANCE and LOVE through their relationship changes, or could even come to an end. The NEEDS that their relationship fills shift to that of only VARIETY and CONNECTION as the relationship deteriorates. In the area of CERTAINTY, they go from knowing their partner loves them to certainty that they made a mistake picking this one.

In reality, it is not healthy for anyone to look to a relationship to fill all psychological NEEDS. If people do this, they are setting up themselves, and the one they love, for disappointments. This is never done intentionally, and when it does happen, it can be surprising to both people. This is why it is good for both people to have interests that are their own and separate from each other. Again, as in everything, balance is key.

A majority of the models today have positioned women in the masculine role. If this is where you find yourself, it is simply where you are. It is not right or wrong. The key is to understand what is happening and why. Understanding opens the door for coming up with a solution, whereas confusion only leads to frustration.

Yes, without doubt, men are different than women. It is my sincere hope that the information contained within this section has been helpful for women to understand the men and boys in their lives. As we have explored, men and women are complex individuals who operate on many different levels at the same time. As individuals, we all do the best with the resources we have.

Conclusion

It is my hope that this book has provided new insights that have made it possible for you to understand yourself and others at a new level. Men and women are extremely adaptive and capable in what they can overcome. If you doubt this, simply look around at all of the technological accomplishments that you enjoy. Each technological advance is a direct result of someone seeing the challenge clearly and doing something about it for their benefit as well as the benefit of others.

It is important for both men and women to learn how to be congruent with their core nature. A man can be masculine and congruent with his core and still reach out and express compassion, tenderness and love without giving up any of his masculinity. So too, a woman can be congruent with her core nature and still be strong and stand up for what she believes in without sacrificing her femininity. Both of these scenarios are only possible if their models and beliefs do not create conflicts within the human experience.

I thank my Lord for the opportunity to share this information with you. It is truly an honor and a privilege for me to write this book. As I have discovered these insights, and applied them in my personal and professional life, I have been amazed at the difference it has made in my life.

Now that you have new insights, you have the ability to make changes in your life. If you want your world to change, you must change. Life is a continual process of change and growth. The question is, what are you going to do? Remember, to postpone a decision is making a decision to do nothing. Today begins the rest of your life.

If you are interested in additional information and resources, they can be found at TheNeuteringoftheAmericanMale.com and for coaching, go to JimWysong.com.

LaVergne, TN USA
13 February 2011
216356LV00001B/5/P

9 780984 395002